LABOR-MANAGEMENT
CONTRACTS AT WORK

LABOR-MANAGEMENT CONTRACTS AT WORK

*analysis of awards
reported by the American
Arbitration Association*

BY MORRIS STONE

HARPER & BROTHERS · *NEW YORK*

TABLE OF CONTENTS

PREFACE

In an opinion of the United States Supreme Court on June 20, 1960, Justice William O. Douglas referred to the collective bargaining agreement as an expression of "industrial self-government" and to arbitrators as the designers of "private law" for labor and management. The object of this book is to reveal some of the characteristics of that private law as applied to ten critical areas of union contract administration and employer-employee relations.

Almost 150 labor arbitrators are represented in this volume. Their awards were rendered under the Voluntary Labor Arbitration Rules of the American Arbitration Association since January 1, 1959, and were selected from among those reported in the Association's monthly Summary of Labor Arbitration Awards. Although these awards were not written for publication—each having been composed by the arbitrator at the specific request of a company and union and intended only for their use—the Association asked the parties' permission to publish them because they contained material of general interest.

It is customary for an author to say that he alone is responsible for the opinions expressed in his book. In a sense, an exception must be made here. The purpose of this volume is to show how professional arbitrators have solved problems, not how the author would have done so if he had been chosen to solve them. It was his plan to reflect their views accurately, and to suppress his own. As none of the arbitrators whose work is discussed here was consulted in advance, the author tenders apologies for any errors that may have occurred. For these, he does take full responsibility. This also seems to be the appropriate occasion to make it clear that the American Arbitration Association, under whose auspices the awards were rendered, took no part in the substantive decisions of arbitrators. As an impartial administrative and educational agency, the AAA's sole interest was in placing these arbitrators' recognized insight into problems of industrial self-government at the disposal of all.

*Of the many Association staff members who have assisted in the prepa-
ration of this book, two especially deserve mention. Estelle R. Tracy
collaborated with the author in reading thousands of awards during the
past two years and in preparing summaries of those which seemed to be
of educational value. Without those summaries as an index to the cases
themselves, the task of writing this book would have been immeasurably
more difficult. Ruth E. Lyons worked more directly with the author on
the book itself. If the result is an orderly arrangement of the cases, with
accurate citations and cross references, it is largely because of her dedica-
tion to the task. Miss Lyons was more than an editorial assistant; she
was, in fact, the final arbiter on questions of English usage, for which
the author is happy to express his obligation.*

*But the deepest obligation is to the parties who, in the first place, con-
sented to the publication of their awards. There is likely to be at least
one disappointed party in every reported arbitration case. Yet winner
and loser alike have permitted their momentary shortcomings to be ex-
posed to public view. In doing so, they have contributed to a body of
material from which they too can draw. Thus, their waiver of the rules
of privacy which govern arbitration proceedings reflects a maturity in
collective bargaining relations and is, at the same time, one more example of enlightened self-interest.*

JULY, *1961*

LABOR-MANAGEMENT
CONTRACTS AT WORK

1

INTRODUCTION

A quarter of a century has elapsed since collective bargaining was made official national policy in the United States. The right of employees to organize and to negotiate contracts did not, of course, originate in the midthirties. That right had existed long before the passage of the National Labor Relations Act (NLRA) in 1935, but it had also been lawful for employers to interfere with and discourage union organization. Given management's superior economic resources at that time, it was the employer's will that prevailed most often when the two rights clashed.

The adoption of a new labor policy in the United States created a new balance of forces. Collective bargaining was now not only permitted, but advocated. Discrimination by employers against employees for joining unions was declared to be an unfair labor practice. Election machinery was established to determine which union, if any, was desired by a majority of employees in an appropriate unit. By the time the United States entered World War II, over 10 million workers were enrolled in unions.

In 1947, two years after the war's end, Congress tipped the scales again with the Taft-Hartley amendments to the NLRA. For the first time, certain practices by labor unions were also proscribed, along with those of employers. At the same time, some limitations upon the freedom of employers to express their opposition to unions were relaxed. Nevertheless, union membership reached an all-time high of 18 million by 1958.

There are now an estimated 100,000 collective bargaining agreements in effect. Overwhelmingly, the agreements provide for arbitration of grievances arising out of the day-to-day application of their terms. These arbitration clauses mostly are "restricted" in scope; that is, they do not cover all grievances, but only those grievances which involve interpretation of provisions of the contract.

1

Furthermore, arbitrators are usually barred from adding to the contract or changing its terms. But such language does not imply a narrow jurisdiction. On the contrary, the modern collective bargaining agreement embraces such a wide range of subjects that it sometimes seems as though any complaint of a worker can be shown to involve a question of contract interpretation.[1]

Most employers and unions today use *ad hoc*, or case-by-case, procedures of arbitration. Even though their basic agreement provides for arbitration, they anticipate too few actual cases to warrant making full-time arrangements. The parties select an arbitrator only when he is needed. They generally make no commitment to call on him in the future, although this does not exclude the possibility that the same arbitrator will often be asked to serve. Each call to service is for the specific grievance or group of grievances with which the parties are momentarily concerned.

The acceptance of collective bargaining as a permanent feature of American industrial life, and the almost universal use of grievance arbitration clauses in contracts, have given rise to a new "profession"—that of the labor-management arbitrator. Theoretically, this profession is open to any person, for no government license is required, nor is there any formal test of ability to be met. Nevertheless, the profession is a small one. Thousands have served from time to time on an occasional case, but there are perhaps no more than 500 men who earn all or a significant portion of their living by arbitrating labor-management controversies. What the others lack often is not technical qualification, but acceptability to the parties. In a sense, arbitrators perform a highly personalized function for unions and companies. The parties establish the kind of grievance machinery and arbitration procedures that suit them best, and call upon arbitrators whose style of performance and technical skills conform to their particular needs. The concentration of arbitration

---

[1] Often, a complaint is baseless on its face, as may be the assertion that a question of interpretation of the contract is involved. But even such complaints are arbitrable under typical arbitration clauses. This is one apparent effect of a decision by the United States Supreme Court in *American Manufacturing Company*, 363 U.S. 564, and *Warrior & Gulf Navigation Company*, 363 U.S. 574. There it was held that the courts should resolve disputes over arbitrability unless it could be said "with positive assurance" that the parties excluded it from the scope of their arbitration clauses.

work in the hands of a relatively small number makes it evident that labor and management want grievances resolved by persons who can be expected to render predictable decisions within the framework of modern union contract interpretation.

Shortly after World War II, when arbitration was becoming reconstituted on a voluntary basis, there was some controversy as to whether *ad hoc* arbitration provided the kind of service that most parties needed. The really creative role, it was argued, was played by the "permanent" arbitrator, or umpire, named for the duration of a contract. Only he was in a position to become fully familiar with the viewpoints, problems, and conditions of the particular union and company, or industry. He could, therefore, participate in some aspects of contract-making, an area usually closed to the *ad hoc* arbitrator.

The fact that both the permanent and the *ad hoc* systems are widely practiced in American industry supports the conclusion that there was, and is, room for both. It would be pointless to say that, in general, one set of procedures is better than another. Nevertheless, it is important to note that *ad hoc* arbitration is not exactly the institution that it was two decades ago. The intensive and continuous preferential selection of arbitrators, creating a relatively small corps of full-time professionals, has itself wrought a change. It would be anachronistic to say that today the *ad hoc* arbitrator is necessarily a stranger to the parties, or they to him. A number of factors combine to overcome whatever strangeness might have existed fifteen years ago. Thousands of arbitration awards have been published. They are widely read by labor and management representatives and by arbitrators, encouraging a trend toward standardization in collective bargaining and in the performance of arbitrators. The parties to a particular case may be calling upon an arbitrator for the first time, but it is unlikely that they do not already have an impression of his work from his published awards. Furthermore, there is a considerable interchange of information among unions and among companies.

The arbitrator, too, precisely because he *is* a professional, learns as much as he can about his prospective clients. It is unlikely that he presides over his first case for a set of parties without knowing a good deal about their bargaining history. But the most important reason for the familiarity of *ad hoc* arbitrators with the parties they serve is simply that the latter often are reluctant to select new arbitrators. In principle, company and union representatives favor the training and use of newcomers. But, faced with a particular grievance, they tend to select those who have decided cases for them in the past. This tendency keeps the profession small, but well informed. In short, many *ad hoc* arbitrators are acquiring some of the attributes of the permanent arbitrator, except that their unit is not a single company and union, but the labor-management community of the area.

If the interpretation of collective bargaining agreements has become a field of specialization in the United States, it is partly because the union contract is like no other. For one thing, it is necessarily vague in many critical areas of the employer-employee relationship. Union and company negotiators might confer endlessly without agreeing on circumstances under which the discharge of an employee would be justified. The usual formula, acceptable in most cases, is that "employees shall not be discharged except for just cause." What this is to mean in practice is left to the grievance procedure and, if there is no agreement, ultimately to arbitration. Similar general phrases are found in other areas of the contract. Promotions will go to the senior employee, provided he is "reasonably" qualified to do the work; call-in pay will be given, except when work is unavailable because of an "emergency"; employees will be given their choice of vacation periods "whenever possible";— these and countless other phrases may have represented a meeting of minds at the time of negotiations, but are obviously too inexact to answer every practical problem that arises later. Even the most common words may prove to be of uncertain meaning. Does a probationary period of thirty "days" mean calendar days or working days? Does the right to bid for another "job" give an employee the right to bid for transfer to another machine within the same classification? Is a day when no work was scheduled a day of "absence," within the meaning of a holiday-pay clause? Thus, the problem of contract interpretation often becomes a matter of discovering whether words were used with their common meaning, or with a special meaning derived from practices in the particular establishment.

Union contract interpretation is difficult enough when negotiators intended to express full agreement. But it becomes more difficult when language was meant not to express agreement, but—for pragmatic reasons—to conceal the absence of agreement. Many examples will be found in the chapters of this book. In one case it was found that the parties had discussed proposed changes in their seniority clause during 1960 negotiations. But "in the final rush and heat" of the settlement, this question was "swept under the rug." In another case, parties could not agree on the basis for holiday pay for certain employees. Not wanting to hold up conclusion of the contract, they agreed upon an ambiguous phrase. Each then put a memorandum into his own files containing his own interpretation of that language.

In a third case, the history of bargaining on a seniority clause revealed that the negotiators had tacitly agreed to remove certain seniority restrictions, so that the employer would have more flexibility in scheduling production. If that agreement had been expressed in writing, however, the union officers might not have been able to win a majority membership vote for ratification. The expedient adopted permitted the employer to proceed in accordance with the new understanding, but to leave the language of the old contract unchanged. Obviously, this gave rise to an erratic way of doing things—one more reason why the whole question of past practice plays such an important part in grievance arbitration.

Collective bargaining agreements are often the product of slow accrual of language. An ambiguous clause may be permitted to stand unchanged for years because of apprehension that an unsuccessful attempt to revise it in one direction would be evidence that it really meant what the other party said it did. But disputes eventually arise under such clauses, and fixed interpretations become necessary. During the negotiations that follow, parties may correct obscure language or bring the clauses into line with practice, thus avoiding the possibility of further grievances. Unfortunately, however, the correction of one clause without a review of the contract as a whole often only opens the way for disputes over the meaning of other provisions.

This volume contains many examples of situations where the internal consistency of an agreement as a whole was disturbed by new language added to one clause; or where a new meaning, perhaps not intended by either party, was given to a seemingly unrelated section. In a dispute over whether incentive employees were to be given pay (in lieu of overtime opportunities missed) at their incentive rate or at the base rates, the decision turned, in part, on the fact that stewards who were paid for time spent in negotiating grievances—another form of pay for time not worked—received the incentive rate. Quite possibly the employer who agreed to the incentive rate for grievance-processing time never anticipated that the clause governing this condition of employment would be used to support an overtime-pay grievance. But that is precisely how some grievances arise. Conflicts between clauses also produced questions such as: Does a new clause giving employees time-and-a-half for working on Saturday "as such" mean that they are entitled to premium holiday pay when the holiday falls on Saturday? Does a cost-of-living bonus recently added to base pay increase vacation allowances by that amount? Does a provision giving a steward immunity from layoff also mean that his rate cannot be cut? These are a few typical questions that have arisen because of an apparent conflict between clauses in the same agreement.

The omission of words may be just as critical as their presence. When a contract provides for seniority in layoff, recall, promotion, choice of vacation dates, and a half dozen other provisions of the agreement, was it purposeful or an oversight that there is no mention of length of service in the overtime clause? The answer may depend in part on the history of bargaining. A long-standing relationship between the parties, and a contract that shows a high degree of refinement, may well lead to a presumption of sophistication —the conclusion that the contract said exactly what the parties intended it to say and that the omission of seniority in the overtime provision was deliberate. A first agreement, on the other hand, especially one negotiated by inexperienced persons, might well lead an arbitrator to the opposite conclusion. Modern collective bargaining agreements, however imperfect, are not the primitive documents that they once were. Undoubtedly, this has something to do with the fact that what is known as the "doctrine of sophistication" is expressed more often in recent awards than in decisions of arbitrators shortly after World War II.

Partly for the reasons indicated above, but mostly because collective bargaining agreements are administered by scores of individuals who may have special interests to serve, past practice always plays an important part in union contract interpretation. But past practices are of many kinds, and not all equal in persuasive force. Where the contract is silent on a matter, for instance, an arbitrator will be most reluctant to upset an established practice. Similarly, where language is ambiguous, so that no clear intent of the parties can be derived from it, consistent past practice will be taken as some evidence of the parties' probable intent. At the other extreme—that is, where the contract is seemingly clear—past practice will certainly have less influence upon the arbitrator's decision. But even here, if the past practice was known to both parties and was consistently applied over a long period of time, arbitrators may sometimes find that it had the effect of modifying the written terms of the agreement.

The purpose of this volume is to illustrate contract interpretation problems resolved by arbitrators in ten critical areas of employer-employee relations. The source material consists of several hundred awards rendered since January 1, 1959, by arbitrators in tribunals conducted under the auspices of the American Arbitration Association. The awards discussed were chosen because they highlighted typical problems of contract interpretation. Many available awards were omitted because they were too brief, or too lacking in detail to be useful for the instruction or guidance of others, or because they did not contain sufficient reference to the controlling contract language. Others were omitted because the decision turned almost entirely upon credibility of witnesses or upon subjective impressions on the part of the arbitrator. Such cases are unlikely to have much meaning to any but the parties directly concerned.

It should also be clear that no adverse inference is intended about the performance of arbitrators whose awards are not represented in this volume. Arbitration is a voluntary and adaptable process, responsive to the needs of the parties. The arbitrator who purposefully omits certain details or impressions from his written opinion because he knows such omissions will contribute to more harmonious labor-management relations is doing his part just as surely as the arbitrator who, with the same motives, finds it expedient to trace the background of the grievance in detail and show the reasoning process by which he came to his conclusion. In short, service to the particular parties, rather than the prospect of publication, is the primary concern of the arbitrator. Thus, the selection of awards for publication can hardly result in a scientific or completely balanced sample.

The cases are limited to those administered by the American Arbitration Association in accordance with the agreement of the parties to use this particular administrative agency. Parties fashion their arbitration procedures to suit their needs. Some permit "any grievance" to go to arbitration. Others prefer arbitrators to resolve only grievances over "interpretation and application of the contract." The latter, of course, creates a narrower jurisdiction.[2] Similarly, most parties specifically bar the arbitrator from adding to or modifying the agreement, a prohibition usually repeated by both sides at the hearing itself. But this limited view of the arbitrator's function is not shared by all. Arbitrators are sometimes specifically permitted to recommend new procedures or contract clauses; indeed, at times parties purposely select arbitrators because of their known inclination or ability to mediate as well as arbitrate. No statistics are available on the subject, but it is at least possible that those who prefer administered tribunals do so because they want arbitrators to observe the limits of their office more rigidly. If this be so, contract interpretation problems may be relatively more common in AAA cases than in *ad hoc* cases generally.

The cases discussed here are intended to illustrate problems that frequently arise and to tell how many professional arbitrators have resolved them. This volume is offered to the industrial relations community in that spirit.

---

[2] A typical grievance arbitration clause reads: "Any dispute, claim or grievance arising out of or relating to the interpretation or application of this agreement shall be submitted to arbitration under the Voluntary Labor Arbitration Rules of the American Arbitration Association. The parties further agree that there shall be no suspension of work when such dispute arises and while it is in process of adjustment or arbitration."

2

REDUCTION OF THE WORK FORCE

Few companies in American industry guarantee their employees an annual wage. Almost invariably, when production requirements fall, some employees lose work and wages. The form this loss takes is the subject matter of layoff and recall provisions in collective bargaining agreements.

Virtually every contract calls for the application of seniority in a reduction of the work force. But beyond this common characteristic, there is a great variety of procedures. In some establishments, work is shared to a limited extent before layoffs take place. In others, juniors are let go immediately, giving seniors a virtual guarantee of full time until it becomes their turn to be laid off. Many contracts have not one, but several, sets of procedures, depending upon whether the reduction in work is expected to be brief or of long duration. Seniority systems, too, have an influence. Some permit employees to "bump" into jobs of juniors only within their departments, while others make it possible for long-service workers to claim any job in the plant, provided they are capable of performing it with reasonable efficiency.

Especially in industries where the incidence of layoffs is high, union contracts tend to be more specific on the order of layoff and recall than they are about most other matters. Nevertheless, unanticipated questions inevitably arise, bringing matters of contract interpretation before arbitrators.

REDUCTION OF THE WORKWEEK AS AN
ALTERNATIVE TO LAYOFFS

At the *Socony Mobil Oil Company* (Independent Oil Workers)[1] the method used in reduction of force was made to depend upon

[1] 2 AAA 13.

the extent of that reduction: "Should conditions become such that a reduction in hours of work or a general reduction in the number of employees is necessary," the contract read, "there will be no general layoff until the number of hours of the workweek have been reduced. The amount of the reduction in the workweek shall be discussed and be a matter for negotiation between the company and the union."

In June 1958, 75 hourly paid employees out of a total of 1,950 were laid off. This followed by one month the "early retirement" of 68 employees, an action which the union called an "indirect layoff." Taken together, the union said, these constituted a "general" reduction in force, which should have resulted in discussions with the union, leading toward reduction of the workweek as an alternative. The employer denied that the layoff was general in nature.

"At this point," wrote Arbitrator Israel Ben Scheiber, "it should be obvious that the key word in the grievance is 'general' and that it is the Arbitrator's duty and responsibility to define and interpret that word, in the light of all the facts presented."

The arguments at the arbitration hearing began with what Mr. Scheiber called a "battle of semantics." The union produced five dictionary and legal definitions of "general," stressing its meaning as "miscellaneous," or as the antonym of "specific." Not to be outdone, management produced an encyclopedia definition by which "general" meant "related to a whole genus, kind or class."

Returning to the industrial relations issue at hand, the union said that the layoff was general in that it affected all employees in two particular categories. They were (1) all employees who were eligible for early retirement in 1959 and 1960, and (2) all employees hired on or after January 1, 1956.

The employer answered that whether a layoff was general or not depended upon the number of individuals affected in relation to the population of the bargaining unit. A mere 75 out of 1,950 employees was not a sufficiently large proportion.

It was significant that company and union representatives had on several occasions in the past discussed this very issue, and had not been able to agree on a definition of "general." At one point during contract negotiations a management spokesman had suggested that a layoff affecting 10 per cent would be "general." This figure was arrived at on the assumption that a reduction of the workweek from forty hours to thirty-six hours would amount to 10 per cent. The union favored a figure closer to 1 per cent. As no meeting of the minds was reached, the contract was permitted to stand without a precise definition, the parties apparently hoping it would not be necessary to invoke this clause.

Although the parties had not reached precise agreement, the nature of the discussions gave a clue to Mr. Scheiber's decision: "From the record, it is clear that the yardstick which both parties had in mind in measuring the meaning of 'general layoff' was 'numbers,' 'extensiveness' and 'proportion,'" in contrast to such categories as the union had called attention to. Furthermore, the union had cited an award by another arbitrator for other parties in which the adjective "mass" had repeatedly qualified the word "layoff." Thus, the very material which the union presented as favorable to itself established the criterion of numbers. "By no stretch of the imagination can the 3.8 percent layoff involved be regarded as a mass layoff," Mr. Scheiber concluded. "In any event, being convinced that numbers, rather than categories, was the determining factor in the thinking of the parties, this Arbitrator is impelled to the conclusion that the layoff of the 75 hourly rated employees was not a 'general reduction' in the number of employees."

Shortened Week Upheld

Roles were reversed at the *Lummus Company* (Office Employees International Union, AFL-CIO),[2] where the employer reduced weekly hours from forty to thirty-five, with a corresponding reduction in wages, while the union insisted that the proper way to deal with a reduction of business was to lay off an appropriate number of junior employees.[3]

The union contended that work-sharing in this manner violated provisions of the agreement which (1) declared it to be the intent of the parties "to set forth herein the basic agreement covering rates of pay, hours of work and conditions of employment to be observed between the parties hereto"; (2) defined "standard working days

---

[2] 5 AAA 24.

[3] Management had consulted the union about reducing the workweek, but on failing to get concurrence, directed the change unilaterally.

of the work week" as Monday through Friday and "standard working hours" as eight per day; and (3) provided for layoffs based on seniority. If the company were permitted to reduce the workweek in this manner, the union said, it would create the basis for still further reductions, with the result that all advantages of seniority would be lost.

Elsewhere in the contract, however, there were several provisions, seemingly unrelated to the work reduction problem, which shed light on the issue. Lloyd H. Bailer, the arbitrator in this case, found that (1) the holiday provision called for a full day's pay "not exceeding eight hours"; (2) the vacation clause defined a full working day as "not less than seven and not more than eight hours per day"; and (3) the sick leave clause referred to "the number of hours regularly scheduled for work up to a maximum of eight hours."

"These contract references," he said, "present a strong implication that a work day of less than eight hours is contemplated as permissible under the agreement. In any event it is apparent that the contract does not provide in clear and unambiguous terms that the minimum work day the company must schedule is eight hours, nor does it provide in those terms that the workweek may not be reduced below forty hours."

Finally, the language of the contract was observed to be identical with the language of the agreement of the same union and company for a unit of clerical employees in another city, where the agreement was applied in a manner urged by the company in the instant case.

Shortened Week Not Upheld

At the *Florence Pipe Foundry and Machine Company* (United Steelworkers of America, AFL-CIO),[4] the conclusions reached were quite different from those in the *Lummus* case, discussed above, despite management's reliance on arguments and reasoning similar to those presented by Mr. Bailer.

The fact that the *Lummus* case involved hourly rated employees, while the *Florence* case dealt with weekly salaried clerical workers, may have made the difference. Here Edward A. Lynch ruled that under a contract which (1) established "weekly salary rates" based on a forty-hour week, (2) barred changes in such rates "unless the

[4] 7 AAA 8.

parties mutually agree," and (3) called for departmental seniority in layoff, the company did not have the right to schedule clerical workers for thirty-two hours and pay them only for the hours worked.

The company's defense was that the phrase "scheduled for forty hours of work" in the workweek clause of the contract[5] implied that employees could be scheduled for hours other than forty as well. Furthermore, it was argued, a management prerogative clause, reserving to the employer "the right to relieve employees from duty because of lack of work," permitted reduction of the workweek.[6]

The grievance was upheld. However logical the company's contention might be, Mr. Lynch wrote, the result has been a schedule of thirty-two hours per week, resulting in less pay than the "weekly salary scale." This was in violation of a clause that read: "It is further agreed that no change in existing rates shall be put in effect unless the parties mutually agree." Therefore, the arbitrator concluded, "all the company's arguments must fall before the predominating mandate of the agreement that the grievants are granted a standard weekly salary rate when they work, which can only be changed by mutual agreement."

The remedy in this case is of considerable interest, although it does not appear from Mr. Lynch's written opinion that he regarded it as unusual in any way. The company was directed to compensate "all . . . bargaining unit employees who were scheduled and paid for less than forty hours per week, for the week of January 12, 1959 and thereafter for the difference between the rates at which they were paid and the standard weekly salary rates to which they were entitled in accordance with this award."

Thus, all employees, *including the juniors, who should have been laid off*, were given monetary relief. It was apparently Mr. Lynch's

[5] The text read: "Each weekly salary rate established under the foregoing paragraph 1 is recognized as the rate of fair pay for fair performance and is the established weekly rate of pay for an employee scheduled for 40 hours of work."

[6] The text of this clause read: "Management of the plant and the direction of the working forces, including the right to hire, suspend, or discharge for proper cause, or transfer, and the right to relieve employees from duties because of lack of work, or for other legitimate reasons, is vested exclusively in the Corporation."

view that if the junior employees were called in at all, they had a contractual right to a full week's pay.

Limited Remedy for Shortened Week

Rolf Valtin was called upon to arbitrate a similar remedy problem at *L. F. Grammes & Sons, Inc.* (United Steelworkers of America, AFL-CIO),[7] which he solved quite differently. Here, the contract seemed sufficiently explicit on the procedures to be followed in reduction-of-force situations. The agreement stated:

Whenever possible, working forces shall not be decreased as long as it is possible, through an equal division of work, to provide a minimum of thirty-two (32) hours work (Monday through Friday only) to each employee during a calendar week. Whenever it is impossible to divide work equally during any calendar week, employees with most seniority shall be entitled to the additional hours.

. . . .

Any deviations from this policy shall be by mutual agreement of the parties hereto and where there are questions because of a conflict between the rules as stated and the needs of the business so as to minimize changes that would cause higher operating costs, the Union Management Committee will collaborate and try to reach mutual agreement.

Despite this provision, management reduced the workweek in the two departments to less than sixteen hours during a certain week without seeking the union's concurrence. The company explained that the short week was caused by a sudden and unexpected change of orders from a customer; but this was found to be an inadequate defense, since management was specifically obligated to obtain the union's agreement in advance.

This brought Mr. Valtin to the remedy problem. The union had requested that all employees in those two departments be given back pay, so that all would have wages for thirty-two hours that week. This request was granted only in part.

In sustaining the union's position in principle, the Arbitrator is not holding that every one of the grievants is necessarily entitled to the claimed reimbursement. The company's obligation was not one of "finding" 32 hours of work for the entire workforce, but one of laying off a sufficient number of employees so that the *remaining* workforce would be provided with 32 hours of work. As pointed out at the hearing, it may well be

[7] 16 AAA 19.

that some of the grievants—consistent with the Agreement's seniority regulation—would themselves have been laid off.

Those employees who were given sixteen hours of work during a week when they should have been laid off were, therefore, not awarded any back pay.[8]

Shortened Week vs. Shortened Day

An interesting question of contract interpretation arose at *Fairbanks, Morse & Company* (United Steelworkers of America, AFL-CIO),[9] where the contract gave the employer the right to "decrease the scheduled hours down to thirty-two" as an alternative to layoff. But did this give him the right to reduce the workweek to thirty-five hours by scheduling seven hours per day, five days per week? The employer thought so. If hours could be reduced to thirty-two, he argued, why not to "any intermediate point" between thirty-two and forty?

Alex Elson explained why that could not be done. There were other provisions of the contract, he said, that defined a "regular day's work" as eight hours. Those provisions, dealing with overtime, holiday pay, compensation for jury service, vacation pay, and determination of probationary periods, would be deprived of their intended meaning if the company could alter the regular work day.

It is axiomatic in the construction of a provision of a collective bargaining agreement that it should be considered within the framework of the entire agreement and in relation to other provisions in the agreement germane to it. Did the company have the right under Section 6 of Article VII to change the work day from an eight-hour day to a seven-hour day? It is true that Section 6 of Article VII states that the company may reduce the work week "down to" 32 hours per week, but it does not follow that in bringing about the reduction in hours, the company can ignore the other provisions of the Agreement.

Did this decision mean that the contract guaranteed an eight-hour day? He answered that no such guarantee was implied. "All that results from this conclusion," he wrote, "is that the company must

---

[8] No inference is intended that arbitrators Lynch or Valtin would have decided each other's case differently. The former's decision applied to grievants on weekly salary schedules. The latter awarded in a case involving hourly scheduled workers. It may be that this was the decisive difference.

[9] 18 AAA 10.

schedule employees on an eight hour basis. In all situations in which it may now send employees home before the end of the regular work day it may continue to do so subject only to the call-in provisions."

As often happens in such cases, the employer's defense rested in part on his assertion that his actions were motivated by concern for the best interests of the employees. His course avoided a layoff, and made it possible for all employees to work every day. Mr. Elson conceded that management's motivations were beyond reproach. But if that has a bearing on the case at all, he said, it relates "solely to the remedy," not to the basic question of whether the contract had been violated.

No monetary remedy was awarded in this case. For one thing, the union had delayed filing a grievance, some employees having expressed a preference for the course management took. But most important, the arbitrator concluded, to award back pay would result in a "windfall" not warranted by the facts in this case.

The Arbitrator is by no means certain from the facts in this case that there was a loss of pay in the usual sense of the term. Had the company adopted a 32 hour week instead of a 35 hour week, the employees in fact may have received less compensation than they were paid. To now order the company to pay the employees for 40 hours, although they only worked 35 hours, would result in a windfall.

NOTICE OF IMPENDING LAYOFF

Collective bargaining agreements often require the employer to give employees advance notice of layoff. One object is to give employees who have the seniority and ability for it the chance to claim other jobs, and thereby avoid layoff. At the same time, such advance notice helps management discover and correct any errors in scheduling layoffs before a financial obligation is incurred.

The need for layoffs is not always easy to foresee. Sudden cancellation of orders, machinery breakdowns, unexpected shortages of materials, and other such circumstances may interrupt production briefly, giving management itself no advance warning. Contracts, therefore, sometimes distinguish between temporary layoffs and others, expected to be of longer duration. But what happens when employees are laid off for reasons that are permanent and temporary at the same time? That was the circumstance at the *American Radiator and Standard Sanitary Corporation* (United Automobile Workers, AFL-CIO).[10]

The contract seemed very clear. Paragraph 57, dealing with permanent layoffs, read:

When an employee is subject to layoff from the plant caused by reduction in force, he shall be notified at least two working days prior to the date the layoff is to be made, except that notice given any time on the first working day will be considered a full day's notice.

But in case of layoffs of short duration, Paragraphs 95 and 96 applied:

The company may, at its option, make a temporary reduction in force within any occupation in any department on any shift in line of seniority. Such temporary layoffs may be made without advance notice, but shall not exceed five days for any employee in any occupation in any department on any shift in any calendar month. It is understood that if the need for a temporary layoff continues beyond one day (24) hours, the available work will be distributed equally within occupations.

An employee on a temporary layoff shall be subject to the same layoff procedure as other employees who are still working.

The circumstances out of which the grievance arose were interesting. In November 1959, two employees were notified that they were to be laid off "permanently" four days later. A few hours later, however, because of a parts shortage in another department, they were given fifteen minutes' notice of a temporary layoff. As one layoff merged into the other, it seemed to these employees that they had, in effect, been laid off permanently with practically no notice at all.

According to the union, Paragraphs 57 and 95 could not be applied simultaneously. The latter was intended to relieve management of the obligation to put laborious procedures into motion for a temporary layoff, when employees are expected to return to work very soon. It could not be used to deprive employees of the formal notice before permanent layoff. As a remedy, it was requested that the grievants be recalled to work for two days before resuming their layoff status.

Denying that any violation of the contract had occurred, the com-

[10] 4 AAA 5.

pany argued that the union's interpretation would lead to an anomalous result. It was pointed out that, inasmuch as two juniors had already been notified of the permanent layoff when the parts shortage appeared, it would presumably have been necessary to lay off *seniors* temporarily. Furthermore, the union's interpretation would deprive the company of the right to effect temporary layoffs on Wednesdays, Thursdays, and Friday of weeks when a permanent layoff was imminent.

Finding testimony about past practice "conflicting" and "equally convincing," Ronald W. Haughton arbitrated the case entirely on the basis of the contract language:

While the temporary layoff provision cannot be used as a means of subverting the regular layoff provisions of the contract, it can be used if a situation arises which would otherwise warrant a temporary layoff as provided in Paragraph 95. This means that the company cannot arbitrarily and capriciously declare a temporary layoff after it has given notice of a regular layoff, but it can do so in a particular area if shortages, breakdowns or other emergencies occur.

The union had conceded that if a temporary layoff had been caused by a true emergency, such as a plant-wide power failure, there would have been no basis for a grievance. Mr. Haughton answered that the contract did not contain any language distinguishing among reasons for temporary layoffs:

Since there is no language in Paragraph 95 to the effect that a temporary layoff can be declared only in the case of circumstances clearly beyond the control of the company, such as are frequently referred to as "Acts of God," the arbitrator has no authority to read it in. The fact is that Paragraph 95 provides that the company may, *at its option,* make a temporary reduction in force as provided therein.

The very fact that the call-in pay provision of the contract contained "a clear reference to conditions beyond the company's control" made it evident, he concluded, that the omission of such language in Paragraph 95 "must be regarded as significant and meaningful."

Conflict of Notice and Call-in Pay Clauses

The connection between notice-in-layoff clauses and call-in pay provisions is a close one, in ways additional to those noted above.

These two clauses were in apparent conflict at the *Simmons Company* (Upholsterers' International Union, AFL-CIO),[11] where a number of employees, who had started work at 7:00 A.M., were sent home when a power failure occurred at 10:20 A.M.

If they were temporarily laid off, as the union asserted, they would be entitled to four hours' pay in lieu of notice, in accordance with this provision:

It is mutually agreed in temporary layoffs that no less than four (4) working hours notice will be given. On permanent layoffs ample notice is to be given but in no event will the notice of permanent layoffs be less than one (1) week.

On the other hand, if the call-in pay provision were applicable to this situation, the employees would be entitled to pay until 11:00 A.M., and management would have the right to assign them to other work for the forty minutes that remained to complete four hours of work. The call-in pay clause read:

When an employee reports for work at the regular starting time of his shift without previous notice not to report and his regular work is not available for him, he will receive a minimum of four (4) hours work or pay at the rate provided in the applicable local Plant Supplement, pro-vided, however, that at the Company's option, he may be assigned to an-other job for any portion of said four (4) hours, in which event he will be paid the rate provided in the applicable Local Plant Supplement for whatever time is spent at that job. The Company shall have no liability regarding the above paragraph in the event of a breakdown of power outside of plant or if inside of plant and not maintained by the Company, general plant fire, act of God, act of public enemy, or because of conditions beyond the control of the Company.

Murray M. Rohman resolved this dispute in favor of the union. The call-in pay provision, relied upon by the company, was intended for occasions when employees suffered inconvenience through management's failure to notify them not to report. Although the temporary-layoff provision did not define the circumstances under which temporary layoffs occur, he said, such circumstances could include "lack of work arising from insufficient orders, materials not being available, a breakdown of facilities, a lack of skilled labor preventing utilization of existing plant equipment, or any number

[11] 16 AAA 18.

of reasons which, if not excluded, are deemed under the control of management."[12]

"Conditions Beyond Control of Management"

Dealing with a similar conflict between a call-in pay provision and a notice-in-layoff clause at *Rollway Bearings Company* (United Automobile Workers, AFL-CIO),[13] Robert F. Koretz also came to the conclusion that the latter applied. But because work was unavailable for a reason beyond management's control, the company was not required to give employees pay in lieu of notice. Consequently, the outcome of the case was a victory for the union on principle, without any monetary advantage.

Under the notice-in-layoff clause (Article VIII) two work days' notice (or pay in lieu of notice) had to be given prior to a temporary layoff except "where conditions are beyond the control of management." The call-in pay provision (Article XIV), on the other hand, required that "no employee shall be sent home with less than four hours pay, computed at the regular job level rate, unless notified the previous day." This provision, too, contained an escape clause: "This Article shall not apply where conditions are beyond the control of management."

The conflict between these two articles of the contract became apparent on February 12, 1959, when a surface grinder was told that because of material shortage in the heat treat department, he would not be needed the next day. From the employer's point of view, the employee was "notified the previous day," and therefore had no claim for four hours' call-in pay. But the union said the situation was covered by Article VIII, dealing with temporary layoffs. As two days' notice was required and only one day was given, a full day's pay was due.

It was clear that there was "some internal inconsistency" in the

---

[12] Although the grievance was sustained, the union was not upheld in its view that the four hours' pay due in lieu of notice had to be computed from 11:00 A.M. As the employees had been permitted to remain in the plant until 11:00 A.M., and were paid for that time, Mr. Rohman said, "it follows that the company's obligation would be fulfilled if it gave such four hours' notice commencing with 10:20 A.M., when the power failure developed."

[13] 12 AAA 13.

agreement. Consequently, the arbitrator said, it was of little help to argue, as the company had done, that if the union's position should be sustained, Article XIV would be rendered "nugatory and ineffectual." There was "some truth" in that contention, but "it can be argued at least with equal force that acceptance of the company's position would go far toward rendering nugatory and ineffectual the two-day notice provision of Article VIII." Therefore, he concluded, "it becomes necessary to seek other aids to construction in order to determine which of the provisions respectively relied upon controls the dispute."

The determination as to which of the conflicting clauses "is in plain language directly applicable to this dispute," led to the conclusion that the union's position was more valid. For Mr. Koretz pointed out, as had Mr. Rohman in the *Simmons* case, discussed above, that the call-in clause relied on by the employer could be applied to the instant facts only by implication, while the notice-in-layoff clause on which the grievance was based seemed to cover the facts directly.

Part of the employer's contention was found to have merit, but not exactly in the way management intended. It had been argued that two days' notice was required only where, as was not the case here, the layoff was foreseeable. "I cannot find that the lack of foreseeability of itself precludes the applicability of Article VIII," Mr. Koretz wrote. But Article VIII itself contains an exception when conditions were "beyond the control of management."[14] He was

---

[14] Mr. Koretz found nothing in the agreement which defined the phrase "beyond the control of management." But on the basis of his study of arbitration awards and court decisions, he said, the following definition of "beyond control" seems most sensible: "We are of the opinion that the phrase comes nearer to being synonymous with 'unavoidably prevented,' and that it can hardly be the equivalent of what is called the act of God; but it cannot mean less than that there must have interposed some hindrance which the . . . company, as the actor party, could not foresee or overcome by the reasonable exercise of its powers and the use of the means and appliances that were, or in the exercise of commensurate care should have been, available. What is meant is that the happening must not have been occasioned in any degree by the want of such foresight, care, and skill as the law holds one in like circumstances bound to exercise. The words 'beyond control' fairly imply a pledge to exercise human agencies to the point of excluding negligence under the above test, and if this be true human agencies are not excluded from consideration as factors" [*California Spruce Co. v. Black Mountain R. Co.*, 201 S.W. 154, 156 (Tenn. 1918)].

satisfied by the evidence that the cause of layoff was not, as the union had suggested, "negligence of management."

Unusual Conditions

At the *Alan Wood Steel Company* (United Steelworkers of America, AFL-CIO)[15] the clause relieving management of an obligation to give advance notice of layoff referred to "unusual conditions," not merely conditions beyond the control of management. The question which James C. Hill had to resolve, therefore, was whether the low level of ore supplies over a period of months was such an "unusual condition."

Before addressing himself to this question, however, Mr. Hill had to dispose of the union's first contention that layoffs on three separated days were in themselves improper, quite apart from whether advance notice had to be given. The union argued that the layoffs were motivated not by economic necessity but by an attempt to influence new contract negotiations then in progress and to punish certain employees who were accused of engaging in a slow-down. Management denied that this was the reason for the layoffs, but admitted that productivity had fallen during the preceding months. The real reason for the layoffs, company spokesmen asserted, was that "pockets were low in muck" and that, with the low level of production among "trimming crews," there was little prospect of raising the level of muck.

Mr. Hill disposed of this preliminary issue in favor of management. "The union bears a burden of demonstrating that the company has exceeded its broad authority," he wrote, "and it would not be sufficient merely to argue that the company's business judgment was poor or its actions ill-advised."

The arbitrator then resumed discussion of the notice-in-layoff aspect of the case. Was the low level of muck in ore pockets on March 4, July 17, and July 21, 1959, caused by an "unusual condition" such as to make inoperative the usual notice requirement? Mr. Hill said it was not:

If the conditions leading to the layoffs were thoroughly unpredictable, and the company suddenly and without warning found itself with no

[15] 21 AAA 20.

muck to run the mill, the situation might reasonably be considered exempt from the requirement of advance notice. If, however, the company were faced with low supplies of ore to the pockets over a period of months, the situation becomes subject to some prediction and control.

Inasmuch as management had the right to close down operations when materials were not forthcoming, he concluded, "it bears a responsibility of so scheduling the work as to be able to give the notice contemplated in the agreement." In other words, in this case, management *was* guilty of "negligence," as management of the *Rollway Bearings Company* had not been.

Limited Monetary Remedy

But here too, as in the *Rollway* case, the remedy was not exactly what the union had asked for. "The union demands a full day's pay for each layoff to all employees affected," Mr. Hill explained. This, he said, would be an "excessive" remedy for three reasons. First, the union's demand was made in conjunction with the claim that the layoffs were themselves improper. This aspect of the grievance was denied. Secondly, the purpose of the notice-in-layoff clause seemed to be to permit the union to perform its "proper function" of enforcing seniority rules in cases of layoffs extending beyond three days. Here, the layoffs affected single shifts and were caused by "unpredictable" conditions. Even if seniority were to apply to such a situation, only the most senior employees, not all the laid-off employees, suffered damages. And, finally, "to award eight hours' pay for failure to give seventy-two hours' notice would seem to be inconsistent with the reporting pay provision." If the employee reports for work and finds none available, he would be entitled to four hours' pay. "It seems quite inconsistent to hold that the failure to give notice three days in advance should lead to an award of greater damages."

As "equitable relief," Mr. Hill directed that employees affected by the three layoffs should receive four hours' pay for each occasion when they were laid off without notice. This payment was to be "inclusive of, and not in addition to" any call-in pay that might be due under the reporting pay provision of the agreement.

Notice in Layoff Caused by Strike

A strike called by the Mail Deliverers' Union against all daily newspapers in New York on December 8, 1958, made it necessary for the management of the *News Syndicate Company* (International Association of Machinists, AFL-CIO)[16] to lay off truck maintenance employees about a week later. The contract provided for a week's notice in layoff, and contained no language limiting application of this notice provision for unusual circumstances. The employer nevertheless believed that notice was not required in the circumstances of the case. The layoff was made effective at the end of the shift following posting of a notice on December 18. As the phrasing of the notice was to become an issue at the hearing, conducted by Robert L. Stutz, the language is quoted in full.

To Our Employees:

The continuation of the strike by the Newspaper and Mail Deliverers' Union of New York and Vicinity, which commenced December 9, 1958, against the publishers of nine New York newspapers, compels The News to make further reductions in staff. Under existing conditions publication of The News is neither practically possible nor economically justified. As you know publication has been temporarily suspended.

Since there is no work for most of our employees while this temporary suspension continues, you are directed not to report to work until further notice. Your compensation ceased as of the last shift worked.

Employees whose services are required will be notified regarding their assignments and only such employees will be paid for services performed during the period of temporary suspension.

We emphasize that this is not notice of termination of your employment, but is only a notice of a period during which there is no work to be performed. You will be informed when you are to return to work.

The management of The News regrets that this situation has been forced upon it.

The News

Citing the contract clauses which read:

9. The Union agrees that there shall be no interruption of work by strike during the life of this Agreement and the Publisher agrees that there shall be no interruption as a result of a lockout of the members of this Union. In the event of a general layoff because of a labor dis-

---

[16] 17 AAA 9.

pute with another Union, the Publisher shall have the right to cover the garages for maintenance and safety purposes.

11. The size of the force shall be determined by the Publisher. If it becomes necessary to reduce the force in any classification, the men or man with the least seniority in that classification, regardless of location, shall be the first to go. Men so affected shall be given one (1) week's notice. They shall also be offered re-employment in the order of seniority if a restoration of the force takes place within one (1) year.

the union demanded five days' pay in lieu of notice.[17] The issue thus was whether, on December 18, the garage maintenance employees were subjected to a reduction in force, a layoff, or some other kind of separation from work. Mr. Stutz found the answer in the notice the publisher had posted, which spoke of "no work for most of our employees."

It was also significant, Mr. Stutz said, that the one man retained in each garage was selected by seniority. This suggested that the parties were in agreement that Paragraph 11, quoted above, applied at least to this extent, although there was no agreement as to whether the reduction in force was of the kind the contract contemplated.

Returning to the publisher's notice, Mr. Stutz found certain other phrases significant. In particular, he observed that the word "staff" was used synonymously with "force." Although this was "doubtless an inadvertence on the part of the person who drafted the notice," he said, it points up the "semantical dilemma" one faces when trying to explain what happened on December 18 in terms other than of a reduction in force.

It seems apparent that, if upon resumption of publication it was decided by the Publisher that only 50% of the employees in the garages would be required during the first two weeks of publication, the determination as to who should be recalled first would be made on the basis of seniority. Again there is no guide in Section 9 for this determination; rather the guide is found in Section 11.

The final question was whether it would have been impractical or

[17] The union's grievance also requested pay for Christmas and New Year's Day, which fell during the period of idleness. This aspect of the case is discussed in Chapter 7.

"unreasonably onerous" to apply the notice requirement of Section 11 to the fact situation.

Obviously, it was possible for the Publisher to give proper notice on December 10th or 11th, since the employees worked until December 18. The Publisher alone could determine how much repair and maintenance work should be done and how many employees were needed to do it. If the acknowledged purpose of the notice requirement was to be served, these employees were entitled to proper notice as to when their layoff would occur. There is nothing impractical or onerous in this interpretation.

Layoff vs. Staff Reduction

Circumstances brought about by the same strike of the Mail Deliverers' Union resulted in a grievance of editorial and clerical workers at the *New York Herald-Tribune*[18] (American Newspaper Guild, AFL-CIO).[19] Calling attention to a clause requiring up to four weeks' notice of dismissal or "staff reduction," the union demanded pay in lieu of notice to employees who, although willing to cross the picket lines, were laid off without notice a few days after the strike began when the paper suspended publication.

David L. Cole ruled that the clause relied upon by the union was intended to cover force reductions brought about as a matter of management judgment "based on economic considerations." It did not apply to "a complete or partial suspension of operations" resulting from an "effective strike." In particular, he rejected the contention that the grievants were in effect dismissed in a staff reduction. The layoff of the grievants did not constitute "terminations of employment" within the "ordinary meaning" of those words.

"To convert such an obviously temporary suspension into a mass of wholesale discharges or dismissals of the employees would indeed require a maneuver in semantics," he wrote. Furthermore, the reference to dismissals in the clause dealing with notice in force reductions did not mean, as the union asserted, that reductions in force could not be accomplished by means other than dismissals. Finally,

[18] All other New York daily newspapers, organized in the New York Newspaper Publishers' Association, were also parties to this case. The award applied to all, based on the reasoning set forth by the arbitrator in the *New York Herald-Tribune* case.

[19] 23 AAA 1.

Mr. Cole said, this decision is consistent with most decisions in cases of this kind in the newspaper publishing industry.

The union put forward supplementary arguments in favor of paying the grievants for their lost time. It was urged that having been ready and willing to cross the mail deliverers' picket line, the grievants were serving the employer on a "stand-by basis." Furthermore, union representatives at the arbitration insisted, to deny the employees pay for this time would create an economic hardship, inasmuch as they could not know how long their inactive status would continue, and were therefore unable to arrange for other income.

These contentions, too, were rejected by Mr. Cole: "Essentially, this claim of the [union] partakes of the nature of a guaranteed wage," he wrote. "It is possible to have this, but only by affirmative and definite contract provisions. I know of no guaranteed wage achieved by the indirect means of interpretation by an arbitrator."

THE ORDER OF LAYOFFS

When the work force must be reduced, contractual provisions giving senior employees preference for the remaining jobs are put to a severe practical test. From the union's point of view, application of seniority rules are expected to be a guarantee against favoritism and an assurance that the layoffs will be used by management neither as an opportunity to get rid of less desirable employees nor as an occasion to tighten work requirements. Management, on the other hand, needs flexibility to prevent inefficient use of manpower during periods of curtailed production and to avoid payment of wages for time not worked.

Assembly Line Shutdown

The conflicting interests of labor and management and the requirements of a seniority-in-layoff provision proved difficult to reconcile at the *Magnavox Company of Tennessee* (International Union of Electrical, Radio and Machine Workers, AFL-CIO),[20] when whole assembly lines were closed down. As each worker completed his task on the last chassis, he punched out. But employees

[20] 13 AAA 17.

were not assigned to the lines in accordance with their seniority. It inevitably followed that seniors occasionally worked on their last chassis and ran out of work before juniors. According to management, this involved no contract violation as long as juniors and seniors were laid off *during the same day.* In other words, said the employer, it was permissible to lay off a senior at 2 P.M., when he ran out of work, as long as the man junior to him was laid off at 3 P.M. of the same day.[21] The alternative, management thought, would be chaos, particularly as it was necessary to schedule work so that each employee would have at least four hours, if reporting pay penalties were to be avoided.

This problem was not a new one. Company and union representatives had discussed it at least six months before the arbitration hearing, when other grievances had been filed. Recognizing the company's problem, the union had offered, as a compromise, not to process grievances where only one hour was involved. This was apparently not acceptable to management.

The arbitrator, A. R. Marshall, said that the contract undoubtedly means what the union says it does: "in layoffs due to a reduction of forces the youngest seniority employee shall be laid off first." But it also seemed clear to him that when the parties negotiated the contract they were not thinking about seniority problems that would arise when an assembly line is closed down. "Otherwise, some provision might have been made to reconcile the seniority rights of employees with the difficulties encountered by the company in laying off employees without detriment to efficient operations."

His conclusion was that when a senior employee is laid off up to two hours earlier than a junior within a layoff day, it should be regarded as *de minimis.* Any loss in excess of two hours was to be made good by payment for the time. This decision, he said, "indirectly requires that the company shall make an effort to do some advance planning so that the principle of seniority in layoffs will be observed as strictly as possible."[22]

---

[21] According to the union's grievance, there were occasions when juniors worked as much as four hours after seniors were sent home.

[22] In the course of the arbitration, management argued that its practice had been in effect "for a long time," and that the union had not always complained. This did not mean, Mr. Marshall wrote, that the union had accepted a past practice and was foreclosed from protesting now: "The fact that some violation

Intershift Bumping

Another case turning on management's contention that observance of the contract was impractical was that of *Merrill-Stevens Dry Dock & Repair Company* (Industrial Union of Marine and Shipbuilding Workers, AFL-CIO).[23]

The contract called for the layoff and the rehiring of "first class skilled employees" by departments and classifications, "provided the particular employee has the ability and the physical capacity to do the work." Under this clause, it was apparently permissible for a qualified skilled employee facing layoff on one shift to bump into another. But did that mean that the transfer had to be made on the very day the layoff occurred?

The employer's view was that when layoffs affect more than one shift, seniority within the shift applies during the first day of layoff. Only on the next day could a man assert his company-wide seniority to claim a job on another shift. To do otherwise, the company said, would be impractical and would result in absenteeism and loss of production.

If the language of the clause governing layoffs were considered by itself, Paul W. Hardy said, the union would have to be upheld. However, it was necessary to examine other provisions of the contract as well.[24] He found a clause which "clearly sets forth premium pay penalties which must be assumed when they change an employee's shift hours without the benefit of a twenty-four hour notice." As it would create "double jeopardy" to require the employer to permit an employe to take two shifts in one day, it seemed logical that the company was correct in its view of the contract and past practice: "The Arbitrator finds that layoffs resulting from reduction of force can be made on a shift basis in accordance with seniority

---

of the contract has not been protested by the employees or the union does not mean at all that the latter has accepted a procedure whereby the company does not honor division seniority in layoffs arising out of reductions in forces."

[23] 18 AAA 23.

[24] The employer asserted the existence of a practice in favor of his interpretation. The union denied knowledge of the alleged practice and answered that, in any event, actions which constitute a violation of the contract would not be pertinent. Mr. Hardy said that "this controversial testimony" made it necessary for him to look to other provisions of the agreement for help.

for the first day only when such layoffs affect employees working on more than one shift."

CONFLICT OF "SUPERSENIORITY" AND LAYOFF CLAUSES

As will be seen in the chapter on stewards and union officers, unions often obtain superseniority rights for stewards, permitting these employees to remain at work, where they may perform their grievance-processing functions, regardless of their natural seniority. In return for this concession, employers sometimes obtain the right to place on an exempt-from-layoff list an equal number of junior employees who are judged essential to production.

An interesting case growing out of such an arrangement was that of *Sun-Chief Electronics, Inc.* (International Union of Electrical, Radio and Machine Workers, AFL-CIO).[25] The two clauses, balancing each other off, were:

The Union shall have the right to designate from the seniority list a number of employees of the Company with at least one year of seniority, said number in no case to be more than $2\frac{1}{2}\%$ of the total number of employees in the bargaining unit, whether stewards, committeemen, or officers, to be placed at the head of the seniority list for the term of office.

and,

The Company shall likewise have the right to designate a number of employees of the Company with at least one year of seniority, said number in no case to be more than $2\frac{1}{2}\%$ of the total number of employees in the bargaining unit, to be placed at the head of the seniority list, said employees to consist of employees who, because of their special training, or exceptional ability, are deemed by the Company to be essential to the continuance of production.

Shortly after these clauses were negotiated, the employer named a certain junior as essential to production and placed him at the head of the seniority list as Setup Man A in the press department. As a consequence, an employee with ten years of seniority was laid off.

A grievance was filed in which the union asserted that the favored

[25] 19 AAA 19.

junior had no more ability as a setup man than anyone else. Placing him at the head of the seniority list was, therefore, a violation of the agreement. The employer conceded that he was no more qualified than two other setup men with more natural seniority, but insisted that the junior had demonstrated an "aptitude in handling men," which made him "good material for a supervisory job." It was part of management's plan, witnesses testified, to keep the junior at work so that he might substitute for the foreman, if the latter should become ill.

This defense was beside the point, Saul Wallen ruled. It may well have been that the junior surpassed others in qualities of leadership, in which event management ought to have promoted him to foreman, a position outside the bargaining unit. But it "runs counter" to the clause providing for superseniority "to argue that a man is 'essential to the continuance of production' because he may at some time in the future make a good foreman."[26]

Junior with "Specialized Knowledge"

A problem of a different kind was presented at the *Vertol Aircraft Corporation* (United Automobile Workers, AFL-CIO),[27] where superseniority was given to a junior who admittedly had "specialized knowledge of a particular job," within the language of the contract. The question was, however, whether the company had the right to retain this junior during a period of layoff when there was another employee—one with greater natural seniority—who also had specialized knowledge.

The union's view was that management's right to place employees on the layoff-deferral list was governed not only by the clause setting up that list but by the seniority clause as well. The latter stated that "whenever the skill and ability of two or more employees are equal to do the work then required, seniority shall govern." Accord-

---

[26] The man with ten years of seniority who had been laid off was therefore entitled to back pay. But inasmuch as he had declined to bump into a lower-rated job, he was awarded not full back pay, but only the difference between his regular rate and the rate of the job he should have taken. Mr. Wallen said the grievant had an obligation "to mitigate his losses by accepting [the lower rated job] pending prosecution of the instant case." The employer's back pay obligation was further to be reduced by "any sum recovered from unemployment compensation."

[27] 15 AAA 6.

ingly, union representatives argued, the selection of employees for
the deferred list must be based on seniority whenever the junior,
although qualified, was not more so than the senior.

Lewis M. Gill upheld management.

I think it is clear that the union is wrong. The obvious purpose of [the
deferred list clause] is to allow the company a free hand in selecting a
limited number of key people to be *exempt* from the general seniority
principles laid down in Section 1, subject only to the requirement that
those selected fit into one of the specified categories. To say that there
is a *further* limitation on the company's freedom of selection—a requirement that the general seniority provisions must govern the selection—
seems clearly to be reading in something which is simply not there.

In some words of "clarification," expressing a view similar to that
of Mr. Wallen in the *Sun-Chief Electronics* case, he added that an
employee placed on the deferred list must be shown to have "*special*" knowledge for the work. "This means more than simply 'ability
to do the work'—it means that there must be some *special* knowledge over and above the general qualifications possessed by all the
employees in the classification involved." But where two or more
employees have that special knowledge "there is no requirement
that the company follow seniority in making the selection for the
deferred list."

Conflict with "Skill and Ability" Clause

At the *Plume & Atwood Manufacturing Company* (Mine, Mill
and Smelter Workers),[28] management had the right to exempt from
layoff as many employees of "exceptional value" as the union named
on a stewards' superseniority list, which, in the spring of 1960, numbered twelve. The contract also contained another provision, under
which seniority was to prevail in layoffs "with due consideration
given to skill and ability to do the required work."

These two clauses seemed to be in conflict when reductions of
the work force became necessary. The union argued that the company could retain a total of twelve employees exempted from seniority regulations, under all the provisions of the contract. The
company answered that it could retain twelve of "exceptional value"
under one provision, and as many juniors as necessary under the

[28] 24 AAA 2.

other provision, where it was found that the seniors could not do the available work.

James C. Hill, called upon to arbitrate this dispute, agreed with the company. The two clauses were "independent" of each other, he wrote. "This is an inescapable conclusion from every standpoint —logic, purpose and collective bargaining interests and relationship of the parties." Provided the employee is capable of doing the work, the clause calling for seniority in layoffs is "customary" and a "virtually necessary" provision of agreements, he said. Under the seniority provision of the contract, the company's choice "is governed by seniority and ability," with the union having the right to protest that senior men could in fact do the work. But under the super-seniority provision, he concluded, "the company has discretion to choose the men they wish and the union can not challenge the selection."

Deferral from Layoff of Handicapped Junior

When a contract provides for a certain order of layoffs, employers may not be permitted to depart from that order even for an admittedly humane reason. A case in point was that of the *Wayne Pump Company* (United Automobile Workers, AFL-CIO),[29] where the employer wanted to exempt from layoff a junior employee who had lost an arm in an industrial accident. The union, while agreeing with management that the injured worker needed to be helped emotionally and economically, nevertheless feared that its position would be jeopardized in the future if it permitted the contract to be disregarded now. Furthermore, what the employer was trying to do placed the burden on a senior employee, who would be laid off out of turn.[30]

Arbitrator John Perry Horlacher described the union's dilemma:

From the union's comments at the hearing it was clear that it also was fully sympathetic with [the injured man's] special needs and desirous of meeting them, but it was fearful of going along with the company by not

[29] 20 AAA 13.

[30] During grievance processing, the union had suggested that the handicapped worker be transferred to the office (outside the bargaining unit), or be given janitorial work, which was governed by a different seniority system. Management found neither suggestion feasible.

pressing a grievance because of the potential liability under the newly enacted Landrum-Griffin Act.

Regretfully, Mr. Horlacher upheld the grievance. The employer's motives were "laudable," but they constituted "insufficient reason for condoning a deliberate contract violation." He pointed out that an arbitrator is "not free to redraft labor agreements in particular situations in order to accomplish what all parties might consider an equitable and just result." He feared that if he were to uphold the company, it might "open a Pandora's box," freeing either party "to define the extraordinary situation which it thinks will justify disregard of the agreement." Any departure from the terms of the contract, he said, would have to come about through the mutual agreement of the parties, not by arbitration.

The company had a further argument, in addition to the view that this was an "extraordinary" situation, warranting disregard of the contract. It contended that the handicapped worker had been given "made work," which would not have been given the senior employee in any event. This argument was "not sound," Mr. Horlacher wrote. "If, as the company says, it is able in such situations to permit one more man to work, under the contract only the most senior man is entitled to this permissive and optional job. In the contract sense, someone was hurt and is entitled to redress."[31]

---

[31] For a somewhat similar line of reasoning, see Chapter 9 for the decision of Archibald Cox in the *Electric Storage Battery Co.* case, 19 AAA 22, where the employer tried to rectify an error in the assignment of overtime by offering "made work" to a by-passed employee.

3

SENIORITY AND ABILITY

Contract clauses providing for application of both seniority and ability in promotions, bumping, recall, and voluntary job transfers are often difficult to interpret for one chief reason: seniority is capable of exact measurement, whereas ability seldom is. Few negotiators of collective bargaining agreements attempt to describe the ability factor so fully as to eliminate the possibility of future disputes. Indeed, it is doubtful that such precision is possible, for the relative weight of the ability factor in the seniority and ability combination tends to shift, depending on the purpose for which seniority is asserted. An employee may be thought efficient enough to hold his job or return to it from layoff, for instance, but he might be found unfit to bump another out of a similar job.

When parties agree that senior employees will be promoted "provided they have the ability," they may be expressing a meeting of minds which they find more convenient not to describe in greater detail. On the other hand, there may have been no meeting of the minds at all. Under the pressure of having to conclude negotiations on wages, hours, fringe benefits, and other substantive matters, company and union representatives may simply have relied upon a standard phrase, knowing that each side interprets it differently, but hoping that the issue will not arise in practice.

THE RELATIVE WEIGHT OF ABILITY

Contracts providing for both seniority and ability do not necessarily give equal weight to each element. At the *Kidde Manufacturing Company* (International Union of Electrical, Radio and Machine Workers, AFL-CIO),[1] the emphasis was clearly on ability:

The company will, whenever possible, give preference to its senior em-

[1] 15 AAA 18.

ployees and will, subject to the company's final decision on qualifications, discuss possible employee applicants with the union committee.

A problem arose when two applicants for promotion proved to be qualified. Did the company have to select the senior? Could the employer appoint the more qualified junior? The company took the second course, and Emanuel Stein, the arbitrator, said it was correct under the contract. The company had the right to fill a vacancy with the employee who had "greater qualifications," he said, even though the senior "had the ability to do the work." The arbitrator found no basis for the union's interpretation, which would give the job to the senior if he had "minimum qualifications." Neither the contract nor past practice supported that view:

In this case, it appears that the company has in the past exercised its discretion in respect to the qualifications of employees without being bound to select the senior employee who met the minimum standards for a position. Its "final decision on qualifications" has been construed, in the past, to vest authority in the company to select the employee it considered best qualified. Presumably, the union did not like such a construction, but there is no evidence that it ever previously resorted to the grievance procedure and arbitration to get a definitive interpretation of "qualifications."

Although upholding the company on the chief point at issue, Mr. Stein found the company in default of that part of the quoted clause that required discussion of possible employee applicants with the union committee. That management knew the grievant was interested in the promotion and had been promised that his name would be considered did not satisfy the agreement or justify the failure to discuss the matter with the union. "Unilateral consideration, however objective, is no substitute for discussion," he concluded. As the company had the right "to select the employee it regarded as best qualified for the position," however, Mr. Stein said it would be "beyond the power of the arbitrator" to award the job to the grievant.[2]

[2] For another example of a case where the company was found in violation of a contract clause requiring discussion of a matter on which management had the right to make the final decision, see *Alco Products, Inc.* (United Steelworkers of America, AFL-CIO), 6 AAA 5. The arbitrator, Sidney Sugerman, ruled that a contract clause barring subcontracting of work without discussing the matter with the union also barred transfer of work to another plant of the company without such discussion. However, the union's request for a remedy consisting of restoration of work, recall of laid-off employees, and back pay for loss of earnings was not allowed. "Such relief might normally be appropriate

Seniority Decisive Where Ability Is "Sufficient"

In the *Kidde Manufacturing* case, as we have seen, it did not matter that the senior was qualified for a certain job, because the junior was more qualified. At the *National Vulcanized Fibre Company* (Pulp, Sulphite and Paper Mill Workers, AFL-CIO),[3] on the other hand, it didn't matter that the junior had greater ability, because the senior, having sufficient ability for the job, had the right to the promotion.[4] The decision by John Perry Horlacher in the latter case was based upon the following language:

Paragraph 58: Employees with the greatest seniority shall be given the opportunity to fill permanent vacancies in higher rated occupational classifications within the bargaining unit when such openings occur, provided they have the ability to perform the work required, and have indicated their desire, qualifications, and experience for such vacancy on a form available upon request at the Employment Office.

The grievance arose when the employer filled a newly created job (Machinist and Auxiliary Equipment Mechanic) with a junior bidder who, according to management, had knowledge of gasoline engines. The senior bidder, it was thought, lacked the ability to perform all aspects of the job. Mr. Horlacher said the company did not have a sound reason for assuming that the grievant was unqualified; but before discussing that part of the issue, he explained why, under the contract, the company could not select anyone but the senior applicant who met minimum qualifications.

It is natural and quite understandable for a company in filling a job to prefer—consciously or otherwise—the applicant who has the superior qualifications and is likely to turn in the most efficient performance. This tendency however cannot be permitted to displace a different contractual rule governing the filling of job vacancies.

Paragraph 58 of the Agreement does not employ a test of comparative ability. The job is not to go to the best qualified person but to the person

_____

for breach of an agreement not to subcontract at all, or without the union's prior consent, but not for breach of a duty to discuss that which the company is at all times empowered to do anyway," Mr. Sugerman wrote. "It is sufficient that the company be tagged with the finding of violation and a direction in effect to cease and desist from such violations in the future."

[3] 20 AAA 18.

[4] For another case decided similarly see *Paterson Parchment Paper Company* (United Papermakers and Paperworkers, AFL-CIO), 1 AAA 5, decided by G. Allan Dash.

"with the greatest seniority" provided he has "the ability to perform the work." The requirement here is for minimal ability—enough to competently perform the job duties, not relatively superior ability. Essentially this construction of the provision was espoused by the union at the hearing and not denied by the company.

The next question was whether the grievant had minimum qualifications. It appeared that he had had relevant experience with many types of equipment during other employment which, according to Mr. Horlacher, created a "presumption" of qualifications for the job, although it did not establish qualifications "beyond a peradventure of a doubt."

In view of the presumption, although not the certainty, that the grievant was qualified for the job, the award directed a trial period of not less than thirty days "to ascertain fairly whether [the grievant] has the necessary capacities." He added that "the judgment made by the company at the end of the period should be as impartial and objective as the company is capable of making it, but it must be the company's judgment as the manager of the business and not [the grievant's]."

Shifting Standards of Ability

Whether an employee has the degree of "ability" contemplated by the agreement often depends on the kind of job transaction he tries to effect. The local supplementary agreement at a plant of the *General Electric Company* (International Union of Electrical, Radio and Machine Workers, AFL-CIO),[5] for instance, provided for two sets of standards. If a senior wanted to be transferred to an "existing opening," he had to be either fully qualified or capable of becoming fully qualified "with a minimum of training." But if he wanted to bump a junior out of a job, and if he was not already fully qualified, he would have to be able to qualify "within a reasonable period of familiarization."[6]

---

[5] 2 AAA 17.

[6] The text of the clause read: "Layoffs and transfers shall be made first within the affected job classification beginning with those employees who have the shortest continuous service. Employees not retained within their group shall be transferred on the basis of total length of continuous service to existing openings for which they are qualified or can qualify with a minimum of training. If no such opening exists, the affected employee shall be transferred by displac-

It became necessary to interpret that contract language when management refused to permit a senior employee to bump into a maintenance job he had once filled only as a helper. The parties selected Douglass V. Brown as arbitrator. He upheld the company largely because of evidence showing that the grievant had never exercised "independent judgment" and that his experience had given him only "superficial knowledge of some of the operations."

Thus, the factual situation clearly favored management and seemed to present no great difficulties for the arbitrator. But his discussion of the distinction the contract made between different standards of qualification may be instructive:

At the very least, "familiarization" implies that the employee will qualify through his own efforts and perceptions. "Training," on the other hand, implies that he is entitled to outside help. Considering only the literal wording, therefore, it seems quite clear that tougher hurdles were placed in the way of him who would seek to displace another employee than those in the way of a candidate for an existing opening.

The contrast between the two concepts, he said, was sharpened by the history of bargaining on this matter. At one of the bargaining sessions, the company representative had defined familiarization as "a process whereby an employee may refresh his memory concerning details of a job for which he previously acquired skill and ability." In contrast, it was said, "training requires the teaching of new skills or the development of old skills." There was evidence that the union was not pleased with this definition, but there was no evidence that the company retreated from its position. As the phrase originally submitted by the company was incorporated into the agreement, Mr. Brown concluded that the grievance had to be resolved as he had done, in terms of whether the grievant could qualify "within a reasonable period of familiarization."

High Standards of Ability for Bumping

To make it clear that an employee bumping another out of a job must be able to perform it without a period of training, the contract

ing a shorter service employee who is on a job for which the longer service employee is qualified or can qualify within a reasonable period of familiarization. An employee thus displaced shall be considered laid off from his regular job due to lack of work."

at the *Lovell Manufacturing Company* (United Rubber, Cork and Linoleum Workers, AFL-CIO)[7] stated that "consideration" would be given to both seniority and ability, with seniority the "determining factor" where the employee "is able to do the job." Despite the clarity of the language, a grievance arose when management interpreted it to mean that only actual prior experience on a job could qualify a man for bumping into it. This was an error, said the arbitrator, Frank R. Uible.

A senior employee must have the "capacity, skill or competence to satisfactorily perform the job when he enters upon it, and without a training period," he wrote. But this did not mean that the skill could not be acquired in ways other than by direct experience on the job:

In the absence of qualifying or modifying language, we must assume that parties in the use of words in drafting provisions intended the common and ordinary meaning as approved by recognized authorities. As the result of this observation, we conclude the company's conception of the meaning of "ability" is too narrow.

On the other hand, Mr. Uible also rejected the union's view that only "innate ability" was required. In other words, in order to exercise bumping rights, the senior would need more than "a competence to be demonstrated in the future." At the practical level, however, the arbitrator found a meeting ground for the two viewpoints. The company had the right, he said, to take prior experience on a job into account when evaluating an employee's ability. At the same time, consideration should be given to the "occasional employee" who has no prior experience but who does have the "innate talent or skill to step into a job and immediately and satisfactorily perform it."

Ability for Apprentice Job

It would seem, almost by definition, that when a senior employee claims the job of an apprentice, there should be no question about the former's ability to do the work. But that question was raised by management in another case of the *General Electric Company*

[7] 23 AAA 9.

(American Federation of Technical Engineers, AFL-CIO),[8] result-ing in a decision by Robert L. Stutz that an employee who was still in the early stages of a formal apprenticeship program could not be displaced from his job by a senior. The apprenticeship program, he said, is obviously designed to service long-term company needs: "The beginning pay scale, academic aspects and actual company requirements indicate that young men will be involved in the pro-gram, with relatively short periods of service with the company. If their apprenticeship were to be interrupted every time there was a layoff, it would spell doom to the program."

Furthermore, while the two senior employees, who were the grievants in this case, could have taken over the technical work of the apprentices, they could not have replaced the apprentices "in their apprenticeship affiliation," because the "work" done by these trainees was "learning."

Whether Mr. Stutz' decision would have been the same if the apprentices had been in the later stages of their training program, when their tasks would perhaps have consisted of relatively more "working" and less "learning," remains an unanswered question. As most experienced arbitrators do, Mr. Stutz answered the question put to him without expressing opinions on other matters.

"A Reasonable Period" of Familiarization

At *General Electric,* as we have seen, allowance was made for very brief orientation of senior employees who bump juniors out of jobs. At the Eichor Division of the *Scranton Corporation* (Federal Local Union, AFL-CIO),[9] on the other hand, the contract language was less specific. It said only that in the event of layoff, seniors could bump juniors "subject to their ability to perform the available work." Nevertheless, the question of a reasonable period of familiarization could not be avoided.

In short, did the contract mean present ability, or did it mean ability after a brief period of training? That was a question put be-fore Bert L. Luskin, in a case involving the removal from a job of an employee who had bumped into it only two days earlier.

The company argued at the arbitration that there had been dis-

[8] 9 AAA 20.
[9] 14 AAA 16.

cussions during the most recent negotiations about the meaning of the seniority and ability clause. Management had wanted to be more specific about the degree of ability required for bumping, but the union objected to any change in the language. It was asserted, however, that union negotiators agreed that an employee claiming the job of a junior would have to be able to work "at or near the production norm" immediately. Mr. Luskin answered that the decision would still have to turn on interpretation of the contract. "Unless an ambiguity exists," he said, "the basic rules of contract construction would require that all matters discussed during the negotiations leading to the execution of the agreement must be considered to have been merged into the provisions of the contract."

As to the meaning of the critical phrase, he wrote:

An analysis of the provision in question would indicate that the words, "subject to their ability to perform the available work," must be construed to mean present ability, as distinguished from ability to perform the work after a training program. It should be noted that Article XIV (Job Bidding Procedure) provides for the establishment of a trial period of six weeks in cases involving promotions to existing vacancies or to new jobs. If it was the intention of the parties that the words "their ability to perform the work" were to mean ability to perform the work after training and indoctrination, a trial period or a specified period of time would have been established in the same manner as a trial period has been established by the parties under the job bidding procedure article of the agreement. The issue must be determined on the basis of [the grievant's] ability to perform the work at the time that she bumped into the classification.

In view of the facts of the case, however, Mr. Luskin ruled that the company was wrong in removing the grievant from the job after only two days. The grievant had previously performed satisfactorily on that job for two years. Specification changes were made while she was away from that job, and it seemed that she should qualify if given "a reasonable period of time to familiarize herself with the use of new or added tools or devices." A two-day trial period was not sufficient for that purpose, Mr. Luskin said. He added that his decision was based on the particular facts of this case. No inference was intended that a trial period would be required under all, or most, circumstances.

Senior Must Be as Able as the Junior He Bumps

Negotiators of the seniority and ability clause at the *Union Boiler and Manufacturing Company* (United Steelworkers of America, AFL-CIO)[10] tried to be very specific about minimum qualifications for bumping. The contract required that a senior employee who claims the job of a junior must "demonstrate his ability to do the work as well as the employee being replaced." G. Allan Dash ruled that this clause did not justify the employer's refusal of an on-the-job trial to a senior who wanted to bump into a truck driving job. The following facts were found pertinent:

1. The grievant had a state driver's license, authorizing him to drive either of the company's two vehicles
2. He had driven many types of vehicles during military service in Korea
3. The grievant had driven the company's largest vehicle within the plant
4. He satisfied the requirements of the Interstate Commerce Commission's safety regulations

"The background of [the grievant] was such that driving of the company's largest truck should not have been a difficult task for him," wrote Mr. Dash. Management had argued that the company should not be required "to expose itself to considerable monetary loss" that would result if the grievant should prove incompetent. This argument would be persuasive, Mr. Dash answered, if the grievant were "totally lacking in experience." That was not the case here.

As Arbitrator Luskin did in the *Scranton* case, Mr. Dash cautioned that his award did not open the job in question for automatic trial periods.

The Arbitrator's determination to support the grievant's claim to a right to "bump" into the Truck Driver's job is based upon the particular and specific facts of the grievant's background and experience in driving trucks. This finding does not open the Truck Driver job as a classification through which any employee, possessed of a driver's license, can "bump" out of and into the plant. Article 7, Section 5, is not worded so as to imply any such intent by the parties. The Arbitrator's intent here is not to establish the Truck Driver's job classification as a "path" through which

[10] 4 AAA 2.

employees can move out of and into the plant at times of layoff and rehire.

Experience "Comparable" to the Posted Job

At the *American Engineering Company* (United Steelworkers of America, AFL-CIO),[11] the contract contained the usual provision for promotion of the senior "where skill and ability are relatively equal." But the dispute over interpretation of that clause was unusual, in that the union argued that only experience in the posted job was relevant to any comparison between two bidders.

"If only experience in the job being offered can be considered," answered Donald A. Crawford, who arbitrated the case, "the company would have no way of determining whether the skill and ability to do the job are relatively equal. Seniority alone would become the controlling factor in many promotions." The contract stated that in comparing ability of applicants, "only actual experience with the company shall be considered." But this did not mean, Mr. Crawford wrote, that experience with the company on some job other than one posted for bidding was not valid.

In this case, the junior had acquired experience "comparable" to the posted job while he had been assigned to the machine shop. The grievant had not had the opportunity to gain that experience.[12]

Group-Leader Ability Problems

In no area is the concept of ability more intangible than in selection of employees for group leadership. Although such positions are within the bargaining unit, many of the personality traits essential for satisfactory performance are the same as those required by foremen and supervisors. Management generally has a free hand in appointing foremen, but the seniority and ability standards of contracts give the employer less freedom in naming group leaders. Two

[11] 2 AAA 16.

[12] The union's case was also based on the assertion that the grievant had been promised the job ten months earlier, when it had been posted, but not filled. This could not influence the decision in the present case, Mr. Crawford wrote. "The proper action for [the grievant] would have been to seek enforcement of his September 1957 award within some reasonable length of time. The Arbitrator cannot remedy that situation now by violating [the junior employee's] contractual rights to the present vacancy."

cases, one in which the employer was upheld and the other in which the grievant was sustained, illustrate some of the problems.

At *Westinghouse Electric Corporation* (International Union of Electrical, Radio and Machine Workers, AFL-CIO),[13] the contract stated that group leader jobs were to be filled by seniors "who have the ability to organize and direct a group." When management appointed a junior, the union filed a grievance in behalf of a senior who, it was shown, had held positions of leadership in the community and the union. This was proof, the union argued, that he had the personality necessary for the job. Unfortunately for the grievant, he was admittedly deficient in certain technical requirements of the job. This weakness, wrote the arbitrator, John W. May, would detract from his ability to lead others. "Since community and union leadership ability are not transferable to mechanical ability, such evidence is ruled irrelevant to the issue in the instant case," he said.

A group-leader job was also the issue at the *New Jersey Aluminum Extrusion Company* (United Steelworkers of America, AFL-CIO).[14] The contract called for plant-wide seniority in layoffs and bumping; but the employer refused to consider the possibility that a senior employee, who happened to be a union officer, might fill that job. He would be reluctant to exert the pressures necessary, it was argued.

Herbert Wechsler ruled in favor of the union. The argument may appear plausible to management, he conceded, but refusal to consider the senior amounts to discrimination for "union activities," which was expressly forbidden by the contract. "Group leaders are not foremen," he wrote. "They are included in the bargaining unit and have the normal rights of all represented employees."[15]

[13] 6 AAA 2.

[14] 22 AAA 9.

[15] The parties stipulated that if the grievant had been given the group-leader job, he would subsequently have been bumped out of it again through a chain-bumping process. The appropriate remedy for him, therefore, was pay at the laborer's rate, for he would finally have settled in a laboring job. The union made a further request at the arbitration for monetary relief for others who may also have been improperly laid off through the employer's error. This further remedy was denied. "The only grievance submitted to arbitration," Mr. Wechsler wrote, "was that concerning [one employee]. I am accordingly without au-

TESTS OF ABILITY

As the "direction of the work forces" is one of management's functions, the decision as to an employee's qualifications and fitness for promotion is almost always made by the employer in the first instance, subject to review in grievance procedure or arbitration if the decision is questioned. Most of the time, this judgment is based on observation of the employee's performance on related jobs, records of his education and previous experience, or subjective impressions of his general aptitude.

Written Tests as Sole Criteria

There are occasions when management believes a formal written test is necessary. In the absence of any contractual provision dealing with the matter, may such a test be administered, and may an employee be disqualified from the job he seeks solely because of his refusal to take the test? Reported decisions of arbitrators suggest an affirmative answer, with a qualifying "but it depends on the content of the test and on how it is used."

The dispute at the *Nicholson File Company* (United Steelworkers of America, AFL-CIO)[16] was typical. An employee filed a grievance in which it was asserted that his seniority rights were violated when a junior was promoted to Second Electrician. Three men had applied for the job. All were given a set of five questions composed by the plant manager. One of the applicants, able to answer none of them, admitted his lack of qualifications. The grievant answered two correctly and was disqualified by management. The job was given to the third, a junior employee, who achieved a perfect score.

Essentially, three questions were answered by Carl A. Warns: (1) Did management have the right to administer a written test?

---

thority to award relief for others, whether or not they are entitled thereto on the facts respecting their own situations."

On the other hand, for a case in which a remedy was withheld from named grievants because of the possibility that individuals not named in the grievance may have had a superior claim, see the decision of Archibald Cox, *Crompton and Knowles Corporation* (United Steelworkers of America, AFL-CIO), 9 AAA 9, in Chapter 6, note 12.

[16] 9 AAA 2.

(2) Was the test one reasonably designed to determine qualifications for the vacant job? (3) Without regard to his performance on the test, did the grievant have the degree of ability required by the contract for claiming the promotion on the basis of his seniority?[17]

To begin with, Mr. Warns pointed out, the contract established two standards: (1) an employee must have "the ability and physical fitness to perform the work," and (2) the employee "with the longest seniority will be given preference." This was different, he said, from a situation where the job is given to the senior only "where skill and ability are relatively equal." In the instant case, there is no basis for comparison between the junior and senior employees in ability. If the senior is sufficiently competent, he must be given the job even though the junior might be more able.

With this introduction, the arbitrator undertook the answer to the three questions. As to the first—whether the company has the right to administer a written test unilaterally—he answered "yes, but . . .":

In my opinion whether a company can unilaterally give a test to determine "ability" depends on many factors, including the requirement that the test be reliable and a valid one. This means that the test must be consistent and predict job performance with reasonable accuracy. A written test is not the same thing as an oral interview. Many experienced individuals can converse about their experience and aptitudes but on a written examination "freeze." In the final analysis for a written test to meet the standards of fairness and objectivity that the labor agreement demands there must be some proof that the test given will in fact show that success in taking it will probably demonstrate qualifications for a Second Electrician. There are a number of ways this can be done—the test can be given to those who are already second electricians and compare their grades with the applicants'. The point is that the writing and

[17] The text of the relevant contract clause read: "SECTION 16. It is the policy of the management to cooperate in every practical way with the employees who desire transfers to new positions or vacancies. Accordingly, such employees who make application to the Personnel Department will be given preference for filling open jobs, provided employee has the ability and physical fitness to perform the work. Both the employees and the local union shall receive a copy of all applications. In the case of two or more applications for the same open job, the employee with the longest seniority will be given preference. In order for an employee's application to be considered for an open job his application must be on file in the Personnel Office within twenty-five (25) hours after the job becomes open."

giving of tests is a highly technical subject easily abused. There is the
further requirement that the test must be given under the same conditions
and that there must be a valid "norm" for a passing grade. This cannot
be determined arbitrarily but must have some proved relation to the
skill required.

Applying these standards, Mr. Warns found little justification for
the particular test the plant manager had prepared. The five questions were "all general and basic," he said, and there was "no evidence that this examination had ever been given before" or that it
was "related in more than a very general way to the actual job requirements."

The ruling that the test was not a valid one—at least not if it was
to be the "sole" criterion of ability[18]—did not necessarily mean that
the grievant had to be awarded the job. It merely put the grievant
and the junior back where they were before the test was given. It
therefore remained for Mr. Warns to decide whether there was other
evidence supporting management's decision not to give the job to
the senior. On the basis of his analysis of the grievant's experience
in electrical work, he ruled that sufficient ability for the Second
Electrician job was lacking.

"Ability," as used in the contract, he said, means "present capacity
for the job, not simply an ability to learn." It did not appear that the

---

[18] For a case in which test scores were *not* the sole criterion of qualifications,
see *Allied Chemical and Dye Corporation* (United Steelworkers of America,
AFL-CIO), 7 AAA 14. The grievant had sought a promotion as a means of
avoiding layoff for lack of work. The arbitrator, Dudley E. Whiting, ruled that
the seniority and layoff provisions of the contract did not give an employee the
right to a promotion to which he was not otherwise entitled. Secondly, management had not acted "arbitrarily or discriminatorily" in finding the grievant unqualified for the higher classification. Part of this judgment was based on his
performance in a "general knowledge and comprehension test" that the grievant
and other employees had taken. The union objected that the test could not be
used against the grievant because no scores were announced. To this Mr. Whiting replied: "I recognize that these test scores are not made known to the
employees and I understand the objections of the union to their consideration.
If they were the sole factor in a determination of employees' relative ability,
a different question would be presented. Here they are but one factor, among
which are the difference in schooling and the difference in experience in the
Mechanical Maintenance Section, to confirm the objectivity of the supervisor's
evaluation of relative ability. Under all of the circumstances shown and in
accordance with the provisions of this contract, the union's judgment of relative
ability may not be substituted for the judgment of the company thereon, so
this grievance cannot be sustained."

grievant, whose experience was in "house wiring and appliance work," had the "present capacity" for a job requiring knowledge of industrial electrical work. In short, although the five questions were improper as a basis for job selection, the company did not violate the contract when the job was not awarded to the senior, because he did not have "present ability" to do the work.

A conclusion very similar in many respects was reached by Arbitrator Robert G. McIntosh at *The Magnavox Company* (International Union of Electrical, Radio and Machine Workers, AFL-CIO).[19] Here, too, a senior applicant for a job was denied the promotion because he failed a written test. As in the *Nicholson File* case, the union objected both to administering the test and to making it the sole determinant of ability. Mr. McIntosh agreed with the union only on the second point:

There is no question in the mind of the Arbitrator, and this is supported by the decisions of many other hearing officers in arbitration, that the company has a right to give reasonable tests to determine the qualifications of employees. However, the rule is subject to the qualification, that unless the contract provides that the tests shall be controlling, the results are to be used only as part of the basis for management decision. Other criteria, such as the work record of the employee, his attendance, his attitude, and the general and surrounding impressions built up by an employee over a period of service with a company must be considered in making the selection.

The decision that test scores could not be the "sole criteria," he said, followed particularly from the contract language. The seniority and ability clause stated that the employee with the greatest seniority "who bids and who may reasonably be presumed to be able to qualify for the work, shall be given the first opportunity on the job opening." The first three days on the new job would be a trial period, during which the employee may decide to return to his old job or may find that he lacks qualifications after all.

The use of the word "presumed" in the relevant clause, Mr. McIntosh said, made it clear that a test could not be the sole criterion of ability. "A presumption ordinarily arises when proof is lacking," he wrote. "Written tests, used as a sole criterion, however, would not raise a presumption but would be proof of qualification."

[19] 18 AAA 18.

License Requirement

After changing over from the manufacture of radio and television equipment to the manufacture of electronic equipment for the government, management of a plant of the *Sylvania Electric Products Company* (International Union of Electrical, Radio and Machine Workers, AFL-CIO),[20] established a new job: Performance Analyzer. It was to be filled by employees who could pass a written test and obtain a second class radio-telephone license from the Federal Communications Commission.[21] The union objected to these requirements.

The arbitrator, Clair V. Duff, ruled that under the contract clause reserving to management the right to "select, retain, transfer or advance its employees," the company had the right to do so in any manner not "unlawfully discriminatory" or in violation of other provisions of the agreement. "We have searched the contract with care and find in it no provision that either expressly or impliedly prohibits the use of written tests to select personnel for jobs," he said.

A reasonable cause for administering the written test was found in the nature of the job and the urgency of the company's problem:

The company was faced with the difficult problem of selecting properly qualified employees for a new job requiring initiative and resourcefulness —in short, the ability to work with a minimum of supervision. The job required employees who possessed a good working knowledge of electronic theory, so that, individually, they could solve complex problems without the constant presence and aid of Supervisors or Technicians. Under those circumstances the use of a written test was reasonable.

It was also significant, Mr. Duff added, that "the union has not argued that the test was formulated or graded in an unlawfully discriminatory manner."

Once it was established that the company could administer such a test, the arbitrator said, it made little difference that the FCC license was required in addition. The company test was, in fact,

[20] 14 AAA 6.
[21] The union objected to the establishment of the new job on the ground that it was merely a combination of two already existing jobs. The employer was upheld. (The discussion of the job classification aspect of the case is not relevant to the present discussion.)

based on an FCC examination, so that an employee who passed either one of the two could "in all probability" pass the other.

Educational Requirements

In a sense, a requirement that an employee must have achieved a certain level of formal education is no different from a requirement that he pass a test intended to show that he has the equivalent of that education. Not surprisingly, the only reported arbitration case in which an applicant for promotion was disqualified by the employer because he had less formal education than a junior resulted in a decision very similar to those reported above, in which it was held that performance on a test could not be the sole criterion of ability.

In this case, management of the *Long Island Water Corporation* (Utility Workers Unions of America, AFL-CIO)[22] promoted a junior employee to a bookkeeping and clerical position solely on the basis of his experience with the company and his partial college education. There were two senior bidders, one of whom, the grievant in this case, lacked college training. Furthermore, his experience with the company was not quite as relevant to the vacant job as that of the junior.

The difference in education between the two employees was not controlling, said Arthur Stark, "because there is no evidence that [college training] was in any way related to bookkeeping and clerical functions." And as for the difference in experience, this too was not decisive. The senior had experience of his own that would be useful, and he had the "mental qualifications" to familiarize himself with the job quickly.

In sum, it is our conclusion that [the junior's] qualification advantages in terms of specific familiarity with certain accounts and procedures is balanced by the longer experience and training of [two seniors]. The difference in their educational backgrounds, in the present situation, is not substantial enough to be meaningful. Accordingly, we find that seniority should govern since qualifications of the three employees are relatively equal.[23]

[22] 10 AAA 20.

[23] Mr. Stark added that there was no basis for excluding college education "*as such*" from factors that would determine qualifications for a job. "Education, like work experience, constitutes one type of qualification," he said. For

Production Figures as Criteria of Ability

Assuming objective standards are better than subjective ones for weighing the "relative ability" of two employees, management at *Eljer Company* (United Steelworkers of America, AFL-CIO)[24] cited production figures and attendance records in favor of a junior employee. The union objected to the use of these figures and argued that, in any case, the differences they revealed were "insignificant." The arbitrator, Frank R. Uible, agreed with management on both points. The contract's reference to "relatively equal" ability in itself indicated that comparisons were to be made, he said. Furthermore, the words "physical fitness" in the clause also made absences due to sickness a relevant consideration. Finally, the contract made seniority a secondary consideration. Only where ability to perform the work and physical fitness were "relatively equal," was seniority to be the "determining factor." Mr. Uible therefore concluded:

In arriving at its determination, the company considered a series of statistics, applicable to the four employees, and also the collective judgment of the four foremen in the enameling department. These statistics were a compilation of the production records of these employees and their absences due to sickness. We believe these statistics afford a proper and reasonable basis for the comparison of the ability to perform the work and as to their physical fitness.

As the production and attendance figures showed that the junior employee was "significantly better" than either of the two seniors who protested, the grievance was denied.

Unjustified Absenteeism as Criterion of Ability

In the *Eljer Company* case, above, attendance records were cited because they were relevant to an employee's physical fitness for a job. At *Waller Brothers Stone Company* (United Stone and Allied Product Workers, AFL-CIO)[25] excessive absence became an issue in a somewhat different way. Harry J. Dworkin stated the question

---

instance, "it is doubtful that certain types of bookkeeping jobs can be properly performed without a high school diploma." But in view of the nature of the available job, "very little" weight should have been given to the junior's college education, which, in any event, Mr. Stark found "uncertain."

[24] 22 AAA 5.

[25] 22 AAA 2.

before him: "May an otherwise qualified applicant be denied an available job by reason of excessive absenteeism?"

The grievant, bumped from his job by a senior, claimed the job of a "top sander" who was junior to him. There was no dispute as to his technical proficiency, but the opportunity to bump was denied solely because his record of attendance was poor.[26] Management pointed out that an entire department depended upon uninterrupted functioning of the top-sanding machine.

Mr. Dworkin found the answer to the problem in the seniority clauses. Of special interest was one which read:

An employee whose seniority entitled him to consideration for a vacancy shall be given the opportunity to prove he can do the work. If at any time during the thirty day trial period, it is determined that the employee is not qualified, he shall be returned to his former job, if he so desires, without loss of seniority.

This thirty-day trial period, he said, gave management "ample protection" if it should turn out that the grievant's attendance record continued poor.

Furthermore, Mr. Dworkin wrote, a section of the contract dealing with discipline provided a way for the employer to deal with absenteeism. "To permit the company to reject an employee's bid for a job on the ground of absenteeism would add an additional penalty for absenteeism which is not provided for in the agreement," he concluded.[27]

[26] The employer's evidence showed that in the last 135 scheduled days, the grievant was absent 11 partial days and 9 full days, to a total of 15 per cent of his scheduled working time.

[27] For a discussion of six other cases where denial of contract benefits as a form of discipline was an issue, see Chapter 10.

4

STEWARDS AND UNION OFFICERS

Stewards and union officers play a dual role. As employees of the company, they have the rights and privileges of other employees, and are generally bound by the same rules of conduct and conditions of employment. But as representatives of the union, they investigate grievances, negotiate and participate in the day-to-day administration and application of the collective bargaining contract. Because this second function requires the presence of stewards in the shop when grievances arise among their constituents, special privileges are often legislated by the parties, giving stewards "superseniority," which may be asserted to claim assignment to particular shifts, or preferential treatment with respect to overtime, layoffs or transfers. The application of superseniority provisions accounts for most arbitration cases involving stewards and officers. In second place are discipline cases, often turning on whether certain conduct was insubordinate, and therefore punishable, or was privileged by the union officer's status. Occasionally, disputes also arise over the application of clauses granting pay to stewards for grievance-processing time.

OVERTIME PROBLEMS

At the *Elastic Stop Nut Corporation* (United Automobile Workers, AFL-CIO),[1] the contract required the assignment of a steward to overtime when ten or more employees of his group were so assigned, provided that he was "capable" of doing the work. On a certain Saturday, the steward, an expediter, was permitted to work four hours, until he completed a task that had been assigned to him. The other expediters were permitted to work the full schedule of

[1] 21 AAA 2.

eight hours overtime. Benjamin C. Roberts did not accept the union's claim that the steward should have been permitted to take over the work of another expediter. Although the job classification system of the company contained only a single classification for expediters, this job had "special characteristics"; there would be "undue delay" if one expediter was asked to take over the job of another:

> The nature of the job is such that the expediter on the job has a knowledge and intimacy of the immediate status of the work in the department that is not necessarily reflected on the job board and could not be transmitted to another expediter either by the departmental expediter or by the foreman without a substantial portion of the four hours to be taken in bringing the new expediter up to date on the status of the work as of that moment.

Nor was the union persuasive in its contention that interchangeability of assignments was proved by the facts that the grievant had substituted for an absent expediter, and that the employer had assigned a "utility expediter" to substitute for other absent employees in the past. The contract "cannot be interpreted on the basis of an action necessitated by a situation of an emergency nature, where the company must fill in as best it can."

Unlike the *Elastic Stop Nut* case, where the issue was the steward's ability, an *American Bosch Arma Corporation* case (International Union of Electrical, Radio and Machine Workers, AFL-CIO)[2] involved a steward who was admittedly able to do the work. The whole question was whether there were enough of his constituents assigned to overtime to justify his presence.

The contract required that overtime be offered a steward whenever five or more employees of an "occupation" worked overtime. On the occasion that gave rise to the arbitration, the company had assigned three blueprint clerks, one senior blueprint clerk, and two release technicians to extra hours. Thus, while there were six workers, no single classification numbered as many as five. But were there, among these six employees, at least five within a single "occupation"? Because the contract language provided no clear answer,

[2] 2 AAA 7.

Joseph F. Wildebush resolved the dispute in favor of the union, largely on the basis of past practice of the parties.

There undoubtedly were many situations where the five or more employees were of the same occupation as defined by the company, but testimony from union officials revealed that there were times when less than five employees in an occupation were called in and yet a shop steward was also called in. It is true, as the company argues, that no supervisor has a right to vary the terms of a contract, but where the terms of the contract are vague and in dispute, the actions of [supervisors] in carrying out and interpreting the contract have probative value as past practice. Under the circumstances, it is the opinion of the Arbitrator that the word "occupation" in the last sentence of [the contract] means the area of shop stewardship.

At *Hitemp Wires, Inc.* (International Brotherhood of Electrical Workers, AFL-CIO),[3] stewards enjoyed superseniority for purposes of layoff and recall, but the contract did not specifically give them preference over other employees in the distribution of overtime. Nevertheless, the union believed that the purpose for which superseniority was legislated for stewards implied that they would be present in the plant at all times when at least two employees were at work. Consequently, when management assigned some employees to Saturday overtime without a steward, a grievance was filed.

Thomas A. Knowlton agreed with the company that the assignment of overtime to stewards in the manner urged by the union would violate the contractual requirement for "equal division of overtime among the employees normally assigned to the performance of the work in which the overtime is required."[4]

LAYOFF AND BUMPING

In negotiating a contract at the *General Electric Company* (Inter-

---

[3] 21 AAA 15.

[4] The union also asserted that stewards had been given preferential treatment in overtime for the past year and that this constituted a "past practice" which should be continued. Mr. Knowlton rejected this: "For an arbitrator to give weight to a practice such as is claimed by the union as existing in this case, there must be either a 'past practice clause' in the agreement (there is none) or some lack of clarity in the language of the agreement. In this case, all the pertinent sections of the agreement are clear, concise and without possibility of misinterpretation."

national Union of Electrical, Radio and Machine Workers, AFL-CIO),[5] the union asked for superseniority for its stewards, to protect them from layoff if a reduction of the work force should become necessary. Management apparently wanted some assurance against an excessive number of stewards having that privilege. Final agreement was reached that, "in general," there would be one steward for each foreman. The full text of the superseniority clause read:

An employee who is a steward of such local and who has accumulated six months or more of service credits shall, upon written request of the local, and if a majority of the group of employees he represented assents as certified in writing by the local, be deferred from layoff (except temporary layoffs) from his job so long as work for which he is qualified is available on such job among the group of employees he represents. If such work is not available on his job, such employee shall, to the extent necessary to defer him from layoff, be deemed to have sufficiently greater continuous service than other employees he represents so as to entitle him to transfer to other work for which he is qualified within his group. This provision shall, in general, apply to a maximum of one steward for each Company foreman.

The last sentence of the quoted clause became the subject of a dispute when two departments were merged into one. The combined work force numbered more than fifty bargaining unit employees, including such previously unrelated groups as painters and cleaners, on the one hand, and welders, on the other. There were two stewards among them, but one was subsequently laid off, management holding that as there was only one foreman in charge, only one of the stewards could have superseniority.

Thus, two questions were presented: Could that group be represented adequately by one steward? Did the employer have the right to determine unilaterally what situations justified departure from the "general" one-for-one rule?

Paul R. Hays found for the union on both counts. The company itself had indicated in a manual that fifty employees were too large a number for adequate representation by a single steward. Furthermore, he pointed out, "there is no reason to believe that the steward representing painters and cleaners would have been aware of or understood the problems of a group of welders. The work area cov-

[5] 2 AAA 9.

ered by the combined groups was larger than that ordinarily serviced by one steward."

But the principle—that is, whether exceptions to the general rule may be made by one side alone—was at least of equal importance with the solution of the particular grievance. Here, Mr. Hays supported neither the position of the company nor that of the union, for each claimed that it alone had the right to determine when exceptions to the rule governing the ratio of stewards to foremen were to be made.

It is quite unlikely that the Agreement was intended to leave the number of stewards to the sole determination of either the employer or the union. The union would hardly have agreed to a provision which could be used to increase or decrease the number of stewards at the employer's will, and, indeed, even to eliminate stewards who incurred employer displeasure. On the other hand, it is difficult to believe that the employer would leave to union discretion the potential for seniority manipulation involved in the unlimited power to fix the number of stewards, to say nothing of the provision of the agreement for the payment of stewards engaged in grievance adjustment.

He concluded that exceptions to the general rule must be made by mutual agreement, and that where the parties fail to reach such agreement, disputes must be resolved "in the manner provided by the Agreement itself for the resolution of differences involving application of the provisions of the agreement." Among the criteria, or "standards," which should govern, he said, were the number of employees in the group, the character of their work, the size of the area in which they worked, the location of the employees with relation to each other, and the time during which the employees worked.

Downward Bumping of Stewards

A special provision intended to keep a steward in his own department does not necessarily prevent him from being bumped to a lower classification by an employee with more natural seniority, as long as the downward shift does not remove the steward from the employees over whom he has jurisdiction. That was a conclusion reached in a case of the *American Bosch Arma Mississippi Corporation* (International Union of Electrical, Radio and Machine Workers, AFL-CIO).[6]

[6] 13 AAA 15.

When layoffs became necessary, a steward, whose work was claimed by a senior employee, was offered the option of taking either a lower rated job in his own department and retaining his stewardship, or a job at his regular classification in another department, and renouncing his stewardship. The union argued that neither offer was in accordance with the contract, the relevant clause of which read:

The company agrees that a union steward will not be moved from the department or group of departments or shift which he represents as listed in Article 16, Section 2, if there is work in his classification or work in another classification in the department or departments he represents which the company agrees the steward can perform.

Denying that the grievant had superseniority rights to withstand the claim of a senior employee to his job, management downgraded him within the department, in accordance with the first option. As Ralph R. Williams analyzed the contract, this was a proper course of action:

This provision of the contract prohibits the company from moving a steward "from the department or group of departments or shift which he represents," so long as there is work in his classification there. But in the instant case, the grievant was not "moved from his department"; he was downgraded within that department. Hence, it is immaterial that work in his classification remained available in his department.

Article 13, Section 17, of the Agreement does not give a steward the right to work both in his job classification and in the department he represents. It simply gives him the right to stay in his department. He may not be moved from his department, but he may be bumped out of his job classification by a senior employee in the same manner as any other junior employee may be bumped, so long as he remains in the department he represents. The contract, therefore, gives no added job protection to a steward insofar as his downgrading within his department is concerned. The provision falls short of the usually accepted scope of "super seniority" for stewards, because it fails to state that a steward shall hold his job classification so long as work is available therein.

A Stewardess without Constituents

The abolition of a night shift at the *Bigelow-Sanford Carpet Company* (Textile Workers Union of America, AFL-CIO),[7] left the committeewoman in an anomalous position. Did her status as rep-

[7] 4 AAA 1.

resentative of employees in her department survive the department itself? All that the collective bargaining contract said on the question was: "Union officers, the shop chairman and committeemen will be granted superseniority in their occupational group in the event of a layoff for lack of work." Management's interpretation was that when the shift was abolished for lack of work, the committeewoman had to be laid off, together with her fellow workers. The union insisted that her superseniority gave her the right to be transferred to the day shift; at that point she would be entitled to only so much job protection as was warranted by her natural seniority.

Thomas A. Knowlton agreed with the company's interpretation:

The language of the agreement is reasonably clear. There is no limitation with respect to shifts. The only doubt in the arbitrator's mind is whether a committeewoman, without a constituency, remains a committeewoman within the intent of the parties. Quite apparently, the parties are agreed that she does not since the union's belief, upon [the grievant's] transfer to the first shift, is that she would be forced to rely only on her regular seniority standing as a safeguard against layoff.

Under these circumstances, the Arbitrator believes that [the grievant] was not entitled to transfer to the day shift by reason of the fact that her union status ceased upon the dissolution of the second shift. In this connection it is important that the union, which established [her] jurisdiction, made it co-terminous with the second shift—Winding Operation. The union's grievance will be denied.

Rate Problems

Normally, an employee asserting his seniority in order to claim a job in a lower rated classification does not retain his old rate of pay. But does this rule apply when the employee who bumps downward is a steward, and the seniority he relies upon does not derive from length of service but from the office he holds? The question is usually answered by the superseniority clauses, which make clear the limits of superseniority. Where clauses are not explicit on this point, however, disputes may have to be arbitrated. Two such cases were reported.

At the *Marvel-Schebler Products Division of Borg-Warner Corporation* (Allied Industrial Workers, AFL-CIO),[8] Patrick J. Fisher held that where the contract was silent as to the rates of pay for

[8] 5 AAA 18.

stewards and union officers who assert superseniority in downward bumping during a permanent reduction in force, each employee must be paid the rate for the job into which he bumps:

The contractual provisions which gave the grievants their right to work in this situation specify that "stewards shall hold top *seniority*" and "the president, financial secretary and members of the bargaining committee of the local union shall have top plant-wide *seniority*." Since the contract does not give other employees the right to a rate of pay higher than that of the job to which they are transferred, what basis could there be for giving such higher rate to the grievants? If the contract doesn't confer such a benefit, how can the Arbitrator?

The union had tried to show a past practice of paying stewards higher rates when bumping downward, but on closer examination the practice was found to have grown out of situations other than permanent reductions in force, as was the case here. There had been disputes about the rate for stewards during brief periods of reassignment, and two awards, by other arbitrators, had been rendered. Examining this history, Mr. Fisher observed that "the union did not *always* believe that stewards, committeemen and the president of the union were entitled to the rate of their regular jobs when they were downgraded." It was apparently only after receiving the two previous awards, which did not deal with permanent reductions in force, that the union concluded that "perhaps the contract meant something it hadn't meant previously."

The past practice at *W. L. Maxson Corporation* (United Automobile Workers, AFL-CIO)[9] was of a different order, which accounts in part for a decision different from that rendered in the *Marvel-Schebler* case. Here, Rolf Valtin ruled that stewards who assert superseniority in order to claim lower rated jobs are entitled to their regular, higher rates.

The contract seemed to provide for all contingencies and to answer all questions directly, except that of the appropriate rate for stewards who bump downward:

The steward and chief steward will have preferential seniority in their occupation and labor grade in the district that they represent on their shift under the layoff procedure. If a steward or chief steward's job is eliminated, such union representative will be transferred to another job

[9] 17 AAA 4.

in his district which he is capable of performing and he shall retain his preferential seniority. On this new assignment, if the employee is no longer recognized by the company as an active union representative, the employee will enjoy all the benefits of his preferential seniority for ninety (90) days or expiration of his term of office, whichever is earlier. If in the event any job eliminated under this section is reactivated the steward and/or chief steward will be returned to the reactivated job, providing they still retain their preferential seniority.

The company position, very similar to that expressed by arbitrator Fisher in the *Marvel-Schebler* case, was that the quoted clause related to seniority alone, not to wage rates. As far as wages were concerned, management representatives argued, the governing provision was the following, which applied to all employees, including stewards:

Wages at time of transfer or recall will be determined as follows: (a) When an employee is transferred or returns to work from lay-off to an "occupation-labor grade" having a maximum rate which is lower than his current rate or lower than the highest rate he held previously in the "occupation" of such "occupation-labor grade," such employees will be paid the maximum rate of the "occupation-labor grade" to which he is assigned.

If the matter were to be determined on the basis of contract language alone, Mr. Valtin said, the employer's view might be upheld. "Normally speaking," he wrote, "a provision which on its face deals with seniority rights—and which makes no express reference to any rate-of-pay requirement—cannot properly be construed as a maintenance of pay provision. Seniority regulations go to rights of job *occupancy*, and do not govern the wage rate to which a holder of seniority rights is entitled."

But in this case, the language could not be read without taking into account the way the parties had applied it. Two facts were especially significant: (1) the identical clause, during an agreement preceding the current one, had been interpreted in the manner now urged by the union; and (2) the employer had tried without success to modify the language of the contract in the current agreement so that it would mean what management now said it did mean. "To disregard this history is to say that the parties' own, conscious past application under the clause has no bearing on the proper interpretation to be given it," Mr. Valtin wrote. "It would be wholly improper to proceed on that basis. Assuming that the agreement is open to an interpretation which preserves the content and meaning which the parties themselves have given to a particular provision, it is clearly not the function of arbitration to remove such content and meaning."

Another point of similarity between this case and that of *Marvel-Schebler* was that both companies argued that the past practice asserted by the union had to do with "intermittent" displacement of a steward, from his job rather than "permanent" displacement. Mr. Fisher, as we have seen, found the employer's view compelling. Mr. Valtin, on the other hand, thought little of it in the circumstances of this case. "The distinction eludes me," he wrote.

In *both* situations, at the time a union officer is reassigned, *all* work in the particular occupation has run out—for, if any work remained available in it, *he* would be kept on to perform it. In *both* situations, moreover, there is the expectation that work in the particular occupation, sooner or later, will once more be available. If, in referring to the "permanent" type of situation, the company had in mind a situation where an occupation becomes truly extinct—as a result of automation or a change in the company's line of products, etc.—the Chairman could grasp the purported distinction. But this was obviously not the situation in [the instant] case. On the contrary, it was within a scant three weeks that work in [the grievant's] regular occupation once more became available—and this was a far shorter period than several of the intervals in which [a grievant in an earlier case], in the fifteen months in which he is said to have been affected by an "intermittent" situation, did not work in his regular occupation.

Mr. Valtin expressed one more reason why he could not accept as valid the employer's distinction between "intermittent" and "permanent" displacement. Whether a displacement is permanent or not is a matter of "expectations," which do not lend themselves to objective determination. Subjective impressions and beliefs do not provide a sound basis for determining which union officers are to keep their regular rates, and which are to have their rates reduced to the level of the jobs into which they bump.

While finding the company's view untenable in general, Mr. Valtin thought it was quite reasonable of the company to ask whether there was not *some* point at which it would be proper to pay a union officer the rate for a job in a lower classification. Did a union victory in this case mean that union officers are *indefinitely* guaranteed the rate of the job they once held? *"Elimination"* of an occupation, he said, would create a situation justifying reduction of a union officer's rate, if he should be downgraded as a result. As the instant case was one in which the union officer had worked in a lower classification for three weeks, it was sufficient to say that the grievant was entitled to the higher rate; and it was not necessary to say "what precise duration attaches to the rate protection here in question."[10]

PAY FOR GRIEVANCE-PROCESSING TIME

Because a steward or union officer is often obliged to leave his job to investigate grievances or to attend grievance committee meetings with management, provision is frequently made in contracts to pay him for that time. Apparently, most contracts are quite explicit on the circumstances calling for grievance-processing pay, since only two disputes over that issue have been reported since January 1, 1959. These cases, while not necessarily typical or representative, are nevertheless interesting and instructive of problems that may arise.

At the *Philadelphia Transportation Company* (Transport Workers Union, AFL-CIO),[11] the contract provided "pay to working employees who are union representatives for loss of work time when attending scheduled grievance meetings with company representatives during their regularly scheduled working hours."

Although there was nothing in the language requiring payment to employees who were waiting for a case to come up at the meeting, the company had, in practice, always paid for waiting time as well as for grievance-processing time. But on a particular occasion, two union representatives waited for a case which was never heard because the union forced adjournment of the meeting. Were the stewards entitled to pay for waiting time under those circumstances? John R. Abersold said they were not, his decision resting, to a large extent, on the reason for failure of the parties to reach that case.

[10] In the course of the arbitration, the union agreed that the "rate protection" it was urging was "good" only for the union officer's current term and would not continue in the event he was re-elected.
[11] 9 AAA 4.

It seems that the union had been dissatisfied with the company's failure to pay for grievance-processing time when meetings ran into overtime. When a grievance meeting with management on a certain afternoon dragged on to 4:30 P.M., the regular quitting time, the union abruptly withdrew, causing adjournment of the meeting. This was the factual background for the two stewards' claim to waiting time pay.

The only issue recognized by the arbitrator was the question of pay for their waiting time, not whether the company had to pay for grievance-processing time on overtime. Nevertheless, his comments had implications for both aspects of the case. The grievants had forfeited their right to waiting time pay by an "unnecessary" postponement of the meeting. "The matter of overtime could have been resolved by merely protesting the company's refusal to pay overtime and then filing a grievance charging the company with a violation of the labor agreement. This is the very purpose of the grievance procedure."[12]

As to grievance-processing time during extra hours, the arbitrator said it was "very important to note" that union officers attending "third level grievance meetings" on their scheduled off-days were not customarily paid for that time. "This is very strong additional evidence that the union's section officers' refusal to attend the third level grievance meeting beyond the normal quitting time of their regular work was not justified." However, a "rule of reason" would have to be applied in determining "how long section officers should be required to remain at such grievance meetings."

As the *Philadelphia Transportation* case illustrates, an agreement to pay for grievance-processing time may, in its operation, produce claims that go beyond management's original intention. Another example was seen at *Waterbury Companies, Inc.* (United Automobile Workers, AFL-CIO).[13]

The grievance procedure called for consultation between the "department steward and the foreman" at the first step, and provided further that "union stewards and other personnel required to attend

[12] The two stewards had been put on notice at the grievance meeting that they would not be paid for waiting time if the union should postpone the hearing.
[13] 15 AAA 19.

meetings in any of the steps will be granted absence-permission from their regular duties" and will be paid "at their regular hourly rate for time lost."

A dispute over application of this provision arose when the "plant chairman" participated in a first-step meeting with the foreman of a department where there was no steward. After his discussions with the foreman, the plant chairman also spent some time writing up the grievance. This, too, became an issue in the union's demand that he be paid for all time spent at first-step grievance processing.

Saul Wallen found unconvincing the company's argument that, as the first step of the grievance procedure required participation of the "department steward," no other union officer could be paid for first-step processing, even where the department had no steward. It was obvious to him that the shop chairman "assumed the role of acting department steward" in this case. Concerning the time spent in writing up the grievance, "it would be contrary to universal practice as well as contrary to the obvious intent of the clause to restrict the scope of Step 1 to the meeting itself and to rule that the subsequent written grievance and reply are external to Step 1 and lie in some nebulous no-man's land between the first and second step."

DISCIPLINE

When a steward or union officer is disciplined for violating some rule of conduct, there may be a dispute as to whether there was just cause for the penalty. To that extent, a steward's case may be no different from that of any other employee. But when the union asserts that the disciplinary action was motivated by an attempt to frustrate collective bargaining, or that the steward's violation occurred during the course of negotiations and was, therefore, beyond the reach of the employer's power to discipline, a different sort of problem is presented.

At the *American Can Company* (International Brotherhood of Pulp, Sulphite and Paper Mill Workers, AFL-CIO),[14] the local union president was discharged for leaving his work place without per-

[14] 12 AAA 18.

mission, engaging in "contumely" while doing so, and making "irresponsible strike threats." The incidents leading to the discharge began when an employee in a department other than that in which the union president worked visited him at work about a grievance. The foreman ordered the man back to his own department. Although versions differed as to exactly what conversations passed between the foreman and the union president, it was clear that the latter left his work place without permission to investigate the grievance.

Looking into the background of the discharge, Daniel Kornblum found that the union and management had been holding joint meetings to review procedures for conducting union business. The president attended those meetings and knew that "unauthorized leave taking" was the chief subject of discussion. Union committeemen had been admonished particularly against "loud and boisterous" talk in the presence of customers of the employer and against "running around the plant on union business both during on-duty and off-duty hours." Thus, the grievant in this case was on notice that repetition of such conduct would lead to disciplinary penalties.

When the discharged local president's case came before a grievance committee meeting, the union admitted that he was in the wrong, and an apology was offered. This offer was refused, however, by management, which held that the grievant's truculent attitude, as well as his role in a wildcat strike several years earlier, precluded leniency. The arbitrator agreed with management. "The grievant would have it appear that at most his talk and tactic was headstrong, aggravated by a feeling that his immediate supervisor as well as top management retained a grudge against him because of his part in the illegal job action of April 1957. [But] the grievant's pronounced disregard for managerial authority was obviously more deep-rooted and long-standing than his vocal scorn for his immediate supervisor on the morning in question."

In upholding the discharge, Mr. Kornblum refused to take a position as to whether a union officer should be treated more or less leniently than others. "The business of splitting the personality of the grievant into that of either union official or company employee is a doubtful exercise," he wrote. "The grievant's conduct and his entire role must be viewed in its whole setting." From this point of view, he concluded, the discharge had to be upheld. This did not necessarily mean, he added, that a lesser penalty might not have been more appropriate. His function was not to determine the most appropriate penalty, but to rule on whether management had "abused its discretion."[15]

Another case involving a steward who left his department without permission to investigate a grievance occurred at the *Vertol Aircraft Corporation* (United Automobile Workers, AFL-CIO),[16] but here there were no collateral offenses and no history of irresponsibility. The penalty was a one-day suspension, which was upheld by Lewis M. Gill.

The steward had asked his foreman for a pass to leave the department three times within two days, and on each occasion permission was refused. Believing that permission was improperly withheld, the steward finally went to investigate the grievance without the pass.

Mr. Gill said there was "very serious question" as to whether the foreman had acted properly in denying the grievant a pass. But "strictly speaking," that was "beside the point." Furthermore, by the time the arbitration convened, the parties came to an agreement on procedures to be followed in the future. This was an additional reason why the arbitrator did not have to rule on whether the steward should have been permitted to leave his department. But as to just cause for the suspension, he wrote:

Orders of supervision must be carried out, and the grievance procedure used to challenge their reasonableness if that is questioned. When the supervisory order in question appears to be impeding a shop steward from carrying out his function as steward, the situation becomes more touchy, since it enters a sensitive area of labor-management relations. However, I think it is important that the principle be observed in these situations no less than in others, and for the same reasons. Actually, it can be persuasively argued that it is even *more* important in the case of a steward; part of his responsibility is to promote orderly observance of the contract grievance procedure by the employees, and he can scarcely do that by setting a bad example.

At the *National Carbon Coated Paper Company* (United Paper-

---

[15] For similar expressions of view as to the limited nature of the arbitrator's review powers, see note 47 in Chapter 10.

[16] 17 AAA 11.

makers and Paperworkers, AFL-CIO),[17] a local union officer was found in a department where the employer thought he had no business to be. The problem was not one of leaving work without authorization—the officer was off-duty at the time—but of improper plant visitation. Believing that he had failed to contact the forelady on entering the plant, the company sent him an official letter of warning. When the fact that he *had* reported to the forelady on entering the department was disclosed, management insisted that the letter of warning should nevertheless stand because the employee "had no substantial reason" for going there at all. The grievance the officer was there to discuss had to do with workloads, the company said, and this was something that was not within his jurisdiction. Finally, management said, while the contract gave international union officers the right to visit the plant for grievance negotiations under certain conditions, this permission did not extend to local union officers.

Russell A. Smith found, first, that there was "serious question" as to whether it would be proper to uphold disciplinary action taken on one ground, shown to be mistaken, when another ground might have been asserted.[18] In addition, the employer's view was immaterial, because the forelady neither objected to the officer's entry into her department nor refused to talk to him about the workload grievance. "The company cannot very well complain of a conversation with a member of supervision in which the supervisor willingly participated, especially when the union official was off duty."

It would be "unrealistic" to interpret a contract giving high union officers the right to visit the plant in such a way as to exclude local union officers, who are permitted to visit other departments during their working hours. "That which these officials are privileged to do during their working hours they are privileged to do during their off-duty hours." The letter of warning to the local union officer was ordered "expunged from the files of the company."

Discipline for Illegal Work Stoppages[19]

Whether a shop steward who had instigated an illegal work stop-

[17] 11 AAA 6.
[18] For comments on this problem by James J. Healy, Chapter 10, see note 91.
[19] Discipline of stewards and union officers for alleged misconduct in the

page can be singled out for disciplinary action while the other participants go unpunished was a major issue in a case of the *International Smelting and Refining Co.* (United Steelworkers of America, AFL-CIO).[20]

The grievant denied that he had instigated the work stoppage, but Burton B. Turkus was persuaded that he had.[21] As to the contention that it was an act of discrimination to discipline one employee alone, Mr. Turkus answered that what the company had done was in fact laudable. "It is to the credit of management that it limited its action to the discharge of the 'ringleader.' It would be unconscionable to accord [the grievant] immunity from discharge because the company deems it unwise or improvident to penalize an entire shift or to make a 'goat' of the employee who trustingly but unwisely relied on the advice and counsel of his shop steward in refusing to undertake the work assigned."

There had been other wildcat strikes in this establishment in the past, for which no employee had been discharged. But this did not affect the employer's right to discharge in this case, the arbitrator said, because there was no proof that the company had ever had such clear evidence as in the instant case.

As Mr. Gill pointed out in the *Vertol Aircraft* case, stewards and union officers are expected to uphold the integrity of the collective bargaining agreement and to instruct employees to use the grievance procedure for resolving disputes. When workers walk off the job in protest against some real or fancied injustice, union leaders are expected to do all they can to terminate the stoppage. When they do not, and particularly when there was evidence that they played a leading role in instigating the strike, discipline may result.

One of the strongest rebukes to union officers was given by Peter Seitz at *Hudson Pulp and Paper Corporation* (United Papermakers

---

course of legal strikes presents issues different from those discussed in this chapter. For cases of that kind, see Chapter 10.

[20] 18 AAA 7.

[21] In an argument with management over a work assignment dispute, the steward had said: "If that is the way you are going to run the plant, we might as well all go home." This admission, Mr. Turkus said, was "self-incriminating" proof that the steward led the walkout which subsequently took place.

and Paperworkers, AFL-CIO).[22] The two grievants were formerly chief shop steward and local union president and had been discharged for leading a two-day illegal work stoppage. As the contract had a clause stating that "any employee who participates in such prohibited activity shall be subject to discharge or other disciplinary action at the sole discretion of the company," it would seem that there was little basis for a grievance, once the fact of their leadership of the strike had been established.

But a grievance was filed, the two former officers presenting four points in their defense, at least two of which were unusual in this type of case:[23]

1. They were misled into improper strike action by a representative of the international union;
2. The employer had provoked the strike by his conduct;
3. They had proceeded with diligence to call a membership meeting for the purpose of calling off the strike after being advised by the international union that the stoppage was illegal; and
4. It was one of the grievants who cast the deciding vote to end the strike.

Mr. Seitz upheld the discharge. First, he said, these two former officers were not merely members of the bargaining unit "swept up in the movement for an illegal strike" and powerless to resist it. "They were leaders and official representatives of the local union, and as such they bore a special burden of responsibility." Furthermore, they were "initiators as well as participants."

Second, there was "no evidence" that they had been misled by international union officers. "As representatives and spokesmen for the membership they may not hide behind the improper counsels of the international representative which, although alleged, were never proved."

Third, in view of the official status of the grievants, their separate

[22] 14 AAA 4.

[23] The local and international union were represented at the arbitration by counsel. However, as the grievants preferred not to be represented by that attorney, the latter announced that he would not actively participate in the case as attorney for them. One of the grievants acted as counsel for himself and the other employee.

responsibility, and the broad discretion conferred on the company by the contract, "I see no occasion, on the record made at the hearing, to inquire into the question whether, in not discharging other participants in the strike, the company unfairly discriminated" against the grievants.

Fourth, "I have no evidence before me which would support a finding that the company provoked the strike."

Fifth, although "it does appear" that one of the grievants cast the deciding vote in favor of terminating the strike, in view of the latitude given the company in discharging leaders of wildcat strikes, "I am not convinced that I should substitute my judgment for that of the company as to whether this should mitigate the penalty."

5

FOREMEN AND SUPERVISORS

Excluded by union contracts and law from bargaining units composed of non-supervisory employees, foremen and supervisors represent the first echelon of management.[1] At the same time, there are many points of contact between foremen and production workers. And at every point of contact, disputes arise.

The most frequent source of dispute is performance of bargaining unit work by foremen. Contracts often permit such work when it is incidental to the foreman's primary functions of instructing rank-and-file workers or directing the flow of work. Whether the extent of allowable work was exceeded in any given case becomes a question both of fact and of contract interpretation.[2]

[1] At *Central Die Casting Manufacturing Co.* (Mine, Mill and Smelter Workers), 23 AAA 13, the union tried to obtain jurisdiction over a foreman who had been supervising only one and occasionally two employees for several years and who had been performing bargaining unit work for a substantial part of his working time, performance of such work by him not being barred by contract. Arbitrator Pearce Davis denied this request to absorb the foreman into the bargaining unit. "It is of little value to the union case to cite the fact that [the foreman] did production work," Mr. Davis wrote. "He has been doing this, along with other foremen presumably, for many years. It is permissible under the contract." Although he agreed that the need for this foreman was at a "bare minimum," he remains "more of a supervisor under the present contract than not. In reality [the foreman] is not now in an appreciably different position from that obtaining since 1957. If [he] was a supervisor for all the time since then—and no one then complained that he was not—he is still a supervisor, under this contract."

[2] In one case, *Oxford Paper Company* (United Papermakers and Paperworkers, AFL-CIO), 5 AAA 16, where there was no clear-cut contractual restriction on the type of work a foreman might do, arbitrator Saul Wallen held that an acting foreman had not violated the agreement when he performed certain repair and maintenance operations while getting a machine ready for production. "The fact that duties of a similar nature were sometimes performed by foremen" in the past was one factor in the company's favor. Another was the "emergency nature" of the repairs, although the need for repairs was "foreseeable," and "greater prudence" might have been shown in assigning another

73

Another point of contact between foremen and bargaining unit employees is the accrual and use of seniority. Foremen are often former bargaining unit workers who have retained or accrued seniority that might be asserted to claim jobs in the bargaining unit if there should be no more need for them in managerial capacities. Thus, they are at least potentially in competition with rank and filers.[3]

BARGAINING UNIT WORK OF FOREMEN

Disputes over performance of bargaining unit work by foremen seldom involve a large volume of such work. On the contrary, there are times when so little forbidden work is involved that the employer relies chiefly on the doctrine of *de minimis non curat lex*—"the law is not concerned with trifles." But unions are seldom satisfied by this defense, for even a small amount of production work,

production worker to the repair task. Mr. Wallen concluded: "This grievance arose out of the fact that [the acting foreman] impresses the men in the unit as a little too 'eager beaver' and that he fails to exercise the forbearance that other supervisors have shown under similar circumstances. While he was close to the line drawn by Company policy between proper and improper activities for foremen, I do not believe he crossed it on the occasion complained of."

[3] Generally, a foreman, being outside the bargaining unit of production workers, may be hired and fired at the will of the employer. The standards of "just cause," which must be observed with respect to rank-and-file workers, do not apply to supervisors. But where the foreman is an ex-bargaining unit employee who has residual seniority rights in the unit, the union may take an interest in any action the company takes against him. That is what happened at *Merrill-Stevens Dry Dock & Repair Company* (Industrial Union of Marine and Shipbuilding Workers, AFL-CIO), 23 AAA 5.

The contract permitted a foreman promoted from the bargaining unit to accumulate seniority in the unit. When the employer discharged such a foreman for negligence, the union protested. It was argued that management could do nothing but reduce him to the ranks. Arbitrator Harold T. Dworet disagreed with this view.

An employee who becomes a foreman leaves the jurisdiction of the union, he said. He then becomes subject to discharge for "justifiable cause," no less than bargaining unit employees. The purpose of the clause relied upon by the union was to permit a foreman to accrue seniority against a time when, due to reduction in force, he might find it necessary to return to the bargaining unit. "There is a great difference [between] a man being out of a job by reduction in force and another employee discharged for negligence," he reminded the parties.

when performed by one who is forbidden to do it, seems to be an attack on the integrity of the bargaining unit as such.

A case in point was that of the *Foote Mineral Company* (Oil, Chemical and Atomic Workers, AFL-CIO).[4] "It is agreed that foremen and supervisors shall not do production or maintenance work customarily performed by hourly workers, except for the purposes of training and emergencies," said the contract. Nevertheless, management believed it was not improper to let a foreman receive materials for less than fifteen minutes at a time on occasion after 4:30 P.M. or on week ends, when a regular storeroom attendant was not on duty. On such occasions, a foreman who did the storekeeper's work would sometimes enlist another bargaining unit worker to assist him; but this did not make the invasion of the forbidden area, as the union saw it, more acceptable. Although the company had the right to change job content, union representatives conceded, work could not be taken from one classification and given to another on an overtime basis only, with the object of avoiding call-back or overtime pay to the storekeeper. But above all, the union found the company's argument of *de minimis* repugnant. A few minutes work now and then contained a threat that the volume would grow in the future. Furthermore, by proper planning, the work could have been done during regular hours by the person properly classified to do it.

Laurence E. Seibel, who resolved that dispute, agreed with the union. He was not persuaded by the employer's view that a small amount of work, since it did not deprive hourly rated workers of jobs, was not within the contract's limitations. Nor did the fact that production might be interrupted if the foreman did not receive the materials constitute an "emergency" within the contract's meaning:

While it is true that the entries into the storeroom appear to be of short duration, they equally appear to be regular and recurring in nature, and, accordingly, it is at best questionable whether the *de minimis* concept advanced by the company is applicable. The better view, in my judgment, is that the contract plainly and unambiguously provides that supervisors shall not perform hourly rated employees' work "except for the purposes of training and emergencies" and that, therefore, the work here in question of a regular and recurring nature should not be performed by supervisors unless in connection with "training and emergencies."

[4] 19 AAA 26.

As often happens in such cases, it was not easy to find an appropriate remedy for the violation. The union had asked for compensation to the storekeeper, at the rate that would have applied if he had been called in to do the small amount of "regular and recurring" work. This request was rejected not only because of the "somewhat technical" nature of the violation, but because the contract itself permits a degree of flexibility and interchangeability in assignment of tasks across classification lines. Furthermore, as supervisors had been performing forbidden work of this kind "for some time" without opposition by the union, "it can hardly be said that the company's violation of the agreement has been purposeful."

Thus, the union won a verdict that the company had violated the agreement, but no monetary relief was awarded.

Deliberate "*de Minimis*" Violation

Virtually the same clause and very similar circumstances appeared in the case of the *Huron Portland Cement Company* (Oil, Chemical and Atomic Workers, AFL-CIO);[5] but here the violations were somewhat more deliberate, giving the arbitrator, Richard Mittenthal, the basis for awarding some monetary relief and the opportunity to caution management that if the practice of committing brief violations should continue, "it might become necessary for an arbitrator to grant compensation in cases of this character."[6]

As in the *Foote Mineral* case, the contract here limited the scope of a foreman's bargaining unit work rather strictly:

Employees not subject to this Agreement shall not perform work regularly assigned to the classifications covered under this Agreement, except in cases of emergency or for the purpose of instruction, training, inspection or investigation.

---

[5] 13 AAA 18.

[6] It is not entirely clear what Mr. Mittenthal meant by this. It is well established that arbitrators may award *damages*, where an employee can be shown to have suffered losses by management's error. But no penalties may be awarded unless the contract so provides. One may doubt whether an award granting some employee pay for a few minutes' work would be regarded by the union as an adequate remedy for a deliberate invasion by a foreman of an area forbidden to him. For comments on the distinction between penalties and remedies, see *Bearings Company of America* (United Steelworkers of America, AFL-CIO), 20 AAA 19, discussed in Chapter 7.

Despite this, it was admitted by the company that supervisors had "lent a hand" to repair crews for a few minutes on several occasions. One of these incidents involved about five minutes' work to finish a job. It would have taken longer than that to find a repairman to do it. The most serious violation, at least in time spent, consisted of "cable pulling" by three supervisors, who devoted a total of thirty minutes to the task.

The arbitrator awarded four hours' pay to the senior man on lay-off because that is what he would have been paid if he had been called in to do the cable pulling. For the "trifling amount" of repair work done, there was no remedy to award aside from the possibly futile warning quoted above.

"De Minimis" Defense Upheld

In one case, *Consolidated Paper Company* (United Papermakers and Paperworkers, AFL-CIO),[7] Mark L. Kahn, the arbitrator, upheld management on a *de minimis* plea; but that was because the contract was not as restrictive as those in the two cases described above. Here, the bar against foremen working was not absolute; it applied only if performance of bargaining unit work by supervisors would "result in lost time or pay to the employees covered by the agreement." Moreover, even if lost time were a consequence, foremen would still be privileged to work "in extreme emergencies to prevent serious company losses."

On a certain day, a paper-making machine was shut down for repair. Five employees, including three millwrights, a pipefitter, and a welder, were assigned to the task on a Sunday. They completed the work within forty minutes of the end of their shift, but apparently not without "an hour or so" of help from the foreman. From the beginning, the union had believed that a fourth millwright should have been asked to work. A grievance was therefore filed, protesting the assistance the foreman had given to the repair crew.

In view of the contract language, the critical issue was whether the work the foreman had done had caused the fourth maintenance man to lose any work. Mr. Kahn said it had not:

The Arbitrator is satisfied that the millwrights who were at work could

[7] 13 AAA 19.

have completed their task well within the eight hour shift even if the foreman had entirely avoided all millwright work. Although the maintenance crew finished its work on April 20, 1958, by no later than 1:50 P.M., the men were paid and could have been required to work until 2:30 P.M. on that day. The Arbitrator therefore concludes that the effect of any bargaining unit work the foreman may have done was simply to let the maintenance crew finish up somewhat earlier than would otherwise have been the case, and did not cause [the grievant] to lose work time or pay.

Furthermore, the evidence showed that the foreman had "got into things" only to the extent he customarily did, without objection by the union, during non-overtime hours. The foreman's work was thus "incidental" to his managerial function.

Bargaining Unit Work during Emergencies

Even where foremen are strictly barred from performing bargaining unit work, exceptions are usually made in case of emergency. But the parties are not always in agreement as to what constitutes an emergency. And even where the fact of emergency is undeniable, the extent of production work permitted to foremen may be in dispute.

At a plant of the *Celanese Corporation of America* (Textile Workers Union of America, AFL-CIO),[8] for instance, a drain line became clogged, causing water to back up and soak several hundred bales of cotton. It became necessary for a foreman to examine each bale and determine which had to be scrapped. All the trucking and re-baling incidental to this operation were performed by warehouse employees, but some slitting open of bales, weighing, and handling of the material was done by the foreman.

The union grieved, demanding fifteen hours' pay at time-and-a-half for an employee next in line for overtime when the incident occurred. The company rejected the grievance, citing a "company policy" adopted nine years earlier, to which the union had allegedly agreed, that foremen could engage in production work "as a temporary measure in case of emergency."

While this grievance was pending a second incident occurred. It seems that a sprinkler head broke in the same area, wetting close to 200 bales. The process of weighing, examining, and determining

[8] 14 AAA 2.

which bales could be salvaged was repeated by the foreman, bringing the total of bargaining unit work performed by him to 31 hours.

When the matter came before Samuel H. Jaffee, the union argued that even if the first incident could be considered an "emergency," the same could not be said of the second. Apparently, the union was most concerned about the weighing operation, a task normally performed by hourly rated employees. Three questions were before the arbitrator: (1) Had the union agreed to the policy statement cited by the company? (2) Did the two flooding incidents constitute an emergency? (3) Could the weighing of bales have been separated from the managerial tasks performed by the supervisor? The arbitrator upheld the company on all points:

1. It is unnecessary to determine whether the policy referred to above, claimed to have been agreed to, is still in existence. Even if it is not, it is the general rule that a supervisor can in any event do unit work "as a temporary measure in case of emergency." So to this extent the policy changed nothing.
2. Do we have an "emergency" here? I see no escape from the conclusion that there was an emergency in both incidents. The fact that it happened twice made the second incident no less an emergency on the facts presented. Among these facts were (a) that time was of the essence, and (b) the large amount of money involved in connection with salvage operations. The fact that the flooding happened twice did not convert the abnormal into the normal.
3. I conclude on the facts peculiar to this case that it was impracticable to require [the foreman] to have separated the weighing from the rest of the work, and that, on the whole, the weighing portion of the work was in any event *de minimis*.

"Man-made" Emergencies

An emergency, according to one dictionary, is "a sudden need for immediate action." But if the need is sudden because of previous neglect, it may be regarded by a union as a "man-made" emergency, and therefore not within the meaning of a contract clause permitting foremen to do bargaining unit work during emergencies. Several cases illustrate this point.

One was at the *Corn Products Company* (American Federation of Grain Millers, AFL-CIO).[9] A heavy rainfall occurred during one

[9] 16 AAA 21.

night, and suspecting that part of the plant might be affected, a foreman made an inspection tour at 1:00 A.M. He found the water level in an electrical manhole dangerously high, threatening to cause a short circuit. Furthermore, water was draining into the basement of the plant. Enlisting the help of a production worker, he installed a pump and operated it for thirty minutes.

This would clearly seem to have been the prudent thing to do, for damage to the electrical system might have resulted if pumping had been delayed until the start of the day shift. Nor was it possible to call in a bargaining unit employee within a short time. But the union filed a grievance, based on the assertion that management was aware of the probability of seepage after a heavy rainfall. By failing to take timely precautions, the union argued, the company had forfeited the privilege of relying on the "emergency" exception to the rule barring foremen from production work.

Bert L. Luskin, who arbitrated the case, found the facts not exactly as the union had portrayed them. The dangerous condition had been "closely checked," he said, and had been corrected on all occasions "when it became evident that the pit had to be pumped out in order to keep the water from flowing into the conduit."

In substance, it is the opinion of the Arbitrator that the condition which existed required immediate attention to the extent that the water should have been pumped out as quickly as possible in order to avoid or prevent the possibility of serious and extensive damage. In view of the fact that sufficient unit employees were not available to perform the function, and in view of the fact that the work should not have been delayed until the start of the first shift or until unit employees could be called in or perform the work, the supervisor was justified in performing the 30 minutes of manual functions within the permissive language of Article IV, Section 15.

Tight Scheduling

Man-made circumstances were illustrated more clearly at another plant of the *Celanese Corporation of America* (United Construction Workers).[10] Here, no natural catastrophe or danger of damage to property was involved. The question, rather, was whether failure of an employee to report for work created an emergency situation

[10] 3 AAA 15.

such as to justify the foreman's performance of his job. The union's case, in essence, was that management had created the emergency by scheduling only thirty-one employees for a shift that required a minimum of twenty-nine employees to operate. Such a schedule was too tight, the union argued. It didn't leave room for normal absenteeism. Thus, when only twenty-eight employees appeared, the foreman substituted for the absent man to keep the shift running.

The company's defense was based on the contract, which read:

It is agreed that supervisory employees, excluded from the bargaining unit, shall not perform work usually performed by the production . . . employees of the bargaining unit, except: 1. In case of emergency . . . 2. In the absence of regular employees when no other qualified employee is available . . .

and on the fact that there seemed to be a concerted refusal of employees on an earlier shift to "double over" and fill the vacant job.

Although scheduling of thirty-one employees for a shift requiring at least twenty-nine might be "tight," Samuel H. Jaffee ruled, the company could not be blamed for not anticipating that there would be a "concerted refusal" of employees on other shifts to respond to a work call.

At any rate, I cannot on the evidence before me find that there existed a "company-created emergency" in the only sense that might be an effective answer to the company's reliance on [the quoted contract clause]— that, right or wrong, it deliberately or perhaps recklessly brought about the situation which resulted in the events of the night of July 19.

Effect on Layoff

Protection of bargaining unit employees from loss of earning opportunities is, of course, the most obvious reason for limiting the amount of production work foremen and supervisors may do. At the *Badenhausen Corporation* (United Steelworkers of America, AFL-CIO),[11] this motive was expressed in a clause permitting supervisors to perform unit work "in accordance with past practice," provided such work would not cause any employee in the unit to have less than forty hours' work.

In January 1959, a factory clerk, who happened to be the most

[11] 12 AAA 20.

junior in the plant, was bumped out of his job by a third-shift time-keeper, whose job had been eliminated with the cancellation of that shift. As there were supervisors who, according to the union, spent about 75 per cent of their time at various kinds of factory clerical work, a grievance was filed demanding that they discontinue this work to the extent necessary to bring about the recall of the laid-off man. The hypothesis was that if work were taken from the supervisors, a vacancy would be created which the junior employee might have filled.

To the company, this seemed to be irrelevant speculation. Bumping is a "calculated risk" which employees must take in view of the union's insistence on bumping procedures in the contract, management said in a fourth-step answer. Furthermore, even if supervisors abstained from bargaining unit work, creating a "vacancy," there would be nothing to require the employer to fill it. "The possibility of such a series of hypothetical circumstances, each developing in favor of the grievant, especially in the present period of reduced shop activity, is entirely too obscure and intangible to be used as a basis for consideration in this case," the company concluded. Finally, it was pointed out in answer to the grievance, the man who bumped into the factory clerk job was working forty hours per week, and the reason for bumping had nothing to do with the amount of bargaining unit work supervisors were doing.

In summary, the union's argument was that supervisors may not do bargaining unit work if *any* union member is reduced to less than forty hours per week. The employer's position was that supervisors may not do production work if *such* work would reduce the workweek of any member.

Arbitrator Irving K. Kessler found the union's viewpoint too "tenuous" to support.

The union did not demonstrate that the work performed by production supervisors was in any way related to the layoff of [the grievant]. He was "bumped" by a senior employee when the third shift in the Weld Shop was discontinued. There has been no change in the complement of the office so that the percentage of time worked by the supervisors was not a factor in the layoff.

In the course of the arguments on the grievance, a secondary issue appeared in the company's statement that the percentage of time supervisors spent at non-supervisory duties was "a flexible matter." On this point, the company was not sustained. "It was unmistakably the intent of the parties to maintain the existing duties of supervisors, but only so long as no unit employees were adversely affected, and certainly not to extend such responsibilities," Mr. Kessler wrote. The company was directed to "remove from the work assignment of supervisory employees any duties whose nature or duration would exceed the percentage of work time of such duties in effect as of the date of the signing of the agreement."

Work during Absence of Bargaining Unit Employee

At the *Celanese Corporation of America* (United Mine Workers, District 50),[12] the contract permitted foremen to do bargaining unit work "in the absence of regular employees when no qualified employee is available." The union thought this clause meant that if the foreman was to do bargaining unit work, he had to take over the absent employee's job and no other. Management believed that the absence of an employee was the condition precedent to a foreman's working; but once that condition was met, the foreman could rearrange assignments, so that he would do the work of an employee who was not absent, permitting the *latter* to do the absent employee's job.

The arbitrator, B. Meredith Reid, upheld the company view, particularly because of the fact that, under the circumstances before him, the rearrangement of work gave bargaining unit employees more work than they would otherwise have had.

In this particular case, it is interesting to note that far from trying to breach any contract right which the employees might have, the company sought the other extreme by giving to the hourly paid employee the greater amount of work available. This was consistent with the usual and customary desire of hourly paid employees that members of supervision not perform their work, or perform no more than is necessary under the circumstances.

Remedies for Forbidden Work

In the *Huron Portland Cement* case, as we have seen, four hours' call-in pay was awarded as a remedy for thirty minutes' work by a

12 23 AAA 21.

foreman. G. Allan Dash made a similar award for *Ball Brothers Company* (United Glass and Ceramic Workers, AFL-CIO),[13] where a foreman on the third shift had done forty minutes of forbidden work. Conceding the error, the employer had offered to "make whole" an employee with forty minutes' pay. But Mr. Dash said this would be inadequate. The fact that the foreman decided to do the work himself implied that there was no bargaining unit employee on hand capable of performing it. That being so, an employee should have been called in specially, in which case he would be entitled to four hours' call-in pay.

Another case involving an admitted violation and a disputed remedy was that of the *Borg-Warner Corporation* (Allied Industrial Workers of America, AFL-CIO).[14] A foreman having performed certain experimental millwright work for three hours, management offered three hours' pay to a bargaining unit employee. The union demanded three hours at time-and-a-half. When the controversy came to arbitration, Russell N. Sullivan upheld the grievance. The evidence was "uncertain," he said, as to whether the work was done during straight time or overtime. As the area in which it was done was not open to union representatives, the company had the "burden of proof" to show that only straight time hours were involved. That burden was not met, in Mr. Sullivan's judgment. As all millwrights were working full time, and none were on layoff, proper application of the agreement may have necessitated overtime, unless other work was postponed. For all these reasons, the more costly remedy was awarded.

"Cease and Desist" Order

The difficulty arbitrators, and the parties themselves, encounter in fashioning remedies for contract violations of the kind discussed in this chapter has led at least one union to seek a "cease and desist" order, presumably as a deterrent to future violations.

In this case, *The Budd Company* (Independent Workers Union of the Budd Company),[15] the contract said that supervisors would not perform work "regularly performed by non-supervisory employ-

[13] 12 AAA 14.
[14] 21 AAA 6.
[15] 10 AAA 8.

ees" except for instructing new employees or when the work requires a supervisor's "special skills." In the past, foremen had occasionally dispensed supplies, a task principally performed by hourly rated workers. But in May 1958, a new foreman assigned to a department began making this task principally his. This, said Lewis M. Gill, was a contract violation:

> The evidence establishes that the *bulk* of the work *was* performed by the office clerk in the bargaining unit. . . . If the foreman had merely continued to do this work to the same degree that foremen had done it in the past, I think no violation would be established. By the same token, I think there *is* a violation to the extent that the foreman's share of this work has been expanded, and the bargaining unit employees' share of it has diminished.

This brought Mr. Gill to the "rather elusive" question of an appropriate remedy. The union had asked for eighty hours' pay to a factory clerk, then on layoff. This figure was arrived at by estimating that the foreman had spent about one hour a day at the work in question, or five hours per week multiplied by the sixteen weeks which had elapsed since the most recent layoff. The arbitrator said this estimate was "about right," as far as the time spent by the foreman dispensing materials was concerned. The difficulty was, however, that only part of this time represented an expansion of the customary amount of such work done by a foreman:

> No exact calculation is possible here, but my best estimate is that if 80 hours is the *total* amount of time spent by the foreman in handling the supplies, probably about one-half of that time represents a continuation of what the foreman had done in the past, and the rest represents an expansion of the foreman's activities in this area. Under these circumstances, an award of 40 hours' pay to the appropriate bargaining unit employee (identity to be left to the parties), seems in order.

Thus, arithmetic and a rule of thumb led the arbitrator to a monetary remedy of forty hours' pay. The more unusual problem was presented, however, in the union's request for a "cease and desist" order against the company. "I am not inclined favorably to that type of award," answered Mr. Gill. "While I do not doubt that it is within the scope of an arbitrator's authority, it is relatively rare to find cease and desist provisions in arbitration awards."

Presumably that is due to the fact that an arbitrator, unlike a court, does not possess any authority to rule upon questions of compliance with his awards, unless of course the parties agree to submit such issues to him. In practical effect, it is probably not very important whether an award does or does not contain a cease and desist provision; it is normally a fair assumption that action found violative of a contract provision will not be continued, since to do so would be merely to invite another dispute.

If a company *should* for some reason continue to do what has been found to be violative of the contract, perhaps a cease and desist provision in the award would provide a basis for seeking enforcement of the award in court and then enjoining any continued violation of the award. However, the basic purpose of arbitration is to avoid resort to the courts, as well as strikes, and I am disinclined to include in awards any provisions which might encourage further litigation.

At least part of the reason for the arbitrator's "reluctance" to issue a cease and desist order in this case was that "there is no indication of any sort that this company is likely to continue the activity complained of, should it be found violative of the contract."

Monetary Remedy Paid to Union

The contract at the *Waller Brothers Stone Company* (United Stone and Allied Product Workers of America, AFL-CIO)[16] was unusual in that it specifically authorized a remedy for violations, *de minimis* or otherwise, even where it was not possible to identify any employee who lost earnings opportunities when foremen did forbidden work. The contract required that an appropriate sum be turned over to the union treasury on such occasions:

Violations of this section shall be penalized by the company paying to the employee injured by such violation the wages for such work in addition to any regular earnings, or, if no individual employee is injured, then the company shall pay the sum into the union treasury. All violations shall be penalized at a minimum of one hour's pay for the job, or longer, if the violation continues for longer.

On the basis of this clause, Bert L. Luskin, the arbitrator, directed that one hour's pay be given the union because a foreman pushed a load of stone from one location to another, in violation of a clause forbidding him to do bargaining unit work "except in case of emer-

16 22 AAA 13.

gency" or when bargaining unit tasks are "incidental to supervision or the continuous operation of the plant."

Although the work was "minimal," Mr. Luskin wrote, it was a violation because there was nothing to indicate that an emergency existed. Furthermore, he said, this was not an "isolated instance of momentary oversight," the same foreman having done such bargaining unit work in the past over the protest of employees.

SENIORITY RIGHTS OF FOREMEN

Almost invariably, foremen who have never been in the bargaining unit have no seniority standing.[17] If they should be removed as foremen and transferred to bargaining unit work, they would be as new employees. But with those who were promoted from the ranks, the situation may be different. Under some contracts, they may retain seniority already accrued, but not add to it during the time they are outside the unit. In others, full accrual may be permitted. Collective bargaining agreements also occasionally limit the circumstances under which a supervisor may assert seniority for return to the unit. Thus, for instance, he may be permitted to return to his old classification only if it does not involve displacement of a worker presently employed.

Retention vs. Accrual of Seniority

Arbitrator William E. Simkin resolved a typical dispute at *Joseph T. Ryerson and Son, Inc.* (United Steelworkers of America, AFL-CIO).[18] The issue was the seniority status of a foreman who had once been in the bargaining unit. Demoting him to the ranks, the company credited him not only with the seniority he acquired in the

---

[17] See, for example, *The Cared Corporation* (United Steelworkers of America, AFL-CIO), 8 AAA 6. The contract granted accumulated service credit to "employees in the bargaining unit who are promoted to the position of supervisor" and who thereafter are returned to the bargaining unit. The company thought this provision also justified crediting a downgraded supervisor who had never been in the bargaining unit with seniority for the time he spent as a supervisory employee. Lewis M. Gill disagreed. "Whatever may be said of the merits of granting accumulated service credit to ex-supervisors who did not originate in the bargaining unit," he wrote, "it is clear that this contract did not provide for it."

[18] 22 AAA 17.

bargaining unit, but also with seniority for the time spent outside the unit. The union believed he had lost his seniority when he left the unit; on coming back to a bargaining unit job, he was a new employee, without seniority.

Mr. Simkin noted that the contract did not deal with the question specifically. But there was one clause which listed a number of circumstances under which seniority would be terminated. Accepting a promotion to foreman was not one of the circumstances. From this he drew two conclusions:

1. The ex-foreman was properly credited with the seniority he had once acquired in the unit. His past service was "money in the bank" as far as seniority was concerned. Consequently, his return to the unit was not as a "new employee."

2. On the other hand, it was an error for the company to credit the ex-foreman with seniority for time spent outside the unit:

In the absence of a contract clause or a clear understanding as respects supervisors, seniority for job rights purposes is a concept that is related realistically only to bargaining unit work. Supervisors normally have no formal job rights seniority on supervisory positions while they are supervisors. If prior bargaining unit service is not lost under this contract when a man becomes a supervisor because it is not terminated by any contract provision, it is just as difficult to find a contract provision that provides for accumulation.

The employer had relied on a clause defining seniority as "length of continuous service in the warehouse," but Mr. Simkin said the company was overlooking the real meaning of "continuous service" in that context. "It would be reading a great deal into this [language]," he said, "to conclude that the words 'continuous service' mean continuous service as an employee or as a supervisor or as a clerk." Management had also referred to another phrase in the contract which, without mentioning the bargaining unit, spoke of terminal dates of employment. This was "admittedly in the company's favor," the arbitrator wrote; but it could still not be controlling, because it was clear that "the parties have never grappled with this issue directly in negotiations." Instead, the question of seniority status of foremen was "swept under the rug," leaving the unclear language of the contract unchanged.

The question of whether foremen retain already acquired seniority or accumulate seniority while in a managerial capacity also arose at the *Mississippi Lime Company of Missouri* (United Glass and Ceramic Workers, AFL-CIO).[19] The contract read:

It is agreed that an employee who is promoted to an administrative, clerical, or supervisory position, shall in case he is returned to his former job, retain his seniority and privileges in the line-up he left, provided he takes a withdrawal card from the union.

As the union read the sentence, seniority was "frozen" when a man was promoted to a supervisory capacity. It thawed again and resumed accrual when he once more became a member of the unit. The use of the word "retain" in the clause absolutely barred any possibility of accumulation by a foreman. To this the company answered that a man cannot realistically "retain" his seniority unless he maintains the "relative status" he had when he left the unit. This required accumulation.

Robben T. Fleming, who had been selected to arbitrate the dispute, found both answers possible in a reading of the contract clause itself. "We have not learned to use words so precisely that they can have only one possible meaning." As there was doubt in his mind as to what the negotiators had meant when they drafted the agreement, he turned to the past practice of the parties. Here he found support for the company position. The quoted clause had been in effect for four years, during two contracts. "Under both there had been a uniform practice of according accumulated seniority to supervisors."

While disposing of the grievance before him largely on the basis of past practice, Mr. Fleming expressed five general principles which, he said, usually apply in cases of this kind.

1. Seniority is a valuable right with a long history in American Trade Unionism and it ought not to be lightly discarded.
2. Seniority is clearly a creature of the contract and the parties may give it whatever form they desire. Moreover, seniority rights, once given, do not vest and may be changed from time to time as new contracts are negotiated.
3. Where the contract says nothing about seniority for supervisors, but lists the usual ways in which seniority may be broken, an individual

[19] 1 AAA 16.

does not lose the seniority rights acquired up to that time simply because he becomes a supervisor. He does not, however, continue to accumulate seniority thereafter because he is no longer covered by the contract and the contract says nothing about seniority for supervisors. He can keep what seniority he acquired as a production worker because the contract does not state that he loses it by becoming a supervisor.

4. A production worker who is promoted to supervision retains the seniority acquired prior to promotion, but he may not exercise it while in the supervisory ranks because he is not covered by the contract. If the company returns him to the production force he may then exercise the rights which were frozen when he was promoted.

5. Where the contract is not silent but specifically grants seniority rights to supervisors, the question becomes one of contract interpretation.

Past Seniority Protected in New Contract

The premise that "seniority is a creature of the contract," in the words of Mr. Fleming, quoted above, and that parties may measure seniority in any way they wish, was also illustrated at the *American Radiator and Standard Sanitary Corporation* (International Molders and Foundry Workers, AFL-CIO),[20] where the arbitrator was Robert G. McIntosh. Under contracts negotiated in 1955 and 1956, an employee was credited with "full seniority," despite his supervisory position outside the bargaining unit. In 1957, however, the agreement was modified, so that a foreman returning to the bargaining unit would have accrued seniority only in the classification or department into which he was demoted.

When a foreman was demoted in 1959, making it necessary to compute his accrued seniority, the critical question became whether the 1957 modification had erased the seniority he accrued under the 1955 and 1956 contracts. Mr. McIntosh did not question the right of parties to wipe out previously accrued seniority by newly negotiated rules, but he ruled that in this case they did not do so. His conclusion was based on the fact that the 1957 contract contained a clause stating that "the provisions and conditions set out in this Agreement shall supersede the provisions and conditions as set forth in any previous Master Agreement, but shall not be retroactive beyond its effective date."

"Thus it is obvious," Mr. McIntosh wrote, "that both parties

[20] 7 AAA 24.

agreed that whatever rights, privileges or advantages an employee obtained under a specific contract should not be taken away from him by a subsequent contract or an interpretation of such subsequent contract." Therefore, he concluded, the foreman, having once been credited with service in a certain department, could not be stripped of that seniority retroactively.

Bidding for Unit Jobs

A foreman may have residual seniority rights in the bargaining unit, but as a general rule, he must be in the unit to assert them. He may not be permitted to do so from his position outside the unit. That was a finding of L. G. Lichliter in *Maier's Bakery* (Bakery and Confectionery Workers, AFL-CIO).[21]

A vacancy occurred in the cake-mixer classification and was posted for bidding on the company bulletin board, in accordance with the contract. One of the foremen thereupon notified management that he was resigning his supervisory position in order to get that job. Two other employees, not in supervisory capacities, also entered bids. As the foreman had more seniority, he was awarded the job, whereupon the union filed a grievance. Both sides agreed that the issue turned on interpretation of this clause:

ARTICLE V. An employee employed in a supervisory capacity by the Employer and, therefore, ineligible for Union membership, upon ceasing to hold such supervisory position shall be entitled to membership in the bargaining unit and upon becoming a member of the bargaining unit shall have seniority based upon his original date of employment by the Employer regardless of prior Union affiliations.

The union's position, briefly, was that the foreman's bid could not be honored until after his application for membership in the union was received. This occurred after the closing date for determination of the successful bidder. Management answered that the resignation from the supervisory position occurred before the closing date for bids and that nothing else mattered.

The arbitrator upheld the grievance, but on grounds different from those asserted by the union.

In the first place, the article nowhere deals with the question as to who

[21] 1 AAA 17.

is eligible to bid on a posted job, nor can we find any mention of that subject elsewhere in the contract. All that this article does is to provide that *"upon becoming a member* of the bargaining unit" a former supervisory employee's seniority shall include those years of service he has previously spent with the company outside the unit. It does not say *how* a supervisory employee can become a member of the unit, and certainly a resignation from the position of foreman, with nothing more, could not of itself have put [the foreman] among the classification of jobs which comprise the bargaining unit. It goes without saying that to be eligible to bid on a posted job in the absence of any governing contractual language, the bidder must at that time be a member of the unit.

The argument of the union that union membership is a requirement of bidding is equally erroneous. If an employee, holding a job with the company which is within the unit, seeks to bid on a posted job, he has every right to do so even though not a union member, provided he applies for membership within thirty days, as required by Article I.

In view of the foregoing, we must conclude that under the contract, (1) Only employees who are part of the collective bargaining unit may bid for posted jobs, (2) Resignation as foreman did not, of itself, constitute [the foreman] a member of the unit, and (3) Awarding the job of mixer to [the foreman] was erroneous.

It would appear, therefore, that in order to compete with bargaining unit employees for the posted job, the foreman would have had to resign his supervisory job unconditionally, taking any job open within the bargaining unit. From that vantage point, he could then bid to become a cake mixer. Whether this could be accomplished within the few days during which bids were open, however, was not clear from the facts of the case as revealed in the arbitrator's written opinion.

TRANSFER OF WORK OUTSIDE UNIT TO FOREMEN

As we have seen, when a foreman steps across the line separating him from non-supervisory work, the union may see in it an attack on the integrity of the unit and a threat to the earnings of its members. Understandably, therefore, resistance becomes even stronger when work is transferred away from the bargaining unit altogether, making it part of managerial duties. Nor is an employee promoted to foreman usually permitted to take bargaining unit work with him.

Redesignation of Work as "Managerial"

A case in point was that of the *Rockwell Standard Corporation* (United Steelworkers of America, AFL-CIO).[22] One of the bargaining unit employees, classified as an adjustment and correspondence clerk, was promoted to chief of the accounts receivable department, a job excluded from the bargaining unit. In this capacity, he continued to perform a substantial part of the job he held in the past. The union apparently had no objection to the promotion as such, provided the work was left behind in the unit. Management answered that it had the right to change the content of any job and that the duties involved were essentially supervisory in nature.

Donald A. Crawford's award upheld the union completely:

Even on the basis of its premise that the Adjustment and Correspondence Clerk Job is supervisory, the company cannot successfully contend that it could not have bargained away its contractual right under Article II to exclude this supervisory job, and that it can therefore now unilaterally remove the job from the bargaining unit to correct an alleged error of judgment. The classification in question was established as a bargaining unit job in 1954 and remained so after the renewal of the contract in 1956. Thus the job has been a matter for collective bargaining by the parties, and the company has in fact given up its right to remove the job from the bargaining unit unilaterally. Any problem the company may now have as a result of the job being in the bargaining unit, is a matter for discussion and resolution by the parties—especially since the current contract is about to expire.

Work Never Firmly in Unit

At *Strick Trailers* (United Automobile Workers, AFL-CIO),[23] the decision was in favor of management; but there was a significant difference from the *Rockwell* case, in that the work in question had never become a "historical function" within the unit.

The facts, as described by the arbitrator, Lawrence R. Van Deusen, were simple. In January 1959, certain record-keeping tasks were assigned to a timekeeper in the machine shop. At the time, this employee protested that these tasks were unfamiliar to him and not within his classification. He was overruled on this point and

[22] 13 AAA 12.
[23] 13 AAA 8.

directed to perform those tasks. Three months later, however, the clerical functions were taken away from him and given to an employee who was not in the bargaining unit.[24] Instead, additional timekeeping duties were given the timekeeper. Again he protested, this time asserting that the clerical tasks, although burdensome, belonged to him and could not be transferred out of the unit.

Mr. Van Deusen defined the question before him as follows: "Has the company violated the agreement with the union by taking away assigned functions from the timekeeping classification and assigning them to a classification outside the union?" He saw no violation of the agreement, but for very special reasons. "If the assigned work which was withdrawn had become an historic function, then there would be a violation of the contract," Mr. Van Deusen wrote. As the work had not become an historic function, its removal became "an exercise of the management function and, therefore, not a violation of the agreement."

Moreover, he said, the grievant knew, when the clerical tasks were given to him, that the assignment was experimental, subject to change. It was also significant that "job security" was not an issue in this case, no layoffs having occurred in the timekeeping department.

"Fragments" of Bargaining Unit Jobs

When a bargaining unit job is abolished and its duties are assigned to other employees, some fragments of the job may fall to supervisory employees. That is what happened at *Erwin Mills* (United Textile Workers Union, AFL-CIO).[25] Arbitrator Robert H. Wettach, who arbitrated the case, held that the employer did not violate the contract when a supervisor-trainee was permitted to perform some duties of an abolished job, where those duties were "not substantial" and where they were performed "to a considerable extent" in the regular course of the supervisor's work. Although the supervisor "may have exceeded his regular duties on some occasions

---

[24] This case involved transfer of work from a bargaining unit employee to a clerk, rather than to a foreman. As the clerk was outside the union, however, the issues presented in this case were similar to those involved in disputes over transfer of work to supervisors.

[25] 4 AAA 19.

and performed duties assigned to operators," the evidence as to this "is not clear and convincing and does not add up to the performance of a substantial part of the duties of the discontinued job." Furthermore, the company's action in "combining the duties of the discontinued job with other regular jobs was in accordance with past practice."

6

CALL-IN PAY

The right of management to direct the work force and to arrange production schedules is acknowledged, openly or by implication, in every collective bargaining agreement. But this right carries with it the obligation to notify employees in advance, when work is going to be unavailable at their normal starting time. The customary contractual penalty for failure to give such notice is four hours' call-in pay. It is also customary, however, to relieve management of its reporting pay obligations when work is unavailable for reasons beyond the employer's control.

When disputes arise as to the interpretation of call-in pay clauses, they almost always involve four separate, but interrelated, questions:

1. Did the employee report for work at his scheduled time without having been told not to do so?

2. Was work unavailable for a reason which relieves management of reporting pay obligations?

3. Assuming that work was unavailable for such a reason, is management nevertheless obligated to grant call-in pay because of failure to give employees timely notice?

4. Did employees forfeit their right to call-in pay, to which they would otherwise have been entitled, by some failure on their own part?

THE EFFECT OF EMERGENCIES

A typical problem arose at the *John Wood Company* (United Steelworkers of America, AFL-CIO).[1] On March 19, 1958, one of the most severe storms on record hit the Philadelphia area, where the plant was located. It began in the afternoon and continued on through the next day, blocking highways, crippling rail service, and

[1] 3 AAA 23.

causing interruption of electric power and telephone service.

Despite this, some employees began reporting for work at 7 A.M. on March 20. They found that the power had gone off an hour earlier. There was no management representative present who could tell them definitely whether to wait for work or go home. As a result, some department foremen told employees to wait, others advised them to leave, and still others merely consulted among themselves, but gave no definite instructions to the men under them. At about 7:35 A.M., power was restored, and some men began working. But a half hour later, one of the top executives of the company arrived and ordered the plant closed for the day.

When the time came to pay the employees for that week, it was found that the work force fell into three categories: those who did not report for work at all on March 20; those who reported but did not actually perform work before the order was given closing the plant; and those who did varying amounts of work until the closing order was given. The employer's solution was to pay nothing to the first and second groups, and to pay the third group of workers for actual time worked. The union conceded that the first group—those who did not report—were not entitled to pay. But four hours' call-in pay was requested for the second group, and the difference between four hours' pay and what they received, for the third group. The contractual basis for this demand was the following provision:

Article VIII

Section 1. Any employee who reports for work in accordance with his regularly scheduled shift, whom the company has failed to notify not to report for work before he has left home to come to work, should be given not less than four (4) hours work; but if four (4) hours work is not available, the employee shall be paid for four (4) hours at his average straight time earned rate.

Section 2. Section 1 above shall be inoperative in the event of a labor dispute or in the case of emergencies such as fires, storms, flood, accidents, power breakdown, or other causes beyond the control of the company.

The union's case was based on three chief contentions: (1) the employees had not been notified before they left home that no work was to be performed; (2) several foremen had told employees to stand by, and others had actually put them to work; and (3) work could have continued for the rest of the day after power was restored. To reinforce the demand for call-in pay, union representatives at the arbitration pointed out that if employees who were told to stand by had gone home before the plant was officially closed, they could have been subject to punishment. It was "equitable," therefore, that the time so spent should come within the reporting pay provision.

The employer's view was that the entire situation was covered by Section 2, quoted above. As the storm made it impossible for top company officers to get to the plant in time to notify employees or to reach the plant and each other by telephone, management could not be said to have defaulted in its obligation.[2]

William N. Loucks, who was selected as arbitrator of that dispute, said that the first question before him was whether there had been an emergency within the meaning of the collective bargaining agreement. He answered this in the affirmative. Furthermore, the "indecision on whether the plant would or would not operate" was also caused by conditions "beyond the control of the company officials," thus accounting for the failure of the employer to notify the work force that the plant would be closed. Finally, in reply to the union's contention that, with power restored, the plant could have worked, Mr. Loucks answered that the circumstances such as the parties had agreed upon in Section 2, quoted above, "were so clearly present" that Section 1, providing for call-in pay, was "inoperative on the day in question." As none of the employees was entitled to call-in pay under the circumstances, the union's grievance was dismissed.

Timely Cancellation of Shift

The fact of an emergency does not by itself always cancel call-in pay obligations. The employer may also have to show that there was no opportunity to tell employees there would be no work for them. When the emergency is created by a power failure and repairs are under way, management may be faced with a difficult choice. To cancel a shift immediately may avoid the risk of having to pay employees for reporting. On the other hand, if power is re-

[2] There was testimony of attempts to have announcements made through radio stations, but the breakdown of communications made these attempts ineffective.

stored quickly, it may prove expensive to have cancelled the shift unnecessarily. That was the dilemma that faced management at the *Downingtown Paper Box Company* (International Brotherhood of Pulp, Sulphite and Paper Mill Workers, AFL-CIO).[3]

The power failure occurred at 12:50 P.M., about two-and-a-half hours before the afternoon shift was due to report. As a crew from the electric power company arrived quickly and expected to effect repairs in about an hour, nothing was done to notify employees that the plant might not operate.

Shortly before the start of the afternoon shift, however, it became evident that power would not be restored in time. The shift was cancelled too late to notify the employees, many of whom had already arrived. A grievance demanding four hours' reporting pay was filed in behalf of the thirty-five to forty employees who had to be sent home.

The arbitrator, John Perry Horlacher, ruled that call-in pay was not due where, as here, there was reason to believe until fifteen minutes before the start of the shift that power might be restored. The union's view that the employer could have escaped call-in pay obligations only by cancelling the shift immediately on interruption of the power was rejected:

It seems evident that the time the company has to notify employees not to report starts to run when it is reasonably sure there will be no work for them. It would be irresponsible for the company to cancel a shift in the face of a genuine probability that the work would be available.

Also rejected was the union's contention that the employees should at least have been given a "stand-by alert" when the power failed. "It is not reasonable to expect or require the sounding of an alert against something one is virtually certain (even if mistakenly so) will not happen," Mr. Horlacher wrote.

Although the particular grievance of these employees was resolved in favor of management, the employer was not upheld in his attempt to get a ruling that call-in pay is not due under any circumstance in the event of a "breakdown." The call-in pay provision, the arbitrator wrote:

is designed to prevent workers from reporting for work when there is

[3] 21 AAA 23.

none. It employs the penalty device of four hours pay to assure that whenever possible the company will see that "such employees are notified beforehand not to report." The exception in the case of emergencies assumes inability to give notification "beforehand" although this is not stated. If this assumption isn't present the company would be free in a major breakdown, known the minute it happened to mean a 24 or 36 hour shutdown, to notify no one even though it had many hours in which to do so. There is no more reason for such latitude in shutdown situations beyond the company's control than in those under its control where *both* allow ample time to notify the affected employees. It would be a questionable construction of Section Four which created such a distinction. The "beyond control" type of situation is the one which by its very nature commonly precludes adequate time for notification, hence the logic of the exception.

ALTERNATIVE OF CALL-IN PAY OR SUBSTITUTE WORK

The contract at the *Harsco Corporation* (United Steelworkers of America, AFL-CIO)[4] permitted management the option of giving four hours' call-in pay or offering substitute work to employees, when they were not given timely notice not to report. It also relieved the employer of its reporting pay obligations when work was unavailable because of machine breakdown. The two provisions seemed to be in conflict on one occasion when a machine broke down before employees had done four hours' work. Employees thus made idle were told to do other work while the machine was examined to determine how long it would take to fix it. As it was quickly apparent that the machine could not be repaired immediately, the employees were sent home.

Were they entitled to the difference between pay for hours worked and four hours? The union said they were because, by directing employees to do other work, however briefly, the employer had waived his right to rely on the provision of the contract relieving him of call-in pay in case of machine breakdown. The arbitrator, J. Charles Short, disagreed with the union:

In the judgment of the present arbitrator, unreasonable results would most likely follow upon any determination that required the company to announce an immediate decision to retain or release the employees in the event of a breakdown. To say that if the employees are retained in serv-

4 22 AAA 20.

ice for a minute, a few minutes, or even an hour, the company forfeits the privilege of asserting the defense permitted [by a clause exempting the employer from call-in pay obligations in the event of equipment breakdown], would be to invoke a clearly arbitrary rule. Such a rule would be based upon nothing more than the lapse of time. Since the company's basic obligation is to seek employment for the employees who do report for work every honest effort to carry out that basic undertaking conforms to the letter and spirit of the agreement.

This did not mean, Mr. Short added, that management could keep workers standing around indefinitely after a machine breakdown. If that were done, it would cast doubt on the "good faith" of any refusal to grant call-in pay. In the instant case, he concluded, there was no tenable basis for a finding of bad faith, although the circumstances were "somewhat suspicious."[5]

Forfeit of Call-in Pay by Failure to Remain in Plant

As the *Harsco Corporation* case indicates, management is sometimes given the right to assign employees to substitute work during the guaranteed period. The eligibility of workers to call-in pay may therefore depend on whether they have made themselves available for such work. That was the situation at *Purolator Products, Inc.* (United Automobile Workers, AFL-CIO).[6] The reciprocal obligations were expressed in the following language:

Section 4. Any employee reporting for his or her regular shift or who is required to report for work and not having been notified to the contrary, shall be guaranteed a minimum of four (4) hours work or four (4) hours pay. If four (4) hours at his regular job is not available, the Company may assign him to another job and he shall be paid on the basis of his regular base rate.

When the morning shift arrived for work one day, they found that a steam pipe had broken during the night, leaving their de-

---

[5] Although denying the grievance, the arbitrator did not uphold one argument of the company, to the effect that the employees did other work "on their own initiative" while awaiting a report on the machine. "Employment is a continuing status so long as employees are on the premises of the employer, subject to his direction and control," he said. "Management has the right and duty to direct the work force and the presumption is that work which employees perform was directed, at least impliedly, by the supervisors and not the workers themselves."

[6] 13 AAA 14.

partment too cold for comfortable work. Without waiting to be re-assigned to other departments, which were warmer, most of the employees went home. They nevertheless expected call-in pay because, in their view, the steam pipe had broken early enough for management to have cancelled the shift and notified them of it by telephone. The company denied that the department was too cold for work to be performed. In any event, the grievants were told, failure to remain on duty, as required by the second sentence of the quoted clause, disqualified them from receiving call-in pay.

Arbitrator Harry J. Dworkin agreed with management.

In light of the evidence indicating that the entire complement of 135 employees which comprised the day shift left the plant shortly after their shift was scheduled to commence, and in view of the fact that only a portion of the plant was adversely affected by the break in the steam lines, and for the further reason that the employees arbitrarily walked off their jobs and refused to consider assignments to other jobs it is the conclusion of the arbitrator that the day shift workers who are involved in this grievance failed to qualify for the call-in pay benefits.

Mr. Dworkin found it noteworthy that among the employees who went home, allegedly because there was insufficient heat, were seven maintenance employees who would normally be working out-of-doors part of the time under all weather conditions.

WEEK-END CALL-IN PAY PROBLEMS

When work on Saturday or Sunday is paid for at premium rates, the question may arise as to the call-in pay rate appropriate for such a day. The employer may regard the premium rate as appropriate only for time *worked*, not for time paid for in lieu of work. The union, on the other hand, may expect premium pay for any time *paid for* on week-ends. That was the situation at the *Merrill-Stevens Dry Dock & Repair Company* (Industrial Union of Marine and Shipbuilding Workers, AFL-CIO).[7]

Primarily, the problem of contract interpretation before Paul W. Hardy was one of reconciling two contract clauses. There was Article 6 (a):

[7] 11 AAA 21.

If an employee reports to work on his regular shift, is not put to work, and has not been notified not to report, he shall receive two hours' straight time.

and Article 6 (d):

Employees called in on Saturdays, Sundays or holidays, shall be paid at the proper overtime differential.

The proper overtime differential was described in Section 3 (b):

Any hours worked by production employees on Saturday shall be paid for at one and one-half times the employee's base rate.

One grievant was involved in this case. He reported for work on a Saturday as he had been instructed to do, but there was no work on hand. He was thereupon sent home, with credit for two hours' pay at straight time. The union demanded two hours' pay at the Saturday rate, which was at time-and-a-half. Thus, the monetary aspect of the dispute came to one hour's pay. Nevertheless, both parties wanted the principle adjudicated.

Mr. Hardy resolved the dispute in favor of the union. "That no time was 'worked,'" he said, "is incidental to the fact that the employee made himself available for work. This placed him under the company's jurisdiction and obligation." He concluded:

The language of Section 6 (d) is of a mandatory nature and makes it incumbent upon the company to pay for call-ins on Saturdays, Sundays and holidays and said call-ins are to be paid for at the "proper overtime differential." There is no disagreement that [the grievant] was called in (ordered to report) on Saturday morning. Therefore, it is incumbent that [he] "shall be paid the proper overtime differential."

At the *Tileston and Hollingsworth Company* (United Papermakers and Paperworkers, AFL-CIO),[8] the contract was very clear on the matter of Sunday call-ins:

. . . If any worker is called into the mill on Sunday, he will be guaranteed a minimum of four hours' work at double time.

Seemingly, this left little room for dispute. Yet, a controversy did arise when employees were called in at 10:00 P.M. on Sunday, two hours before their regular shift. After working these two hours, they

[8] 16 AAA 17.

continued in accordance with their regular schedule. In their next pay checks, they received double time for the two hours worked on Sunday, double time for the first two hours worked on Monday, and straight time for the remaining six hours on Monday. Thus, they received no pay for time not worked. According to the union, they should have received eight hours' pay for Sunday (four hours guaranteed at double time) plus straight time for the eight hours of the regular shift.

Management's position was that the contract guaranteed a minimum amount of *work*, not a specific amount of *pay*. As long as the work proceeded from Sunday into Monday, contractual obligations were met by giving double time for four hours and straight time for the rest of Monday.[9]

Donald J. White, the arbitrator, upheld the grievance:

The Sunday call-in pay provision here imposes the obligation on the company to provide a minimum of four hours work at double time for any worker called in on Sunday. The company has the complete right to schedule. Consequently, the company can call a man at four o'clock for an eight hour job, eight o'clock for a four hour job, or at ten o'clock for a two hour job. The company's job is not easy; it may miscalculate; it may not be able to determine the time required with precision. But it has both the responsibility and the right to make the decision. In any case, however, the company must be prepared to pay for a minimum of four hours work at double time because that is what the contract says must be provided.

CONFLICT BETWEEN CALL-IN PAY AND OVERTIME

Two employees at *Socony Mobil Oil Company, Inc.* (Oil, Chemical and Atomic Workers, AFL-CIO)[10] were given one-hour notice by telephone to report an hour early for their regular shift. They worked that hour and continued with their regular schedule. Was this situation covered by the call-in pay clause or the overtime provision? The union said it was a call-in pay situation, giving the em-

[9] The employer also asserted that his interpretation of the contract was supported by the fact that it was the practice in another department. The arbitrator found this argument not persuasive, because the department referred to by the employer was "specially structured to take care of those kinds of problems." Thus, it was not relevant to the call-in pay dispute.

[10] 23 AAA 16.

ployees the right to four hours' pay for the one hour of work. The employer contended, on the other hand, that the employees were entitled only to time-and-a-half for the hour worked before the start of the shift. This interpretation, management said, was compelled by one of the overtime clauses which read, in part: "An employee required to report for work in advance of his normal scheduled starting time shall be permitted thereafter to complete his normal scheduled shift."

Bert L. Luskin upheld the union's view largely because of the way the call-in was accomplished. If the employees had been scheduled in advance to report early, it would have been overtime. Having been given short notice, the call-in pay provision of the agreement applied, "even though the call-in required them to work for a period of time preceding the start of their shift and to thereafter continue to work their regular scheduled shift."

Furthermore, Mr. Luskin wrote, the sentence upon which management relied did not answer the problem. It merely said that employees called in early will be permitted to complete the normal schedule. It did not "in and of itself make any provision for the payment of premium pay for employees who are either called in to work or are otherwise required to report for work in advance of their normal scheduled starting time." The employer had also cited past practice, going back several years, in which employees were allegedly paid in the manner urged by management here. This practice was not controlling, Mr. Luskin said, because it was not consistent with the "clear and unambiguous language" of the contract.

CALL-IN PAY AS A REMEDY FOR OUT-OF-CLASSIFICATION ASSIGNMENT

Although call-in pay is intended to compensate employees for the inconvenience of reporting for work when none is available, the presence of such a provision in a contract may result in reporting pay for employees who have not suffered any inconvenience. A case in point was that of *Harbison-Walker Refractories Company* (United Stone and Allied Products Workers, AFL-CIO).[11] The arbitrator was Harry J. Dworkin.

[11] 13 AAA 1.

As in most other call-in pay problems, there was very little dispute as to the facts. A mechanic, the grievant in this case, had at first been scheduled to work on the midnight shift of a certain day. This work call was cancelled in advance, even though there was, apparently, a total of fifty minutes' work for a mechanic to do during that shift. Management's solution was to assign this task to two employees who were not mechanics. This was admittedly an error on the employer's part, for out-of-classification assignments of that kind were barred by the contract. The issue between the parties in this case was not the error, as such, but the remedy. The mechanic whose work call was cancelled demanded four hours' call-in pay, to which he would have been entitled if he had been asked to do that small amount of work. Management answered that contractual requirements would have been met if a mechanic from the earlier shift had been held over for fifty minutes' overtime. In the employer's view, fifty minutes at time-and-a-half was the extent of his monetary obligation.

Mr. Dworkin said he had to resolve this question in the union's favor. Under the contract, he pointed out, his authority was limited to the specific question which went through the steps of the grievance procedure. As the grievant was the mechanic who was first scheduled to do the work, he "is therefore entitled to be reimbursed in an amount equivalent to four hours by way of reporting pay at his hourly rate."[12]

[12] If the union had prosecuted an overtime grievance in behalf of a second-shift mechanic, it appears likely that fifty minutes' pay at time-and-a-half would have been the remedy. This is one illustration of situations where the financial burden on the employer for violation of the contract depends upon the union's choice of grievants. As Mr. Dworkin pointed out, the issue before him had to be decided in terms of the grievance that went through grievance procedure. For a case in which it appeared that the union, perhaps due to thoughtlessness, asked for a smaller remedy than it could have had, see *Electro-Mechanical Products Company* (United Automobile Workers, AFL-CIO), 17 AAA 10. The holiday-pay aspects of the case are discussed in Chapter 7. A comment on a relevant remedy issue will be found in Chapter 10, note 112.

To the same effect, see also *Merrill-Stevens Dry Dock & Repair Company* (International Union of Marine and Shipbuilding Workers, AFL-CIO), 11 AAA 14, in Chapter 4. Arbitrator Paul W. Hardy upheld a demand for monetary award in favor of a steward, although it seemed likely that this employee was not the one who had suffered the loss by the employer's error.

On the other hand, for a case where arbitrator Archibald Cox declined to

In disputing the grievant's right to call-in pay, the employer also relied on a provision of the contract which said that call-in pay

shall not apply in cases of major breakdown or other causes beyond the company's control or when the employee has been notified not to report for work.

As the grievant had been given more than twenty-four hours' notice that he was not to report, management representatives argued, he had no proper claim for call-in pay.

This contention, too, was rejected by the arbitrator. The provision of the contract exempting the employer from call-in pay when timely notice is given does not apply in this case, he said, because "the substantive basis for the issue and grievance is the assignment of work out of classification as distinguished from a situation where the employee has been so notified, and where in fact no work is performed within his classification on the shift in question." He added that "the right of a member of a particular job classification to be secure in his work area as against the encroachment of others" is a "separate and distinct right." Observance of that right is "in no manner inconsistent" with the provision excluding from call-in pay those who have not been notified not to report.

EFFECT OF SHIFT CHANGE ON CALL-IN PAY

In the *Harbison-Walker* case, call-in pay had to be given to an

---

award monetary damages in favor of a named grievant because he was not necessarily the one who lost by a contract violation, see *Crompton and Knowles Corporation* (United Steelworkers of America, AFL-CIO), 9 AAA 9. Here, the employer should have awarded a job to a senior employee, after examining the qualifications of the bidders and those on layoff. It was improperly awarded to a junior, the employees on layoff having been disregarded altogether. The senior bidder grieved, and convinced Mr. Cox that he had a better claim to the job than the junior employee. Nevertheless, the arbitrator did not award the remedy to the grievant. He wrote: "The job should have been awarded to the senior employee among the bidders and the employees on the layoff list who were willing to take the job. The company should now proceed to fill the job in the correct manner taking [the named grievant] as the senior bidder apart from those who were on layoff at the time of the bidding." No back pay was awarded because "the violation was unintentional and confined to an interpretation which the company had been following for several years. Under these circumstances it would be inappropriate to grant damages merely for the sake of penalizing the company."

employee who suffered no inconvenience. In a *Tileston and Hollingsworth Company* case (United Papermakers and Paperworkers, AFL-CIO),[13] out-of-shift call-in pay had to be given to employees whose shift was changed as a positive convenience for them.

The circumstances were interesting. Following a vacation shutdown, the company had scheduled certain employees to resume work on the midnight shift. During the preceding week, however, it became apparent that only four days' work would be available on that basis. So on the Saturday before these employees were due to start, the personnel office telephoned, and instructed them to report at eight o'clock Monday morning instead. On Tuesday, they resumed their regular midnight schedule, and had a full week's work following the vacation.

As all of this was done for the convenience of the employees, and particularly as adequate notice had been given of the temporary shift change, management saw no obligation to give premium pay. But the union demanded time-and-a-half for Monday, on the basis of the following clause, which dealt with both call-in and change-of-shift situations:

Section 10 B of the July 1, 1957 Agreement—If any worker is called into the Mill and works less than three (3) hours on the call, he shall, nevertheless, receive four (4) hours pay at straight time. If he works three (3) hours or more, he shall be paid time and one-half for hours worked outside of his regular work shift. In both cases, time actually worked will count as time worked on the computation of weekly overtime. If any worker is called into the mill on Sunday, he will be guaranteed a minimum of four (4) hours work at double time.

Commenting on the employer's argument that premium pay was intended only as compensation for the inconvenience of having to work unexpectedly at irregular times, and that the change in schedule was directed mostly for the convenience of the employees, William J. Fallon said that "insofar as intentions are concerned" the company has "the better of the argument." However, he added, the contract does not state the intention the employer relied upon.

There can be little doubt that generally, call-in pay provisions have as their purpose the reimbursement of employees for undue inconvenience or deprivation of proper rest between periods of work at a time when

[13] 6 AAA 4.

their labor is urgently needed by the employer because of production schedules or some other emergency. There is no question but that this type of situation was envisioned by the company and probably the union as negotiations evolved the present language of Section 10 B. However Section 10 B does not state this intention. There is no modifying or qualifying language restricting the application of the clause to a short notice, or to an emergency situation. . . . This is clear, unambiguous language. If an ambiguity existed the intention of the parties could be employed to clarify the ambiguity. Where no ambiguity exists the prior intentions of the parties notwithstanding, the language must speak for itself. To rule otherwise would constitute a modification and an addition to the terms of the call-in pay provision.

The employer also cited an incident about three years earlier, when the same scheduling problem arose and the union did not demand out-of-shift call-in premium pay. Mr. Fallon agreed that the facts were identical, but he denied that it constituted a past practice which could override contract language. "The fact that the union slept on its rights in that case is insufficient grounds for holding that the clear contract language of Section 10 B does not apply now," he wrote.

New Shift on Return from Absence

When an employee reports for work after a period of absence, only to learn that his shift has been changed, his right to call-in pay may depend upon whether he has observed procedures for determining his schedule. Two cases, one resulting in a decision for the grievant and the other for management, illustrate some of the problems involved.

An employee at the *Lebanon Steel Foundry* (United Steelworkers of America, AFL-CIO),[14] who had been out sick since the previous Monday, was notified on Friday that he was due to be laid off. As he felt able to resume work the next week and had sufficient seniority to bump into another job, he visited the personnel office immediately to claim a job in another department.

His claim approved, he then tried to find his new foreman and verify the shift he would be on. According to his testimony, however, the supervisor was not immediately available. Feeling tired and not wanting to spend too much time in the shop, he went home,

[14] 3 AAA 13.

assuming that if there was to be a change in his shift he would be informed of it before Monday morning.

On Monday, he reported at his usual starting time in the morning, only to be told he was not due until two o'clock in the afternoon. This created the question of whether he was entitled to call-in pay for his early morning arrival. The company said he was not. It was the grievant's obligation, management representatives argued, to find out what shift he would be on when he bumped into another department. A clause was cited stating that an employee who "is not put to work . . . due to his own fault . . . shall not be paid for any hours not worked." The union answered that it was management's responsibility to inform an employee of a change in schedule; the grievant therefore committed no "fault" justifying denial of call-in pay.

Donald A. Crawford said the answer turned on the clause governing procedure in bumping. The critical language was:

When an employee has been laid off and made claim to another job he shall present such claim to his foreman or to the Personnel Department.

Thus, the grievant fulfilled his obligations under the contract when he filed his claim with the personnel department, Mr. Crawford wrote. In fact, according to his "uncontradicted" testimony, he did more than was required of him when he tried to find the foreman, for this was "a responsibility he was not required to assume under the contract clause." The award therefore granted four hours' call-in pay.

The outcome was different at *Bird & Son, Inc.* (United Papermakers and Paperworkers, AFL-CIO),[15] where, because of an erroneous assumption on their part that a certain schedule would continue through their vacation period, two employees reported back from vacation at the wrong time. The employer had posted a revised shift schedule on the bulletin board during the previous week, and in doing so, had satisfied contractual requirements governing scheduling of shifts, according to the arbitrator, Thomas Kennedy.

If the call-in pay provison were the only relevant part of the contract, he wrote, he would be inclined to agree with the union that the two employees were entitled to call-in pay. However, when

[15] 19 AAA 6.

schedules were referred to elsewhere in the agreement it was always as a "posted schedule." Thus, the posting of a schedule was all that was required of management.

This interpretation is supported by the fact that the parties appear to agree that under non-vacation conditions the term "scheduled for" in Section I means "listed on the posted schedules." It is only with respect to vacation conditions that the union demands a different interpretation. There is nothing in the contract, however, which calls for an exception to be made in the case of vacations.

Furthermore, Mr. Kennedy said, judging by past practice, "employees on vacation at this plant have assumed the responsibility for determining what they are 'scheduled for' before reporting on the day following a vacation." The grievance was therefore denied.

7

PAID HOLIDAYS

Virtually every collective bargaining agreement, according to the Bureau of Labor Statistics,[1] contains some provision for paid holidays. But in only about 15 per cent of the establishments covered by those contracts do all members of the bargaining unit automatically receive pay for the named holiday.[2] In what is generally regarded as an attempt to discourage absenteeism or "stretching" of holidays, two-thirds of the agreements require attendance on one or both of the scheduled days surrounding the holiday as a condition for receiving the contractual benefit. This limitation, however, is often waived when absence is caused by illness or similar circumstances. An additional 18 per cent of the agreements, according to the same source, require work during more extended periods before or after the holiday. The object here may not be so much to curb

[1] *Paid Holiday Provisions in Major Union Contracts, 1958*, Bulletin No. 1248, U. S. Dept. of Labor, Bureau of Labor Statistics.

[2] An interesting example of difficulties arbitrators face in interpreting union contracts was the case of *Canada Dry Corporation* (International Brotherhood of Teamsters), 24 AAA 3. The contract required pay for "any holiday declared as a legal holiday by the State." At the same time, the agreement named eleven paid holidays, Good Friday not being among them, although Good Friday has been a legal holiday in the state for half a century. It had not been the practice for the employer to pay for that day, and apparently the union entered no protest until 1960. Looking at the history of bargaining, the arbitrator, C. F. Mugridge, found "ample evidence" that neither party had regarded Good Friday as a legal holiday, regardless of the contract and the state law. Furthermore, the union had "traded out" its Good Friday holiday demand for other concessions during negotiations. Thus, the parties had established a "mutual understanding" as to that day, Mr. Mugridge said. He concluded: "If Good Friday had been enacted as a legal holiday after [the holiday clause] had been negotiated and made a part of the agreement, there would be no question as to the company's contractual obligation. Or, if the State did enact new and additional holidays, over and above the twelve already recognized by law, the company would automatically be obligated to consider them as legal holidays."

absenteeism as to restrict holiday pay to only those who would have been scheduled for work on the holiday. This type of clause maintains normal earnings of employees during weeks when holidays occur, but offers no "bonus," in the form of holiday pay, to those who are not in a current pay status. Employees on layoff or unpaid leave of absence are thus excluded from the benefit, although workers who take their vacations during holiday weeks are usually given an extra day.

Not surprisingly, when a dispute arises over the right of an employee to holiday pay, the issue is most likely to be one of eligibility. Only secondarily do there arise such questions as the appropriate rate for holidays, or the right of employers to modify practice with respect to observing holidays.

SURROUNDING DAY ELIGIBILITY PROBLEMS

Identification of the surrounding day for holiday-pay purposes is not always an easy task; seldom is the answer given by the calendar. The problems that may arise were illustrated at *AVCO Corporation* (United Automobile Workers, AFL-CIO).[3] The holiday in question was Thanksgiving Day, 1959. Part of the work force was scheduled for the next day, but others, including the grievant, were not. The grievant was in a class by himself, however, in that he asked and received permission to be absent on the Monday following the holiday. But he absented himself for the rest of the week without permission. When the employer refused to give him holiday pay, a grievance was filed.

The following were the conflicting contentions:

1. The union said that, as the contract required work on "the first scheduled day after" the holiday, all employees who were not scheduled on Friday automatically qualified for holiday pay regardless of other circumstances.

2. The union argued further that even if Monday were held to be the "day after" for the plant as a whole, the grievant satisfied that requirement by having been excused for that day.

3. The employer argued that Friday was a day of "shutdown,"

[3] 22 AAA 16.

making each employee's next scheduled day the critical day for holiday-pay purposes.

Alexander H. Frey, who decided this case, agreed with the union's first contention:

The disagreement in this case arises not from any ambiguity in the contract language in issue, but from the innocent but mistaken assumption of the company that the wording of [the contract] means something other than that which it clearly states. To substantiate the company's position it would be necessary to substitute the phrase "the first day upon which the company schedules work for the entire plant" for the contractual expression "the first scheduled work day." This I am not authorized to do.

Having determined that the first scheduled day after Thanksgiving Day was Friday, the grievant's subsequent work history was irrelevant. But it still remained necessary to determine whether, not having been scheduled on Friday, he lost his eligibility for holiday pay. Again, the union was upheld. If an employee does not in fact work on the first scheduled day after a holiday, Mr. Frey pointed out, he becomes ineligible for holiday pay under the contract unless the reason for the absence was (1) substantiated personal illness, (2) temporary layoff, or (3) other circumstances considered meritorious by the company. Clearly, he said, the grievant was "deprived of a work opportunity" on the Friday in question. He was therefore on "temporary layoff" that day and eligible for holiday pay.

Proof of Illness to Establish Eligibility

A case involving both fact and contract interpretation arose at *Doeskin Products, Inc.* (United Papermakers and Paperworkers, AFL-CIO).[4] Here, an employee telephoned on his first scheduled day after Christmas to report he was sick. The employer asked for a doctor's certificate, and refused to pay for the holiday unless it was produced. The clause under which this action was taken required work on the surrounding days, but also provided that "the company may excuse failure to work on such preceding and following days if the employee has an excuse which is justifiable and is acceptable to the company."

In the view of management, the use of the words "may" and "acceptable to the company" placed acceptance of excuses entirely

[4] 20 AAA 22.

in the hands of the employer. Arbitrator John Perry Horlacher disagreed. Despite the phrasing of the clause, he wrote, the employer's action remained subject to review, if the union protested it.

An "excuse which is justifiable" surely implies some reasonable, non-arbitrary, non-capricious standard to be employed in judging the validity of excuses for absences. It necessarily connotes that an undoubted disabling illness would give rise to a justifiable excuse. The company could not capriciously accept such an excuse in one case and reject it in another simply because of the language "acceptable to the company."

Nevertheless, he said, the holiday provision of the contract could not be interpreted in such a way as to deprive the phrase "acceptable to the company" of all meaning. These words were significant: they precluded the arbitrator from "substituting his judgment for the company's" where management's decision was "reasonable and non-arbitrary." The phrase "acceptable to the company" meant that the arbitrator had to uphold a reasonable determination by management even though it was not exactly what he might have preferred to see.

Although he sustained the grievance, Mr. Horlacher denied the union's request for an award barring the company from requiring a doctor's statement under any circumstance involving interpretation of the holiday provision. "The standard of reasonableness in determining the presence of justification for absence on a surrounding day," he said, "would allow for the necessity of a certificate in certain situations where this would be the reasonable method of resolving a bona fide doubt." The grievant was awarded holiday pay without the necessity of producing a doctor's certificate because, under the facts, there was no reason to doubt he was telling the truth about his illness.

Effect of Extended Absence for Illness on Holiday Pay

At the *Dieters Foundry* (United Steelworkers of America, AFL-CIO)[5] there were three employees who were out sick not only during the two days immediately surrounding a paid holiday, but for several weeks before and after. The contract contained the usual surrounding day eligibility requirement (exempting from it those

[5] 14 AAA 10.

whose absence was caused by "sickness or injury"), but did not specifically provide for long-term illness.

When the grievance of these three employees, who were denied holiday pay, came before Edward A. Lynch, the employer argued that the purpose of the work requirement was only to discourage absenteeism, not to result in holiday pay for employees absent for extended periods of time. The arbitrator found for the union, holding that the contract must be interpreted exactly as written. "We can appreciate the company's argument that a literal application [of the holiday provisions] could go on indefinitely," he wrote, causing hardship for a small company, as this one was. However, "if the parties intended the holiday provisions as the company claims, they failed to so indicate in the applicable agreement. They placed no time limits thereon."

A similar award was rendered by Lloyd H. Bailer at the *Perkins Machine & Gear Company* (International Union of Electrical, Radio and Machine Workers, AFL-CIO),[6] where contract provisions and the fact pattern resembled those at the *Dieters Foundry*. Here, too, the contract required work on the surrounding days, but said nothing about what would be done when surrounding day absences occurred as part of an extended illness. Mr. Bailer said that to uphold the company would amount to amending the contract by the addition of language limiting the duration of absences.

An element in this case, not present in that of the *Dieters Foundry*, was the employer's assertion that employees on extended absence had been denied holiday pay in the past without protest on the part of the union. This could not affect the decision, Mr. Bailer said, because in nearly all of the cases cited by management, the reasons for absence were not given. Furthermore, even if some of those absences were due to reasons recognized in the holiday-pay clause as non-disqualifying, "the union's failure to challenge past violations does not preclude it from insisting upon compliance with the contract thereafter. The necessary ingredients for a plea of estoppel do not exist here."

A dispute at *The Brooklyn Club* (Hotel, Restaurant and Bartenders Union, AFL-CIO),[7] like the two above, involved a situation

---

[6] 21 AAA 19.
[7] 23 AAA 8.

where the contract did not state clearly what was to be done about holidays falling within a period of sick leave. But unlike those two cases, this one was complicated by the fact that employees were entitled to a certain amount of sick leave.

What did this provision mean with respect to two employees who were on extended sick leave, spanning the July Fourth and Labor Day holidays? The employer said the sick leave provision was "self-contained" and could not be construed to give additional benefits not expressly mentioned. The union argued that the holiday-pay provision required an additional day's pay for each holiday to all employees on sick leave, without regard to whether they were still drawing sick leave pay.

The arbitrator, Daniel Kornblum, found the answer in the company's practice with respect to holidays falling within periods of lay-off, on one hand, and vacation periods, on the other. In the former, holidays were not paid for; in the latter they were. Thus, only those on the "active payroll" were paid for holidays.

His conclusion, therefore, was that no employee on paid sick leave *did* have a contractual right to holiday pay. However, it was not to be given in the form of "dual pay," that is, an employee was not to receive both sick leave and holiday pay for the same day. Rather, the holiday was to be debited as an additional day of allowable paid sick leave, thus "preserving paid sick leave in full."

Applying this interpretation, Mr. Kornblum ruled that two grievants who were drawing sick leave pay on July Fourth were entitled to an extra day of paid leave in compensation for the holiday. By the same token, one of the grievants was not entitled to a compensating day of paid sick leave for Labor Day because, by that time, he had already exhausted his paid sick leave.

Partial Absence on Surrounding Day

The effect of partial absence on the day before a holiday was presented at the *Charles Lachman Company* (Textile Workers Union of America, AFL-CIO).[8] Here, the contract required that employees be "not absent" on the surrounding days, but did not otherwise define the term. On the day before Christmas, thirteen employees

[8] 7 AAA 21.

punched out at noon, after only five hours of a scheduled eight-hour shift. There had been some practice in the past of working short days before Christmas, but on this occasion management required a full shift and denied holiday pay to the employees who didn't comply. John Perry Horlacher upheld the company. The distinction between presence and absence, he said, must be understood in terms of the "principle underlying the requirement to be at work." That principle, he added, is that absence from work and consequent loss of production are to be confined to the holiday itself. They must not "spill over" into the day before or the day after. In short, "the worker's personal benefit and the employer's production loss are *both* to be limited to the holiday."[9]

Somewhat similar to the *Charles Lachman* case was that at the *Downs Carpet Company* (Textile Workers Union of America, AFL-CIO).[10] J. Charles Short, the arbitrator in this case, came to substantially the same decision as did Mr. Horlacher.

Because of illness in her family, the grievant in this case had worked only five hours of her scheduled eight on the day before Thanksgiving. Relying on the clause barring holiday pay to employees absent on the surrounding days (except for certain reasons not applicable here) the employer declined to pay for the holiday.

Mr. Short said the company had acted in accordance with the contract. The requirement of work on the "previous day" and the "succeeding day" could not be construed as if the language were "*a part* of the previous day and *a part* of the succeeding day."

The normal meaning of the work day is apparent from the contract itself and the agreement does not contemplate that employees will be regularly scheduled for portions of days.[11]

[9] Whether a day of partial absence is a disqualifying circumstance also arose in a dispute at the *Oil Heat Engineering Company* (International Brotherhood of Teamsters), 17 AAA 2. The issue here was eligibility for vacation pay, rather than holidays. Consequently, the problem of "stretching" or "spilling over" of holidays was not involved. Nevertheless, the decision of the arbitrator, Peter Seitz, may be of interest (see his discussion in Chapter 8; that case is also discussed in Chapter 10).

[10] 20 AAA 24.

[11] As often happens in such cases, there was contradictory testimony as to what the negotiators of the contract had intended. Mr. Short decided the case chiefly on the language itself, without regard to "mental understandings" not expressed in words. "The case cannot be decided on the individual mental

There was "undoubtedly some reason and merit" in the union's view that partial absence amounted to "substantial compliance" and should not be a disqualification, but "the contract is not directed against absence alone; there is a specific requirement of having *worked.*" Although the reason for the grievant's partial absence made it seem "somewhat inequitable to deprive her of holiday pay," Mr. Short concluded it would be wrong "to deviate from the contract standard and substitute in each case the intangible yardstick of 'what is reasonable in this particular instance'."

Partial Absence on a Non-Scheduled Surrounding Day

The question of partial absence on a surrounding day also arose at *J. Chein and Company* (United Steelworkers of America, AFL-CIO),[12] where one employee was scheduled to work on the day after Thanksgiving, while the rest of the plant was scheduled off. Did the lateness of the employee on this day disqualify him from Thanksgiving pay under a clause which required work on "the regularly scheduled workday" after the holiday? Irving K. Kessler answered that question in the negative. The Friday was not a regularly scheduled workday, and the rule about full attendance didn't apply, he said. But even if it were a regularly scheduled workday, he added, it is doubtful that the company could withhold holiday pay. Although the contract speaks of the "full regularly scheduled workday," it does not mean that "an employee must work the full day" of that schedule. "Lateness, therefore, is not a reason for removing from an employee a benefit bargained for, unless it is specified in the agreement that lateness shall be a disqualification for holiday pay."

Refusal of Employer to Permit Employee to Work on Surrounding Day

An unusual set of circumstances occurred at the *Electro-Mechanical Products Company* (United Automobile Workers Union, AFL-CIO),[13] where two employees were refused admittance to the plant

understandings of either party," he wrote, "but must be judged on the basis of the standard which they have incorporated into their written agreement."

[12] 19 AAA 3.
[13] 17 AAA 10.

on the day after Labor Day because they had arrived more than two hours late. The contract did not specifically disqualify partially absent employees from holiday pay, and Ronald W. Haughton ruled that it was "more reasonable" to interpret the language to mean "work on the day rather than work for the whole day." This, he said, was the interpretation placed on similar contracts "generally," in the area where the plant was located (Garden City, Michigan). But the question nevertheless remained as to whether these employees, who might have worked as much as six hours if they had been permitted to enter the plant, were entitled to holiday pay. Mr. Haughton answered this question, too, in favor of the union. The employer's citation of a rule requiring employees to obtain passes when more than thirty minutes late was not an adequate defense, because this rule had been "loosely applied" in the past.

The weight of the evidence is that, in the department in question, permission to proceed to work has been given if the production schedule has been tight. It apparently was quite routinely granted during the period immediately prior to the instant cases because of production demands. There is nothing in the record to show that the situation was any different on the day in question; or that work was not available; or that it would have been a disrupting factor for the aggrieved to have started to work at the time they reported.

The two grievants in this case were awarded call-in pay for the day on which they reported for work and, inasmuch as they would have worked "as much as six hours," holiday pay for Labor Day.[14]

Refusal to Work Scheduled Overtime on Surrounding Day

The holiday provision in the contract of *The Schoonbeck Company* (United Furniture Workers of America, AFL-CIO)[15] required work for "the full number of hours" of the surrounding days as a condition of eligibility. Under this clause, John H. Piercey's award was that employees who refused to work more than eight hours had disqualified themselves from the contractual benefit. The union's contention that eight hours' work should be sufficient for qualification because the holiday itself was paid for on the basis of eight hours was not persuasive. Nor did it matter that the employer had

---

[14] This case is also discussed in Chapter 10.
[15] 19 AAA 5.

failed to give twenty-four hours' notice of overtime as required by the contract. The language of the holiday clause, the arbitrator wrote, compelled a decision in favor of the company. The "imperfect performance" by the employer of his obligation to give notice of overtime could not affect the decision because the union had not required such notice in the past. "To suddenly demand that the Company give 24 hours of notice of any overtime worked after having acquiesced with the practice and policy of the Company would be unreasonable," Mr. Piercey said.

Unilateral Waiver of Surrounding Day Requirement

It is well established in labor relations that where the employer is under obligation to bargain collectively with a union representing his employees, he may not alter the terms of employment, not even to improve them, without the union's consent.

This rule was recalled in two cases in which the employer waived the surrounding day work requirement unilaterally. They were *Perkins Machine and Gear Company* (International Union of Electrical, Radio and Machine Workers, AFL-CIO)[16] and *American Bifocal, Inc.* (International Association of Machinists, AFL-CIO).[17]

In the *Perkins* case, the contract required, as a condition for holiday pay, that employees work "on the scheduled work day immediately prior to such holiday or on the scheduled work day immediately following such holiday, unless such absence was an excusable absence." When holidays occurred during periods of layoff or vacations, the practice was to withhold payment for the holiday until the first pay day following return to work, thus making certain that contractual requirements for eligibility were satisfied.

May 30, 1958, fell within a period of layoff which began early in May and ended on June 6. During this time, the employer advised state unemployment compensation officials that the employees would be paid for the holiday. This notification, however, was erroneous in that it failed to include the information that a return to work on the scheduled day was a condition that still had to be met. Because of this error, it seemed advisable to management that the day-of-return requirement be waived. This, said Lloyd H. Bailer, was improper:

[16] 2 AAA 18.
[17] 9 AAA 16.

The company's unilateral waiver of the contract requirement regarding eligibility for holiday pay, with the consequent payment of this amount to some employees otherwise not eligible for such pay for Memorial Day, was a violation of the contract. The company is not entitled to unilaterally alter the terms of the contract. However, the effect of this action was to increase its liability for holiday pay. Meanwhile, no employees suffered any loss either in pay or in benefits provided by contract, or in benefits to which they were entitled under the New Jersey unemployment compensation statute. Thus there was no basis provided for awarding any compensation to the employees involved in this case.[18]

The facts were somewhat different at *American Bifocal*, but the same principle was involved. Facing the need to reduce forces in December 1958, the plant superintendent posted a notice advising the employees that the plant would be closed from December 19 to January 5. The notice also warned that employees must report for work on the scheduled day of return or they would forfeit pay for the Christmas and New Year's holidays.

Under the contract then in effect, however, employees were *not* entitled to pay for holidays falling within layoff periods of that duration. This was apparently discovered some time after the layoff began. When the employees returned, the employer refused to pay for three holidays (the last half day before Christmas and New Year's Day and those two days), but offered a compromise of one-and-one-half days. The union rejected this, which brought the matter before Jerome A. Klein.

Mr. Klein ruled that if he based his decision on the collective bargaining agreement alone, he would have to say that the employees were not entitled to holiday pay. However, the notice had constituted an "offer" to give holiday pay under stated circumstances, and when the employees reported on January 5, it constituted an acceptance of the offer. That was one reason why contractual holi-

[18] One of the issues of the case was the union's demand for relief, based upon alleged unemployment compensation losses suffered by the employees. After hearing testimony about the procedures of the unemployment compensation agency, Mr. Bailer found that to the extent the grievants received less in unemployment insurance, they were compensated with pay, which they eventually received, for May 30. If they had received both unemployment insurance and holiday pay for the same day, recoupment action could have been taken by the state. Despite the employer's violation of the contract, therefore, no monetary remedy was directed.

day pay for all was equitable. Another was that management had effectively "waived" the surrounding day requirement.

In view of these facts, it is the conclusion of the Arbitrator that the legal effect of the company's December 18th notice was to waive the holiday provisions of the collective bargaining agreement and to estop the company from relying on that paragraph as a basis for refusing to pay three days' pay for the Christmas and New Year's holidays.

It was also influential in Mr. Klein's decision that, with the expectation of pay for three days during the period of layoff, approximately half the work force did not apply for unemployment compensation benefits.

THE EFFECT OF LAYOFF, LAYOFF NOTICE, AND VACATIONS ON HOLIDAY ELIGIBILITY

Garage maintenance employees of the *News Syndicate Company, Inc.* (International Association of Machinists, AFL-CIO)[19] were laid off on December 18, 1959, and not recalled until after January 1, 1960, because of a strike of the newspaper mail deliverers, represented by another union. Thus, their period of idleness included two holidays, Christmas and New Year's Day. Under the contract, employees "regularly scheduled" to work on holidays were to be given those days off with pay. Those who were actually required to work were to get double time.[20] But what was to be done about employees who were not scheduled to work on holidays? That was the issue of the grievance in this case.

The union's position was that all employees were entitled to holiday pay without qualification. Furthermore, it was argued, the

[19] 17 AAA 9.
[20] The text of the holiday clause read: "The following day or days observed as such shall be considered holidays: New Year's Day, Lincoln's Birthday, Washington's Birthday, Decoration Day, Independence Day, Labor Day, Thanksgiving Day, and Christmas Day. When practicable, employees regularly scheduled to work on any of these holidays shall be given the day off with pay. Any employee required to work on one of these holidays shall be paid double the regular day's pay. Overtime worked within the twenty-four hour period of the holiday itself shall be paid time and a half the holiday rate. When a holiday falls on an employee's normal day off and he is not required to work, he shall be paid at the straight time rate for that day."

holiday clause was negotiated as part of a "package settlement." If employees were not to be paid for those days, they would be deprived of something guaranteed by the contract. The employer answered that the contract gave no guarantees of holiday pay to those who were not in a pay status for the day. And as for the package-settlement argument, the holiday clause was first negotiated in the 1930's, long before that style of negotiation became popular.

Robert L. Stutz awarded in favor of the company:

A careful analysis of the language in the holiday clause of this contract reveals that there is absolutely no support for the union position. The first sentence simply enumerates the days that are to be "considered holidays." The second sentence provides that employees regularly scheduled to work on any of those holidays should be given the day off, wherever practicable. None of the employees here were scheduled to work Christmas or New Year's since they had been laid off pursuant to the notice of December 18. The third and fourth sentences set forth the method of pay applying to work on any of the named holidays. The last sentence provides for the method of pay for employees whose "normal day off" coincides with a holiday. The holidays involved here were not the normal day off for any of these employees, since they were all on a layoff status.

If he were to rule for the union, Mr. Stutz concluded, he would be reading language into the contract "which simply is not there."

Application of Surrounding Day Rule When Holiday Occurs during Layoff

In the *News Syndicate* case, the problem was eligibility of employees on layoff for holiday pay. At the *Wayne Pump Company* (United Automobile Workers, AFL-CIO)[21] the issue was not the layoff status as such but identification of the "surrounding days" for purposes of establishing eligibility.

The holiday clause of the contract was a long and complicated one, the first and last sentence appearing to be in conflict. The first sentence read:

An employee otherwise entitled to be paid for one of the designated holidays, even though not worked, shall not be paid for such holiday(s) unless he worked the scheduled working day immediately preceding such holiday(s) and the scheduled working day immediately following such holiday(s).

[21] 1 AAA 15.

The last sentence of the holiday provision read:

An employee who fails to work the day before or day after one of the designated holidays, solely because he was laid off in the week in which, or the week prior to the week in which, the holiday occurred, shall, if otherwise eligible therefor, be entitled to holiday pay.

If the contract was complicated, at least the fact situation was clear. On Wednesday, June 25, 1958, 200 employees were notified that they were being laid off at the close of work on the following Monday, June 30. Fifteen of these employees absented themselves for personal reasons that Monday and were denied pay for Friday, July Fourth. The union's position was that it was the intention of the parties to give holiday pay to employees laid off during the holiday week, or the week before, and that the surrounding day work requirement expressed in the first sentence did not apply. The company's answer was that the phrase "scheduled working day immediately preceding . . . and . . . immediately following," in the first sentence, had exactly the same meaning as "day before or day after," as used in the last sentence.

Arbitrator Donald A. Crawford upheld management on the basis of his own analysis of the holiday provision as a whole. The union was incorrect, he said, in overlooking the phrase "if otherwise eligible" in the last sentence. To be otherwise eligible, "an employee on layoff must have worked on his last scheduled day preceding the holiday," he wrote. The conclusion that an individual had to work on *his* scheduled day before the holiday was reinforced by the history of bargaining, which also shed light on the reason the first sentence spoke of "scheduled working day," while the last sentence referred merely to "the day before." The evidence convinced Mr. Crawford that the last sentence was added to the holiday clause at the initiative of the union, to make possible "accrual of holiday benefits to laid off employees for a specified period of their layoff." He concluded:

Thus, under the current agreement an employee on layoff can acquire eligibility for holiday pay (for a maximum of two weeks preceding the holiday) even though his last scheduled working day does not "immediately" precede the holiday or his first scheduled working day after a holiday does not "immediately" follow the holiday. But as clearly specified in the sentence in question, such an employee must be "otherwise eligible" which requires that an employee on layoff (within the imposed limits) must have worked on his last scheduled working day preceding the holiday or his first scheduled working day after the holiday.

Absence for Circumstances beyond the Employee's Control

An interesting problem in contract interpretation was put before arbitrator Harry J. Dworkin by *Morrison Steel Products* (United Steelworkers of America).[22] The issue was whether an employee on layoff was absent "for circumstances beyond his control," within the meaning of the holiday provision of the contract. As the parties stipulated that the issue turned on interpretation of this provision alone, the arbitrator quoted it in full:

All employees, who do not work on the above-mentioned holidays shall, nevertheless, be paid on the basis of eight (8) hours at the guaranteed hourly rate on the non-incentive curve for the labor grade in which he regularly works, provided, however, that the employee shall have worked the regularly scheduled workday preceding the holiday and the regularly scheduled workday following the holiday. Any employee who fails to work on the regularly scheduled workday immediately preceding and following the applicable holiday, as provided above may, nevertheless, make claim for such compensation provided that his absence was based on circumstances beyond his control. The burden of proof for such circumstances shall rest with the employee and shall be primarily limited to reasons of health, or death in the immediate family, or call for performance of any civic or national duty.

To the union, the fact of layoff was clearly "a circumstance beyond the control of the employees." The employer answered that the grievants, not having been "regularly scheduled" for the surrounding days, could not meet the eligibility requirements. For this reason, the fact that the absence was due to a circumstance beyond the employees' control was irrelevant.

Mr. Dworkin upheld the company's view.

Although absences occasioned by reductions in the work forces are due to circumstances beyond the employees' control, such are not within the exceptions included within the contract terms providing for exceptions to the requirements that in order to be eligible for holiday pay the employee shall have worked the regularly scheduled workdays preceding and following the holiday.[23]

[22] 8 **AAA** 8.
[23] The decision might have been different, the arbitrator said, if it could be

A collateral issue was presented by the union's request for a ruling that employees may be absent on the surrounding days for reasons other than those indicated in Paragraph 44 (". . . primarily limited to reasons of health, death in the immediate family, or call for performance of any civic or national duty") and still be eligible for holiday pay. It was the position of management that this enumeration precluded additional circumstances, even though these might be beyond the control of the employees. On this point, the arbitrator agreed with the union:

The contract employs the term "primarily" which has a dictionary meaning suggesting of principal importance and consideration, or as being fundamental, basic or "from which all others may be derived."

Had the parties intended to limit and restrict the circumstances which would serve to excuse absences for holiday pay to the classifications mentioned in the contract, the use of the adverb "primarily" would be surplusage. It is inconceivable that the parties would have injected this qualification unless it was intended to accord it some meaning and effect. The arbitrator therefore concludes that while basically the parties intended to provide for certain contingencies which would excuse holiday pay, the circumstances enumerated are not exclusive. There may be other absences "based on circumstances beyond his control" which would meet the requirements of the contract so as to constitute an excusable absence.

Mr. Dworkin found it unnecessary to suggest in advance what those circumstances might be, "since the matter must necessarily be resolved on a case-by-case basis."

Holidays during Vacation Periods

Normally, contracts and practices of parties are clear with respect to payment for holidays falling within periods of paid vacations. The usual procedure is for employees to receive either extra days of paid vacation or extra days of pay (which amounts to the same thing). But at the *Bridgeport Brass Company* (United Steelworkers

---

shown that employees were laid off with the express purpose of evading holiday-pay obligations. "Such conduct would constitute an attempt to evade the contractual obligations as to holiday pay and would not receive support or condonation through the arbitration process." In the instant case, the arbitrator found evidence only of "good labor relations" and no allegation of "bad faith" on the part of management.

of America, AFL-CIO),[24] the paid holidays involved were of a special kind.

For a number of years, it had been the practice to give four hours' "bonus pay" for Christmas and New Year's eves. This benefit was granted in the form of extra pay to those scheduled for work. Employees not scheduled did not receive that benefit. Apparently, some grievances were filed by employees who had no work in their own departments on the days in question and preferred to go home, rather than accept temporary transfers. In order to preserve "bonus pay" for them, the contract was amended to read that bonus pay on those two days would also be granted to employees "not scheduled to work." That was the background of a controversy that came before Robert E. Mathews.

The instant grievance involved two employees who received permission to take their vacations during the year-end holiday season. From the union's point of view, they were "not scheduled" to work on the eves of the holidays and were, therefore, entitled to four hours' pay for each of those days, in addition to vacation pay. As the contract language was clear beyond any possibility of misinterpretation, it was said, the arbitrator had to decide in the union's favor and not concern himself with other considerations.

Mr. Mathews agreed that the language of the contract was clear, but he said the intent of the negotiators could not be overlooked. Company witnesses had testified, without contradiction, that the parties had intended to resolve one problem only—that of employees who preferred not to work out of their own departments. "The arbitrator recognized the validity of the rule that in interpreting a contract one must first look at the language itself," he wrote. "But this does not mean merely a phrase, or a sentence or even a section or article. The language of the contract is the language of the entire agreement from beginning to end."[25]

Examining the contract as a whole, Mr. Mathews found many provisions which were "in some respects contradictory" and others

[24] 24 AAA 11.

[25] For a case in which an arbitrator held that the mere fact that contract language was added for a limited purpose did not bar application of the language to other situations, see the decision of John Perry Horlacher in *American Can Co.* (United Papermakers and Paperworkers, AFL-CIO), 4 AAA 17, in Chapter 9.

which, if taken literally, would produce "clearly absurd" results. This reinforced his view that it was "both permissible and necessary to look elsewhere than the language of this agreement in order to determine the meaning of the disputed [clause]." On the basis of his reading of the contract as a whole, the grievance was denied.

Effect of Rotating Layoffs on Eligibility for Holiday Pay

Under any circumstances, the administration of holiday provisions may be complicated by the incidence of layoffs. But when layoff procedures themselves are complicated, difficulties multiply. That was the situation at the *Royal McBee Corporation* (United Automobile Workers, AFL-CIO),[26] where employees were scheduled on a one-week-on, one-week-off rotation plan. Good Friday was a holiday under the contract, with pay to be given only "when the employee would have been regularly scheduled to work on such a day if it had not been observed as a holiday." Thus it happened that some employees worked during Holy Week and were paid for Friday, while those who were scheduled off were denied holiday pay.

The union urged that the contract be construed in "a broad and liberal manner," giving all employees holiday pay providing they worked on the days surrounding the layoff. Arbitrator James J. Healy said he could not support such a construction because it would "render useless" the specific language of the agreement. His decision, he wrote, turned on the intent of the parties:

In holiday pay arrangements, two distinct underlying philosophies may govern: *First*, that the holiday payment is essentially a monetary grant. Under this philosophy if a holiday falls on a Saturday or during a layoff, the employee receives the payment regardless of whether or not he was scheduled to work. *Second*, that the holiday payment is to prevent a loss of income to an employee who would otherwise have worked on that day if it had not been for the holiday. Under this philosophy, holidays falling on Saturday or during a layoff are not paid on the theory that there was no income deprivation caused by the holiday.

As the contract in this case is clearly of the first type, Mr. Healy concluded, "those employees who were not scheduled to work during the week of Good Friday because of the work-equalization rota-

26 1 AAA 10.

tion system and who, in fact, did not work, cannot be found to have satisfied" the requirements of the holiday provisions.

Effect of Layoff Notice on Holiday Eligibility

At the *Lehigh Spinning Company* (United Textile Workers Union of America, AFL-CIO)[27] the contract made employees on layoff eligible for holiday pay "provided that such holiday falls within one week following the start of layoff."

The holiday in dispute was Saturday, May 30, 1959 (Memorial Day). On Friday, May 22, management had notified a number of employees that there would be no work for them during the following week. The question arose: Did the employees have a full week of notice, such as would make them ineligible for holiday pay? As the employer saw it, the layoff began on Saturday, May 23, giving the employees eight days' notice. The union's view was that Monday, May 25, was the first day the grievants would have worked. That was the date from which the time had to be computed for purposes of establishing eligibility for holiday pay. By this method, May 30 was still within the same week.

William N. Loucks, selected by the parties to determine which interpretation was correct, found for the union on the basis of "four sets of considerations." The first was derived from the contract itself. A clause defining the workweek as beginning Monday morning and ending with the close of the last shift that starts on Friday was regarded as "some presumption" that the negotiators had not been thinking of Saturdays and Sundays as working days. For that reason, they could not be counted as days of layoff.

The second consideration contributing to the arbitrator's interpretation was the fact that there was no showing of "industrial practice" one way or another with respect to computing days of notice. The employer's contention that the State Bureau of Unemployment Compensation counted waiting time in the manner urged by management, a contention which was disputed by the union, left the arbitrator with no basis for a decision, unless he undertook an "independent investigation." As the answer would not necessarily be indicative of "industrial practice," Mr. Loucks thought it inadvisable to undertake such an independent study.

[27] 15 AAA 3 and 15 AAA 4.

Thirdly, the union's citations of decisions by arbitrators Harry H. Platt and Harry Shulman[28] "add considerable strength to the union's position in the instant case."

Finally, Mr. Loucks' decision was based on his own "personal consideration of what is a reasonable and logical interpretation" of the parties' use of the words "start of layoff." He stressed the distinction between "notice of layoff" and the actual "incidence of layoff," and concluded:

It is these four sets of considerations, and not any one of them singly, which, on balance, convinces the Arbitrator that a reasonable and logical interpretation requires that the union's position on the matter in dispute be sustained.

Eligibility of Laid-off Employees for Holiday during Week of Vacation Shutdown

Another issue in the same *Lehigh Spinning Company* case concerned eligibility for July Fourth pay. It involved a further degree of complication, resulting from the coincidence of two circumstances: (1) employees were being laid off toward the end of June, some doing no work after June 22, and others performed a day or two after that date; and (2) the contract required the plant to be shut down for a week of vacation during the week beginning June 29.

How, then, did this affect the right of employees to holiday pay under a contract which, as we have seen, permitted no more than a week's gap between layoff and holiday? The employer's solution was to grant holiday pay to those who worked at least one day during the week of June 22, and to deny holiday pay to those who did not. The union objected to the denial of benefits to the latter group, urging that nothing in the contract specifically barred employees on vacation from receiving holiday pay.

Mr. Loucks resolved this issue in favor of management. Had it not been for the vacation shutdown, he said, those who were laid off before June 22 would have remained idle. As far as they were concerned, the holiday occurred more than a week after the date of layoff. The situation was clearly different with those who still had

[28] *L. A. Young Spring & Wire Corporation*, 23 LA 400 (1945), Harry H. Platt, arbitrator, and *Ford Motor Company*, 11 LA 1181 (1948), Harry Shulman, arbitrator.

work to do after the cutoff date of June 22. They worked within seven days of the June 29 shutdown, and were entitled to holiday pay.

If the negotiators of the contract had intended to give employees on vacation more holiday benefits, he concluded, that intention would have been expressed with the "same specificity" as was demonstrated in other aspects of the holiday provision.

HOLIDAY OCCURRING DURING INTERVAL BETWEEN CONTRACTS

In determining whether employees are eligible for holiday pay, there are three critical days—the holiday itself and the two surrounding days. How does it affect the rights of employees when one or all of these days occurs during a period when no contract is in effect? G. Allan Dash answered this question at *Fab-Weld Corporation* (International Union of Electrical, Radio and Machine Workers, AFL-CIO).[29]

The holiday in question was Good Friday—April 15, 1960. It happened that the collective bargaining agreement expired the day before, and no new contract was arrived at until several weeks later. From the Monday following Good Friday to the signing of the new agreement, a legal strike was in progress. After the strike, a grievance was filed demanding pay for the holiday.[30]

For employees to qualify for holiday pay, the arbitrator ruled, all three critical days must fall within the terms of a collective bargaining agreement, *although not necessarily the same agreement.* Consequently, despite the fact that the grievants worked on the first scheduled work day following termination of the strike, they were not entitled to pay for Good Friday.

In order for the union to prove the right of the employees to obtain pay-

[29] 24 AAA 19.

[30] The threshold question of arbitrability was raised by the employer. It was argued that inasmuch as no contract was in effect, there was no dispute over interpretation of the agreement for the arbitrator to resolve. Mr. Dash disagreed with this view. The employees having worked on the first of the surrounding days (the last day of the old contract), they satisfied "at least one-half of the eligibility requirements." This gave them sufficient basis for a decision as to whether they were entitled to holiday pay.

ment for the holiday of Good Friday, April 15, 1960, it would have been necessary to show that the actual day on which the holiday occurred was covered by the May 11, 1959 agreement. If the termination date of the agreement had been April 15, 1960, it would have been possible for the union to show that the holiday fell within the period covered by the agreement, that the employees worked the last scheduled work day before the holiday, also on a day covered by the May 11, 1959 agreement, and that they worked the first scheduled work day after the holiday, which day was covered by the May 5, 1960 agreement. Under this type of reasoning, "scheduled work days" are days of work that occur under an existing agreement, even though the one work day occurs under a prior agreement and the other occurs under a succeeding agreement.

In short, Mr. Dash concluded, "if an employee works the last scheduled work day before a holiday and the first scheduled work day after a holiday (both 'scheduled' during the coverage of an existing agreement) and if the holidays also fall on a day when the former or succeeding agreement is in effect by its terms, such an employee would be entitled to holiday payment."

RATE, PREMIUM PAY, AND OBSERVANCE PROBLEMS

Holidays falling on Sunday, normally a day not worked, are observed in most states on the following Monday. This practice is reflected in virtually all collective bargaining agreements, according to the Bureau of Labor Statistics.[31] The BLS adds, however, that there is no general, nationwide practice regarding holidays falling on Saturday.

As paid holidays are named in advance, and as the calendar is an objective fact that can be taken into account, it would seem that there should be no lack of clarity in collective bargaining agreements as to whether employees must be paid for holidays falling on Saturday. Nevertheless, the BLS points out, slightly more than half of the agreements studied neglected to say specifically what the wishes of the parties were in those contingencies. Not surprisingly, this lapse produces grievances and arbitrations.

Holidays Falling on Saturdays

A case in point was that of the *Tri-Part Manufacturing Company*

[31] See note 1, above.

(International Brotherhood of Electrical Workers, AFL-CIO).[32] The contract provided a premium rate for time worked on Saturdays, Sundays, and six named holidays, and permitted employees "to be absent with regular pay" on those holidays. But the contract did not otherwise specifically provide for pay when an unworked holiday fell on a day when no work was normally performed.

To obtain an interpretation of this holiday provision, the parties put before Louis A. Crane this issue: "Is the company required by the agreement to pay holiday pay for an unworked holiday falling on a Saturday?"

As arbitrators often do in such cases, Mr. Crane traced the history of negotiations to determine whether there had been a meeting of minds by the union and company representatives who drafted the clause. He found that until 1945, the holiday provision called for premium pay for working on holidays, but no pay for unworked days. In 1952, the clause was broadened to provide holiday pay for senior employees. Such employees could be "excused" from work on a holiday, and still receive holiday pay at straight time. Mr. Crane concluded from this that:

It would be peculiar to "excuse" an employee from working on a day on which he is not expected to work at all. Both parties agree that employees normally do not work on Saturday. Theretofore an employee who did not work on a holiday during the work week received no pay. As a result, he suffered a reduction in take home pay. The parties apparently wanted to maintain an employee's take home pay during a holiday week. The language seems no broader than the problem which precipitated it.

Thus, there was no basis for the union's request for holiday pay when no work is performed on Saturdays. Relevant to the history of bargaining was the union's contention that the holiday pay provision was part of "a wage package" and that the employer would be in default unless six holidays were paid for. "Even viewing the holiday pay provisions as part of an economic package," Mr. Crane answered, "they do not unconditionally guarantee to each and every employee six additional days' pay during the year. Before the benefits are payable, the conditions which the parties imposed must first be met. One of those conditions is that the holiday fall

[32] 15 AAA 17.

on a day which gives meaning to the requirement that the employee 'shall be allowed to be absent.' Saturday is not such a day. The grievance must, accordingly, be denied."

Proper Rate for Unworked Holiday Occurring on Premium Pay Day

When labor and management representatives differ on the application of their contract to a particular situation, it is often because each relies on a different provision of the agreement. Such was the case at the *A & P Corrugated Box Company* (United Papermakers and Paperworkers, AFL-CIO).[33]

May 30, 1959, one of seven paid holidays, fell on Saturday. As the contract required "eight hours' straight time pay" for holidays, the employer assumed that was the appropriate rate for this day as well. But the union disagreed. Citing the overtime provisions of the contract, which said in part:

Time not worked in observance of the seven holidays shall be considered as time worked in the computation of weekly overtime, regardless of what day in the week the holidays may occur.

the union demanded premium pay for the holiday.

The arbitrator, John A. Hogan, conceded that "some ambiguity" does seem to appear when the holiday clause is read in conjunction with the overtime provision. He resolved the ambiguity in favor of management by looking into the "intent" of the parties, as revealed not only in the two clauses, but also in the history of bargaining:

The contract conforms to the generally accepted view of overtime as payment of an extra amount to compensate the employee for having to work during hours that are normally set aside as hours for rest and relaxation. Or, viewed from another angle, it is "penalty overtime" levied on the employer to discourage him from scheduling work during hours or days which should be periods of rest.

With this review of the overtime clause in mind we come now to the paragraph cited by the union. This paragraph states that time not worked in observance of the seven holidays "shall be considered as time worked in the computation of weekly overtime, regardless of what day in the week the holidays may occur." In light of the clear language of the holiday pay clause and the overtime clause discussed above the intent of this paragraph was clearly to provide overtime protection for employees who were required to *work* on Saturday, for example, when a holiday had

[33] 15 AAA 9.

occurred during the scheduled work week. During the years when this contract did not provide for overtime pay for Saturday *as such,* but only for overtime after 40 hours of work during the work week, the above clause was necessary to enable the employees to get overtime pay when they were required to work on Saturday during a week in which a holiday occurred.

Proper Holiday-Pay Rate for Employees on Short Workday Schedule

Another conflict, not of clauses but of a basic approach to holiday pay, was revealed in a case of *McQuay Norris Manufacturing Company* (United Automobile Workers Union, AFL-CIO).[34] John F. Sembower was the arbitrator. The issue was whether employees in a department where fewer than eight hours were worked per day were entitled to holiday pay based on the short schedule or on the standard eight-hour day. Taking the view that the purpose of the holiday clause was to "make whole" the employees for loss of normal earnings during a week in which a holiday falls, the employer offered only average daily earnings as holiday pay. The union relied on the language of the contract, which provided:

Employees eligible under these provisions shall receive eight hours pay at their regular straight time hourly rate, exclusive of night shift and overtime premiums for each holiday. In the case of incentive workers, their incentive special rate will apply exclusive of night shift and overtime premiums.

The union urged that the contract was intended not to maintain normal earnings but to provide a definite number of hours' pay, in accordance with the precise words of the holiday clause.

Mr. Sembower awarded in favor of the union. The manner in which he reached this conclusion illustrates techniques of union contract interpretation often applied by arbitrators. To begin with, he said, the holiday clause seems "unequivocal" on its face. The fact that shift differentials and overtime premiums were excluded reinforced the conclusion that no other exclusions were contemplated. It is an "accepted canon of contract interpretation," he wrote, "that if particular matters are included or excluded, it is to be inferred that other matters not so included or excluded are not

[34] 9 AAA 7.

embraced . . ." Consequently, "unless it is clearly established that there are compelling circumstances requiring a special meaning to be attached to the words, they must be given their ordinary meaning in this instance."

Call-in Pay When Shift Extends into Holiday

An interesting conflict between the contract "as written" and the practice of the parties appeared at the *Socony Mobil Oil Company* (Independent Oil Workers),[35] where the holiday clause granted straight time for working on a holiday "and in addition, . . . time and a half for all time worked with a minimum of four hours' straight time pay."

The grievants in this case had the 4:30 P.M. to 12:30 A.M. shift on November 10, thus working a half-hour into Veterans' Day, which was one of the paid holidays. On the strength of that, the union demanded four hours' holiday call-in pay for each of the grievants. The employer denied the request, citing some twenty instances in the past when employees whose shifts similarly extended into holidays were not given holiday pay.

Arbitrator Charles T. Douds found the union's demand precluded by the purpose of the clause. That purpose, he said, "appears to have been to prevent employees from being required to come to work on a holiday except in case of real necessity." That they had to work a half-hour beyond midnight into the holiday did not result "in any significant interference with plans for the holiday."

But the decision seemed to rest mostly on the showing of past practice. Mr. Douds described circumstances where past practice may be regarded as reflecting an interpretation which the parties themselves placed on the contract.

Where there is a question about the intention of the parties as to the meaning of a provision of a contract, one of the best ways to resolve the problem is to examine the practice of the parties in applying the disputed provision in similar situations in the past. From April 19, 1957 to and including November 11, 1958 it was the practice of the company not to pay the four hour holiday minimum under the circumstances described herein. It was the practice of the union during this same period not to protest or grieve the failure of the company to pay the four hour holiday

[35] 7 AAA 5.

minimum under these same circumstances. It seems unlikely that union officers as vigilant to protect the interests of the employees as the officers of this union evidently are, would overlook so many opportunities to protest or grieve a failure to pay what the contract required over such an extended period of time.

Right of Employer to Change Day for Observing Holiday

Because July 4, 1959, fell on a Saturday, management of two companies, *Bearings Company of America* (United Steelworkers of America, AFL-CIO)[36] and *Foster Wheeler Corporation* (International Union of Electrical, Radio and Machine Workers, AFL-CIO)[37] found it expedient to close the plants on the preceding Friday. In the former case, the object was to use the time for installing and relocating certain equipment. In the latter, the purpose was to give executive and supervisory personnel a long week end.

The contracts in both cases required that employees be given holiday pay for July Fourth, despite the fact that it occurred on Saturday. Consequently, the employees, having been given five days' pay for four days' work that week, asked for an extra day's pay. But in both cases, management announced that the closing of the plants on Friday was not in the nature of a layoff, but in observance of Independence Day. Whether the employers had the right to do so, and if not, whether employees were entitled to a monetary remedy, became the subject of grievances and, eventually, arbitration. The decisions of the two arbitrators were quite similar in effect.

John R. Abersold, ruling on the *Bearings Company of America* case, said that the company clearly had no right to alter the day on which a contractual holiday is observed without negotiating the matter with the union. However, inasmuch as a one-day shutdown of the plant was not a violation of the seniority or any other provision of the agreement, the union's demand for "a day's pay for Friday for all people who did not work" had to be denied.

Admittedly, the company would be in violation of [the holiday provision] if it forced the employees to observe Friday, July 3rd as a holiday, but unless it can be shown that the employees suffered some *actual* loss, which the company was not justified under another provision of the Labor

[36] 20 AAA 19.
[37] 21 AAA 14.

Agreement in requiring them to take, they have no recourse. The reason for this is that the process of arbitration is designed for the purpose of *compensating* employees for a *loss* which they have sustained by an action of the company which *cannot be sustained* under any provision of the Labor Agreement. Thus, the damages are *compensatory* in nature and may not be *punitive*. In consequence, the Arbitrator may not penalize the company for an action which, although it may not unilaterally do under one provision of the Labor Agreement, it may do unilaterally under another. If, however, it could be shown that any employee was compelled to perform some service on Saturday, July 4th and the company treated that service as being performed on a non-holiday, simply because it had stated that July 4th was to be observed on July 3rd, then said employee would have cause for compensatory damages against the company. No such action by the company was brought forward by the union.

Although Mr. Abersold found no losses he could make good in the instant case, he did not exclude the theoretical possibility that losses might result from the employer's error. "Should any employee as a result of the company's action be able to show that he sustained a loss, other than the pay not received for not having worked on July 3, he would be clearly entitled to be compensated for such loss," he concluded.

The chief difference between the *Bearings Company* and the *Foster Wheeler* cases was that in the latter, the employer first said the July 3 shutdown would be in observance of Independence Day and later, when the union objected, announced a shutdown on July 3 for lack of work instead. Harry F. Stark, the arbitrator in the *Foster Wheeler* case, was not convinced that a decline in production was "the sole or even the primary motivation" for closing the plant, particularly when it had been announced so far in advance. Nevertheless, as Mr. Abersold did, he found that because management had the right to schedule production, the plant could be closed for the day.

The facts in this case suggest that it is sufficient to clarify the intent of the agreement, and that there is inadequate evidence to support the assessment of a penalty. The contract guarantees paid holidays even though they fall on Saturday. Since in fact the employees received a full week's pay for four days' work and obtained a day of paid leisure, it would seem inequitable to require an additional day's pay without the employer receiving a day of productive effort.

The contract requires an extra day's pay in the event of a Saturday holiday after a full work week. There is no guarantee of such a work week, and the union produced no evidence to show any limitations on the employer's freedom to determine the necessity for production on any given day. The single instance in the present case does not establish the misuse of production shut downs to negate holiday benefits.

Mr. Stark concluded with the suggestion that if further clarification or guarantee is deemed necessary "to remedy a possible conflict between holiday pay provisions and the right to schedule production," the parties might seek such clarification in collective bargaining.

8

VACATIONS AND VACATION PAY

The typical negotiated vacation plan contains three chief characteristics: it defines minimum service requirements for minimal vacations and provides longer vacations for long-term employees; it indicates how vacation pay is to be computed, and occasionally states whether vacation pay is a "vested" right; and it outlines a procedure for the timing of vacations. Every vacation and vacation pay case reported by the American Arbitration Association since January 1, 1959, fell into one of these three categories.

SERVICE REQUIREMENTS

The arbitrator who is asked to determine whether employees have met service requirements for vacation often applies techniques of contract interpretation similar to those relied upon in deciding whether employees are eligible for holiday pay. A case in point was one arbitrated by John R. Abersold, who held that layoff time was not to be counted as time worked for vacation purposes under the special circumstances presented in the case of *Linear, Inc.* (United Rubber, Cork, Linoleum and Plastic Workers, AFL-CIO).[1] The grievants were a group of employees who had been hired in January 1957 and laid off in July, August, and September of that year, after receiving vacation pay corresponding to the amount of work they had performed. They were not recalled during 1958, but they believed they were nevertheless entitled to vacations that year. As contractual authority for their claim, they relied upon the following paragraph:

Temporary lost time during an employee's period of employment with the company of not exceeding twelve consecutive months for layoff or leave

[1] 2 AAA 11.

141

of absence shall not be counted against his record of continuous service for the purpose of vacation payment.

Mr. Abersold said the union had misread the intent of the quoted clause. Its purpose was to measure the "extent" of vacation benefits, not the "qualification" for them. In other words, he said, the fact of layoff would not have reduced the length of the grievants' vacations, if they had established their eligibility for 1958 vacations by work in the current vacation year.

Somewhat similar facts, but different contract language, combined to create a contrary result at the *Stauffer Chemical Company* (Leather Workers International Union of America, AFL-CIO),[2] where 2,000 hours of work by January 1, 1958, were required as a condition for 1958 vacation pay. An employee who accumulated more than 2,000 hours before 1957, but performed no work in 1957 because of illness, was held by Thomas Kennedy to be entitled to 1958 vacation pay.

The company argued that, if the contract were given a logical, rather than a literal, interpretation, at least *some* work was required in 1957 as a condition for a vacation in the next year. But Mr. Kennedy found this view not persuasive. The language of the contract is so clear, he wrote, that it would require extraordinary proof to show a different intent:

If the parties had intended [the vacation clause] to mean 2000 hours in 1957, it would have been easy to have so stated. As the clause stands, it can be interpreted literally only to mean 2000 hours of service regardless of when accumulated up to January 1, 1958.

The employer had also urged that the vacation clause be interpreted in the light of a "change of concept" which has come about, the current view being that vacation is not a "gratuity by management" but a benefit earned by service. The employer's description of the general view of vacations may be accurate, Mr. Kennedy conceded, but it provided "no basis for a change in the application of the agreement."

If the original meaning was to provide vacation gratuitously whether or not an employee earned it in the previous year, the company cannot suddenly change the practice simply because elsewhere other unions and other managements have agreed to a different way of paying vacations.

[2] 6 AAA 8.

Finally, the arbitrator ruled that the company's showing of several occasions in the past when its interpretation was applied without challenge was insufficient "to constitute an accepted past practice and thus negate the clear wording of the agreement" because, among other reasons, it could not be shown that the union was aware of those incidents.

The Effect of Absences on Vacation Eligibility

Past practice was decisive at the *Royal McBee Corporation* (United Automobile Workers, AFL-CIO),[3] where the employer failed to credit employees for layoff time in excess of thirty days. The contract permitted "absences totaling more than thirty days" to be deducted from periods of service for vacation purposes, but it did not specifically say that layoffs were "absences" within the meaning of the contract.

The evidence was clear that for a number of years, operating under similar clauses, the employer had computed vacation allowances in the manner urged by the union in this case; that is, employees were credited with time they did not work because of layoff. Management's answer was that the past practice resulted from errors of payroll department employees who had failed to follow instructions. This defense, said Paul R. Hays, was not valid.

If one of the parties has long applied in practice one of the two or more possible interpretations of an ambiguous provision, the other party may be justified in asserting that it would be wronged by a change in that practice.

The employer's contention that the past practice was a "mistake" would have been a "relevant consideration," he added, if the union's position were merely that past practice sheds light on the intent of the parties. But in this case, the union also had an "equitable claim," in that it had foregone its right to seek a negotiated change in the ambiguous provision. The union's claim, therefore, "cannot be adequately answered by asserting that the practice was the result of an error in procedures which were wholly under the control and direction of the employer."

[3] 5 AAA 6.

The Effect of Partial Day's Work on Credit toward Vacations

The question whether a partial day worked is to be counted as a full day worked for purposes of establishing eligibility for vacations arose in two cases.

The first was at the *Murray Manufacturing Company* (United Automobile Workers, AFL-CIO),[4] where length of vacations was to be determined by the number of months of service, with "each month in which the employee has worked at least one day" to be considered as a month of service. The grievant in this case, who had been on layoff for several months, was recalled for a shift starting at 10:30 P.M. on June 30 and ending at 7:00 A.M. on July 1. The question was: Did he earn a month's credit for vacation purposes by having worked one-and-a-half hours during the month of June? D. Emmett Ferguson was selected to answer the question.

He found the clause "ambiguous" in that the phrase "has worked at least one day" could mean either that the employee had to work "at least one full day" or that "he must have done some work on at least one day." To resolve the ambiguity, he said, "we must search the meaning intended by the parties" when they chose the language they used in the contract. He concluded:

If [the clause] is read as a whole, it is clear that the parties were intending to establish a rule for calculating what is to constitute credit for a years' employment. An employee must work "at least one day" in each month. This does not mean that by working eight hours split over the end of one month and the beginning of the next that he thereby shall be credited with two months of employment. To so hold would mean in effect that eight hours is two days. Our conclusion that he can only claim the service in one month is logical and in harmony with the obvious intention of the clause as a whole.

The second case involving partial days worked was that of the *Oil Heat Engineering Company, Inc.* (International Brotherhood of Teamsters).[5] The vacation clause was an unusual one. It provided for 10 days of paid vacation to every employee who "has worked for the employer and has drawn pay" for 125 days in the preceding year. It happened that one employee had worked exactly 125 days, but on 2 of those days he had left work early without

[4] 3 AAA 8.
[5] 17 AAA 2.

permission. Thus, the issue before Peter Seitz was whether the grievant satisfied the contractual standard for vacation eligibility.[6] He resolved the dispute in favor of the union. "The requirement of 'work' does not specify that eight hours of work in every day must have been performed," he wrote. "The vacation clause does not concern itself at all with the quantum of work, so long as it was performed in a day that is creditable for vacation purposes." The employer had cited contract language (from a clause not dealing with vacations) which referred to "an eight hour day," but this could not sustain management's position because the purpose of the phrase was "entirely foreign and distinct from the vacation clause, which stands on its own feet."[7]

COMPUTATION OF VACATION PAY

As vacation pay is generally related to the wage structure of a plant, changes in the wage level or the method of payment that have occurred since an employee's last vacation may raise questions as to the amount of vacation pay due.

At *E. J. Lavino and Company* (United Steelworkers of America, AFL-CIO),[8] for instance, the contract called for one basis of computing vacation pay for piece workers and another for time workers. The grievant in this case was a time worker on May 1, the day he became eligible for a vacation; but he had been a piece worker during the first quarter of the year. If he had still been a piece worker on May 1, his earnings during January, February, and March would have determined the amount of his vacation pay. The union's contention was that the basis of computing vacation pay for this employee remained the same, despite his change in status to a time worker. The arbitrator, Irving K. Kessler, disagreed. "While there is a definite understanding that January, February and March earnings will be used as a base for the payment of piece workers,"

[6] This case is also reported in Chapter 7, note 9, and in Chapter 10.

[7] As the grievants had violated working rules by leaving early on two days without permission, Mr. Seitz wrote, their wages for the lost time could have been withheld, or they could have been disciplined. But denial of a contractual benefit is not a proper form of discipline. This aspect of the case is also discussed in Chapter 10.

[8] 1 AAA 8.

he said, "this is for the purpose of computation of pay for those employees who are piece workers at the time of vacation. It is not a guarantee that those employees who transfer to a day rated job before the vacation eligibility date will be paid based on piece work earnings."

At least part of this conclusion rested on considerations of what the opposite decision would imply.

For example, if an employee should work during the month of January on a piece work basis and then transfer to an hourly rated job, would he receive his current rate at the time of vacation, or a rate compounded of his average earnings on day work and piece work? The same question might be asked of an employee who had worked on piece work for the first two months and then transferred to an hourly rated job. The union holds that if an employee has worked during the months of January, February and March, regardless of his status, he is entitled to his piece work earnings during his vacation. However, this establishes March 31st as the vacation eligibility date for piece work earnings as contracted with the date of May 1st set forth in [the contract].

Essentially the same problem was presented at the *American Chrome Company* (United Steelworkers of America, AFL-CIO).[9] Vacation pay was to be determined by a formula which took into account (1) years of continuous service, (2) average straight time hourly pay for the period "prior to the anniversary" of the employee's vacation, (3) the length of the scheduled workweek, and (4) the number of shifts worked during the preceding year.

The grievants were on a five-day week at the time of their vacation anniversaries; but they had been working six days a week during much of the preceding year, when vacation credits were being accumulated. The employees sought vacation pay based on the longer workweek, but the employer refused. This brought the matter to John E. Gorsuch. As Mr. Kessler did in the *E. J. Lavino* case, Mr. Gorsuch expressed caution about the consequences of a union victory on this question of contract interpretation.

To give the union what it seeks here, it would be necessary to keep track of every man's work week schedule during the entire year. Such does not seem to be contemplated by the parties or else it should have been included in the contract. The arbitrator believes that the rule which he has adopted here is the one generally followed in industry, unless there is

[9] 5 AAA 8.

a specific contractual provision to the contrary. Although it may work against a man where the workweek is reduced, it seems to be a fair rule because it definitely works in his favor when the workweek is increased.

At the *Industrial Brownhoist Corporation* (United Steelworkers of America, AFL-CIO),[10] computation of vacation pay was complicated by the fact that the contract provided for a cost-of-living adjustment to be added to straight time hourly earnings. The contract called for vacation pay to be computed at the "base rate." To the employer, this meant that the cost-of-living adjustment did not need to be included in vacation pay.

Observing that the same "base rate" phrase appeared in earlier contracts of the parties, the arbitrator, Leon Herman, examined the past practice with respect to vacation pay. He found that vacations were computed on the basis of "straight time hourly earnings," leading to the conclusion that "base rate" and "hourly rate" were synonymous, as used by the parties in this connection. Since hourly rates included the cost-of-living adjustment, he found in favor of the union. Furthermore, it was significant, he said, that the employer added the cost-of-living adjustment to holiday pay and pay for time lost because of injuries, which, under the contract, were also to be paid for at "base rate." It would be "extremely inconsistent," he ruled, if the company were to exclude the adjustment from vacation benefits alone.

The employer's final contention was that the payment of the cost-of-living adjustment was appropriate for holidays and for time lost due to injury, because absences due to these reasons may be regarded as time worked, whereas vacations could not be so regarded. This was an "erroneous theory," based on the notion that vacations are "gratuities," rather than a form of deferred earnings, Mr. Herman replied. "[A vacation] is not a bonus; it is not a gratuity. It has been earned, and it is due and owing subject always to any limiting covenants in the Company-Union agreement."

Effect of Individual Eligibility Dates

When employees become eligibile for vacations on their individual anniversary dates of employment with the company, a general increase in wages on a certain date may create an apparent inequity

[10] 9 AAA 12.

in that those who take vacations just before the increase would be paid at their old rates, while those who become eligible a week or two later would get larger benefits. That is what happened at *Bay City Shovels, Inc.* (United Steelworkers of America, AFL-CIO),[11] where the contract required that employees be given vacation pay based on "the hourly rate the employee was receiving on the date he requested his vacation." If it were merely a question of asking for vacations at the right time, however, there would have been no problem. The date on which a general increase goes into effect is usually known in advance. Employees at work may therefore speculate on the increase (or anticipated upgrading), and postpone the request for their vacations until a more advantageous time.

What complicated the grievance was another provision which required that an employee laid off for lack of work or military service be given vacation pay due him at the time of such layoff. Under this clause, it was the custom to give employees vacation pay based on their status at the time of layoff, whether they requested it or not.

In the spring of 1958, four employees were laid off until after August 1, all getting their vacation pay in the usual manner. During that interval, a 16-cents-per-hour general increase went into effect. Thus, a question was presented as to whether these employees could have elected to ask for their vacations at a later date, as they clearly could have, if they had not been laid off.[12]

It was the union's position that the employees had accepted vacation pay at the time of layoff as a matter of convenience, but as they had not yet asked for their vacations, there was no vacation pay "due" them at the time. Assuming they would have found it more advantageous to ask for vacations in December of that year, the employer owed them the difference between what they received and what they would have been entitled to at the time of their "request" for vacations.

[11] 3 AAA 18.

[12] One of the grievants, whose anniversary date was later in the year, would have received a vacation as a fifteen-year employee if he had been permitted to take it after the layoff. Another grievant was upgraded later in the year. Thus, both would have been entitled to more vacation pay if they had been permitted to take vacations at a time of their own choosing. As the wage question alone illustrates the problem, however, these details are disregarded for purposes of this discussion.

The employer answered that it was his contractual obligation to make vacation payments at the time or shortly after the employee is laid off, at the then prevailing rate. This conflict was referred to Louis A. Crane.

Mr. Crane saw nothing in the contract to distinguish between the amounts of benefits paid to (1) employees who enter the military service, (2) employees who are laid off and never recalled, and (3) employees who are laid off and recalled to work after an interval of idleness.

More particularly, he saw nothing in the contract to permit a temporarily laid-off employee's vacation rights to be diminished. "An employee who works continuously throughout the year may refrain from requesting vacation pay until that time which he deems it most advantageous for him to do so," he wrote. "A layoff for lack of work is not given as a means of reducing the rights of the employee or otherwise disadvantaging him but rather to enable the company to reduce a labor force which is not needed in current operations."

Mr. Crane went on to say that it was "not unreasonable" to continue the usual procedure of giving an employee vacation pay at the current rate when he is laid off. This will "help him maintain himself and his family during the period of enforced idleness." However, if he is recalled to work and "continues at a higher rate for the balance of the work year, it is hardly logical to deprive him of the advantage of requesting vacation pay at such higher rate." At that time he would be entitled to the "excess to which he is entitled above the amount previously paid him."

TIMING OF VACATIONS

Contractual provisions for vacations are intended to give employees time off from work for rest, relaxation, and recreation. It follows from this that, whenever possible, employees should be permitted to take time when they and their families can use it to best advantage. But it is not always possible to oblige employees in this way, because most employees prefer to take their vacations during the summer. Thus, the conflicting needs of employees for their vacations when they want them, and of employers for the efficient operation of their plants, present problems of contract interpretation for arbitrators to solve.

The situation at the *Sutherland Paper Company* (United Paper-makers and Paperworkers, AFL-CIO),[13] was a case in point. The contract gave preference of vacation time to senior employees who submitted their requests by April 1. Those who filed after that date were to be given their choice on a first-come, first-served basis. But acknowledging that further adjustments might be necessary, the negotiators gave management the right to deny a request for a particular period "if it will interfere with production schedules."

Extending the Vacation Period

Applying this clause, management sought to limit the number of simultaneous vacations, and thereby spread vacations over a nine-month period. The arbitrator, Leonard A. Keller, ruled that management had gone too far. The right to depart from the expressed wishes of employees applies only where an individual's absence might interfere with production schedules, he said. "It seems highly questionable that it can be enlarged, or translated, into a broad charter that permits vacation scheduling spread out through the year on the ground that the company will thereby improve overall efficiency during the summer months." Mr. Keller cautioned, however, that his decision did not give employees an "unqualified right" to choose vacation periods "without regard to the effect of their absence on production schedules."

For example, if no adequate replacement were available for a skilled employee, and his work was required to continue, it would seem that the company could demand that he take his vacation at some other time. And, no doubt, limits can be imposed on the number of individuals who can be away at one time, based on production requirements in a particular situation.

The company's position in this case rested to a considerable extent on a showing that the need for summer replacements "had materially affected labor and machine efficiency" and that, together with material wastage, the unnecessary added costs came to about $70,000 in one year alone. This proved only that management had acted in "good faith," Mr. Keller wrote. But the overriding fact, he

[13] 9 AAA 15.

said, was that the contract provided vacations "for the enjoyment of personal and family interests, and this, in the case of a large number, means a preference for the summer months." He concluded: "This preference is a matter of contractual right, as important to the employees as is the necessity for efficiency and economy to the company."[14]

Excluding One Week from Vacation Period

Management at the *Elizabeth Daily Journal* (Newspaper Guild, AFL-CIO),[15] was under contractual obligation to permit vacations during the seven-month period from April to October, but some indication of management discretion was expressed in the phrase that "the vacation schedules shall be arranged by the publisher." In view of this latitude, I. Robert Feinberg said, it was not a violation of the agreement to bar a classification of employees from taking vacations during a certain week in June when three employees in that classification were scheduled to be absent. This constituted "sufficient reason for causing the employer to be apprehensive that the department could not be properly staffed."

The Arbitrator believes that the language of the agreement is clear. [It] provides that the vacation schedules shall be "arranged by the publisher." This language gives the Publishers exclusive discretion. While the contract requires that vacations shall be granted during the period from April through October, it does not require that employees be permitted to take vacations each and every week during that period.

Furthermore, Mr. Feinberg wrote, a contractual provision that "due consideration" will be given to requests of employees did not make it "mandatory" that they be honored in all instances. Nor was the employer under an obligation "to negotiate with the union" on scheduling of vacations. The contract language required only that

---

[14] A second issue in this case was whether preference in vacation time by seniority meant "departmental" or "company-wide" seniority. The company was upheld on this point. "I am satisfied from the proof that departmental lines, as well as classification lines, and in some cases, shift lines, have been employed in the past in granting requests in order of seniority. To use division-wide preference instead, would be, as the company states, extremely difficult in application."

[15] 13 AAA 9.

the employer have a reason for refusing requests, "which reason is not [to be] arbitrary or capricious."

Timing of Third Week of Vacation

The vacation-timing problem was solved for most employees at the *John Wood Company* (United Steelworkers of America, AFL-CIO)[16] by a contractual provision giving the employer the right to shut the plant for one or two weeks in July. However, this did not solve the problem of the senior employees who were entitled to longer vacations. The vacation clause gave them the right to the additional week "according to plant seniority as applied to their department, and according to requirements of production schedules."

A senior employee, entitled to a third week of vacation in 1958, asked for the week beginning December 29, 1958. But as often happens in the case of long-service workers, this employee was skilled at his job; management found it inconvenient to replace him. The year-end inventory would be in progress, and this employee was needed for it, the employer said. He was therefore directed to take his vacation during the week of September 1. The evidence convinced William N. Loucks that at least one junior employee in the grievant's department, who had been permitted to take his year-end vacation, could have performed the inventory work. "The company has not demonstrated that it has a contract right to pick the *best* inventory takers and hold them regardless of vacation choices when juniors in the same department are granted their choice as to a vacation week," he wrote.

Mr. Loucks had to resolve a remedy problem in this case. The original demand for arbitration asked that the grievant be given "pay for lost time." At the arbitration, this request was amended to a week's pay. The arbitrator denied the amended request for a remedy, ruling that he could not go beyond the original demand. The "time" the grievant "lost," he said, was "the difference in earnings between what he earned at the rate at which he was paid while on inventory-taking during the week of December 29 and what he would have earned at his regular production work during the week

[16] 3 AAA 9.

of September 1, if he had worked that week. The arbitrator finds no
monetary damage to [the grievant] beyond this amount."[17]

Compulsory One-Week Shutdown

For a number of years, relatively few employees at a paper con-
tainer division of the *Continental Can Company* (United Papermakers and Paperworkers, AFL-CIO)[18] were entitled to full weeks
of vacation. During that time, the practice had developed of permitting employees to take vacations at any time of the year, subject to
management's approval, under a clause providing that vacations
"will not interfere with . . . efficient scheduling." Later, however,
the work force grew, and became stabilized to the point where
about 700 employees were entitled to more than 900 weeks of vacation.

At this time, management decided that efficient scheduling demanded a one-week shutdown in August. Requiring all to take vacations during this week would do away with the problem of finding
replacements for employees who wanted vacations during other
times of the peak production period, March through August. This
change imposed no hardship on those who were planning summer
vacations at about the time of the shutdown, but it was a considerable inconvenience to those who were planning to take vacations
at other times of the year.[19]

The task for David P. Miller, the arbitrator in this case, was to
apply the following contract clause:

Time of Vacation. Vacations will be taken at such times of the year as
will not interfere with the efficient scheduling of operations in the plant,
and must be arranged and approved by management.

[17] An interesting question might be raised as to what remedy, monetary or
otherwise, the grievant would have been entitled to if his potential earnings for
the week of September 1 had not been higher than his actual earnings for the
week of December 29. Under the circumstances, this remains an open question,
which Mr. Loucks did not have to resolve. In any event, it does not appear that
the difference in pay awarded the grievant really compensated him for the violation of his seniority rights when he was not permitted to take his vacation during the preferred week.
[18] 21 AAA 11.
[19] Production demands were not very heavy from September through April.
Some employees preferred vacations during those months when they might be
on layoff. The union therefore filed a grievance, asserting that the one-week
shutdown was sanctioned neither by the contract nor by past practice.

Insofar as possible, employees with the longer length of service will be given their preference as to the time of their vacations. Should an employee receive a temporary layoff during a slack period, or an emergency layoff (due to shortage of material, etc.) the employee may elect to receive his vacation during such layoff.

Vacations must be taken annually, and are not cumulative.

Mr. Miller concluded that management could "arrange and approve" vacations for weeks different from those requested by employees only to the extent that such rearrangement was necessary to prevent interference with "efficient scheduling of operations."

Consequently, the direction that all employees take vacations during the one week was a violation of the agreement with respect to those who preferred their vacations during the slack season. It was not a violation with respect to those who wanted vacations during the summer months of peak production. He directed that where the granting of off-season vacations "would cause no undue interference with production," employees must be granted such vacations on request, and added that time lost by such employees during the August shutdown was to be regarded as a "period of layoff."

To prevent future misunderstanding as to what constitutes "interference with production," Mr. Miller pointed out that "some" interference with production must be accepted as a "normal and expected consequence" of a vacation plan which, as here, requires that vacations be taken every year. It did not justify "a broad denial of vacation preferences."

VACATIONS AS A VESTED RIGHT

Paid vacations have often been referred to as a form of deferred earnings, to which an employee becomes entitled as a matter of right by having accumulated a sufficient number of hours of work. There is, however, an important difference between vacation pay and wages. The former may become due only at a contractually agreed upon time; so those who lose their status as employees (by having quit or through discharge, for instance) may thereby forfeit vacation pay. Wages for hours worked in the past cannot be forfeited; they must be paid under any circumstance. When a person loses his status as an employee after having accumulated some credits toward vacation pay, but before he has received it, the question may arise as to whether the vacation plan was "vested," that is, whether he has the right to prorated vacation money.

Precisely this issue arose at the *Blackford Glass Company* (Federal Local Union No. 22560, AFL-CIO)[20] before John F. Sembower. An employee who qualified for a vacation in the current year by having worked 500 hours in the previous year died without having taken that vacation. Although the contract said nothing about vacation pay going to the estate of deceased employees, the union demanded that the appropriate sum be given the widow. If death were to be a disqualification, union representatives argued, the contract would have so stated. The employer took the opposite view. If vacation benefits were to survive the employee, the contract would have been as explicit to that effect as it was in the case of employees who became military inductees or pensioners.

These two views, Mr. Sembower held, "cancel each other out," making it necessary to look elsewhere in the contract for guidance in resolving the "ambiguity." What he found was strong evidence of a "linkage" between vacation pay and earnings.

Close examination of the instant vacation plan shows that to a unique degree it corresponds with those plans which are considered as "vested" or deferred payments of compensation already earned. Employees qualify for one week's vacation upon completion of a year or more of service; two weeks' vacation after five years of service, and three weeks after 15 years. This means that they have the privilege of taking as a vacation the specified time off commensurate with their seniority, but vacation pay is linked in direct relationship with the work which they have performed in the preceding year.

The arbitrator added that the "pecuniary linkage" was further indicated by a provision giving vacation pay in December to those who didn't manage to get their vacations during the year. "This seems to indicate that the company is more concerned—and legitimately so—about the scheduling of vacations so as not to impede production, than to withhold payment under certain conditions."

The question of vested vacation pay also arose at the *Alpha Portland Cement Company* (United Cement, Lime and Gypsum Workers, AFL-CIO),[21] but here determination of the issue turned largely

[20] 11 AAA 20.
[21] 13 AAA 16.

on the definition of "discharge." The board of directors having decided to discontinue all operations at a certain plant, management terminated virtually all employees in December 1958. If they had still been employed on the vacation-qualifying date of January 1, 1959, they would have been entitled to vacation pay. But under the circumstances, management refused to grant such pay, relying on a clause which read:

No vacation or vacation pay shall be allowed to employees who have been discharged or who left the employ of the company, except in the case of those leaving to join the armed forces of the United States during wartime.

"The heart of the issue," wrote William N. Loucks, is whether the employees were in the status of "discharged" employees on January 1, 1959. Without saying exactly what their status was, he held it was not that of discharged employees. Mr. Loucks found it significant that a company witness had conceded that the grievants might have been regarded as retaining rights to recall on a seniority basis. This clearly revealed that these employees had not been discharged in the accepted sense of the word.

9

OVERTIME

Almost every modern collective bargaining agreement provides for some method of distributing available overtime equitably among employees who normally perform that work during straight time hours. But, recognizing that it may not always be possible to achieve absolute equality, the typical overtime clause contains such limiting phrases as: "whenever possible," "when it will not interfere with production," and "except in the case of emergencies."

Thus, deviations from the prescribed method of administering overtime inevitably involve questions of fact and contract interpretation: Would it have interfered with production to have assigned overtime to the next man on the overtime roster? Was a rush order toward the end of a shift an "emergency" such as to suspend the normal procedures for distributing overtime? Did a five-hour difference in overtime worked constitute an "imbalance" within the meaning of the contract?

When it is found that the employer has committed some error or contract violation, the question of an appropriate remedy arises. Should an employee who was overlooked, be "made whole" by being offered the next overtime opportunity? Or is pay for the time lost the only remedy?

Other problems arising out of interpretation of overtime clauses may also be indicated briefly: May an employer compel an employee to work extra hours? Does the employer have the right to arrange overtime schedules with a view toward reducing the total amount of premium pay? Answers to these and other questions are suggested in the discussion of cases that follow.

157

"PRACTICAL" AND "POSSIBLE" IN OVERTIME
DISTRIBUTION

When an employer departs from the contractually prescribed way of apportioning overtime, he frequently asserts that the course he took was the "practical" one. This defense does not always prevail with arbitrators. To support a departure from contractual procedures, it may be necessary to show that the contractual requirements were, under the circumstances, impossible or unreasonable. Several reported decisions illustrate the distinction between the "practical" and the "possible."

One example was the case of *C. V. Hill Company* (United Steelworkers of America, AFL-CIO).[1] The contract required distribution of overtime "as equally as possible" among employees by department and classification. To have followed the strict letter of the agreement on a certain Saturday when maintenance painting had to be done, the overtime would have been assigned to a painter who had worked on the third shift during the week just ending. As this would have meant sixteen continuous hours of work for him, management decided to offer the overtime to someone else.

The employer's view, John R. Abersold wrote, "fails to recognize the essential difference between the words 'as possible' and 'as practicable.' The words 'as possible' are much more restrictive than the words 'as practicable.' There can be no question but that it was quite *possible* to assign [the grievant] to day shift operations on Saturday and still stay within the bounds of 'reasonableness.' "[2]

Nor was the employer's contention persuasive that the assignment made was more consistent with "efficiency" and management's obligations to stockholders. Such obligations are "secondary" to its obligations under the collective bargaining agreement. "The aggrieved employee may have rights under the labor agreement that must be fulfilled even though they may interfere with efficiency of operations."

[1] 21 AAA 13.
[2] The arbitrator's written opinion referred to "uncontradicted union testimony" that sixteen continuous hours of work was not an unusual occurrence in the past.

Distinction between "Convenient" and "Practicable"

Procedures required by contracts are not always convenient. But as in the case of "practicality," lack of convenience by itself may not justify disregard of these procedures. That, in effect, was the moral of two cases at the *Decatur Works, Borg-Warner Corporation* (Allied Industrial Workers of America, AFL-CIO), where the contract required distribution of overtime "equitably," by shifts, insofar as "practicable."

The first case[3] came about when a machine broke down at three o'clock in the morning. The foreman in charge thought that the millwright who was due for the next overtime assignment would not be able to report in less than an hour. Furthermore, under the management chain of command, the foreman would first have had to telephone the superintendent to obtain his permission for the call-in. The most convenient solution was to ask a set-up man who was already in the plant to repair the machine, reclassifying him temporarily to millwright and paying him the appropriate rate. When the millwright learned of this, he filed a complaint, demanding pay for the overtime opportunity he missed.

The arbitrator, Samuel Edes, said that the foreman could certainly not be criticized for hesitating to disturb the superintendent at that hour. But a system of command which does not permit "expeditious remedial action" during an emergency cannot be asserted as a defense to a charge of contract violation. "The contract required the company to give [the grievant] this overtime opportunity unless it was impractical to do so. The salient facts as to practicality could only be determined after communicating with [him]." As the foreman had not done so, the grievance was upheld.

The facts in the second case[4] were similarly uncomplicated. When four maintenance men on the first shift worked four hours' overtime on Saturday without finishing the job, management decided it would be practical to let them continue working until the task was completed. This deprived second-shift maintenance employees of their share of overtime.

The employer contended that it would have required "at least one hour of orientation" if second-shift employees were called in

[3] 13 AAA 11.
[4] 20 AAA 14.

to complete the work. Bert L. Luskin found this contention not supported by the evidence. "Each of the four second shift millwrights was qualified to perform the required work on the basis of simple instructions and assignments which would have required minimal periods of time to orient them." The employer's error was in mistaking convenience for practicality. "It may have been more convenient to retain the first shift employees, but the test is 'practicality,' not 'convenience'."

Unanticipated Circumstances Make Equal Division Impractical

On the other hand, a third overtime grievance in the same case involved a circumstance which made it impractical to distribute overtime in the manner prescribed by the agreement. It was the plant engineer's judgment, on that occasion, that maintenance employees would complete a repair job by the end of their shift, or shortly thereafter. Under the circumstances, it seemed impractical to call in maintenance workers from the next shift for the small amount of work that might be available. As things turned out, however, the job took longer than expected. Second-shift maintenance men had to do a considerable amount of work during the third-shift hours. But this did not "in and of itself" warrant a finding that the company had violated the contract, the arbitrator concluded. If the need for much work could have been anticipated, the failure to call in a new crew for a share of overtime would have been a violation. But under the circumstances, management acted properly on the basis of known facts.

NOTIFICATION OF OVERTIME OPPORTUNITIES

A contractual provision for distribution of overtime generally presupposes an orderly way of notifying employees, turn by turn, of overtime opportunities. This raises the question of how much effort management must exert to accomplish such notification. A typical case arose at the *Janney Cylinder Company* (United Steelworkers of America, AFL-CIO),[5] where a foreman, faced with a rush order

[5] 18 AAA 4.

that came to his attention a few minutes after the end of the day shift on Friday, "overlooked" the inspector next in line for overtime, and assigned Saturday work to someone else.[6]

In management's view, the last-minute rush constituted an "emergency," justifying disregard of normal procedures. Furthermore, the overtime distribution provision of the contract itself acknowledged that "strict adherence to seniority may not always be possible." By this language, the company argued, the contract permitted just such discretionary action as the foreman had taken.[7]

The critical question, in the estimation of Wayne E. Howard, was the meaning of the word "possible" as used in the contract. Clearly, he said, a true emergency or the breakdown of a machine might require instant action, and make impossible the observance of the rotation-by-seniority plan. On the other hand, the employer must exhaust "reasonable possibilities from an administrative standpoint." What is "possible" in any circumstance "should be construed within the framework of the operating and administrative difficulties in running a plant." Applying this standard, he found against the company, largely for three reasons: (1) the grievance resulted from the forgetfulness of the foreman, not an emergency; (2) the company would not have had to take time-consuming measures to notify the proper man of the overtime opportunity; and (3) there was no great urgency, as the overtime work was not to be done until the next day.

Notice When Time Is Short

Almost the identical problem—a rush order after the end of a shift on Friday—arose at the *Leader Iron Works* (Allied Industrial Workers of America, AFL-CIO).[8] Here, too, the employer thought an "emergency" existed. But the arbitrator found nothing in the contract permitting exceptions to the contractual method of assign-

[6] The inspector who should have been asked to report on Saturday was working in another department. The foreman testified at the arbitration that, in view of the need for a quick decision, he did not take the time to find out whether the inspector was willing to work overtime on short notice.

[7] The contract also contained a provision for giving employees "by-passed" in distribution of overtime an opportunity to make up the lost time. This too, in the company's opinion, implied some latitude in departing from the overtime roster.

[8] 18 AAA 14.

ing overtime. The only reference to emergencies was in a provision requiring three hours' notice of overtime. Nevertheless, John F. Sembower made these general remarks about what constitutes an emergency:

The test of an "emergency" must be applied strictly, because what is involved here, in effect, is to set aside the agreement in light of it. Courts at law have been very strict when they have been asked to relieve parties of contractual obligations because of an emergency, usually confining such decision to real catastrophes suffered by the party's own facilities, owing to fires, floods, and the like.[9]

Mr. Sembower's definition of an emergency obviously excluded man-made situations. This narrow definition was also favored by Wayne E. Howard in a case at *Bonafide Plastics, Inc.* (United Rubber, Cork, Linoleum and Plastic Workers, AFL-CIO).[10] Here, however, the matter in dispute was not distribution of overtime alone, but the contractual obligation to post overtime schedules in advance. Mr. Howard found that an employee who reported his availability for Saturday overtime, before leaving to visit a doctor at noon Friday, and was told there was no overtime scheduled, was entitled to pay for hours worked on Saturday by another employee in his stead. The employer's defense was that the need for the work arose after the grievant had left and that the situation was, therefore, of an "emergency" nature. Mr. Howard was not persuaded by this, and distinguished between a "truly emergency situation" and one which results from poor planning:

The evidence suggests that while work was unplanned, it was not necessarily work of an emergency nature. The purpose of the agreement that the company will post overtime weekend work schedules is to force the company to plan its work schedules in advance so that its employees will have advance knowledge of weekend work. This agreement must be honored unless it is patently impractical in specific instances for the company to carry it out. The company must show by clear and convincing evidence in each instance where they fail to post this schedule that such failure was caused by the exigencies of a truly emergency situation. In the instant situation, no such urgency was proved. Since this was the case, the company was under an obligation to notify the grievant that overtime weekend work was available.

[9] For a discussion of the differences between true emergencies and critical situations caused by poor planning, see Chapters 5 and 6.
[10] 10 AAA 11.

INVENTORY AND EXPERIMENTAL WORK

When inventory is to be taken, or when experimental work is to be done, management often finds it convenient to select employees for these tasks on an overtime basis, without regard to the methods of assignment normally observed. Whether this type of work is subject to the rules that govern production may depend upon contract language, past practice, and the particular fact patterns.

At the *Electric Storage Battery Company* (International Union of Electrical, Radio and Machine Workers, AFL-CIO),[11] the contract required that overtime "be distributed among all hourly paid employees of that job classification as evenly as is reasonably practicable on a quarterly basis; subject, however, to requirements of production." When the need for taking inventory in the "boosting" department arose, management directed that a "booster attendant" from the shipping and receiving department do the work on an overtime day. The grievant, who was both in the booster classification and assigned to the boosting area, claimed that the work should have been given to him. Bert L. Luskin ruled that this assignment was not a violation of the contract because inventory work was "not the normal type of work which is considered to come within the regular duties performed" by the grievant. Furthermore, he said, the requirement that overtime be allocated evenly among employees in a classification "does not necessarily require that the work be assigned to a particular classification where the work is not normally required to be performed by the employees in the classification in question." In this case, as the employee who performed the eight hours' of inventory work on overtime was classified as a booster attendant, a similar period of overtime would have to be given in the future to the grievant. But the assignment of the work to the employee from the shipping department was not in itself an error.

Within the Scope of the Agreement

Whether inventory work comes within the purview of an overtime distribution clause also arose at the *American Can Company, Dixie Cup Division* (United Papermakers and Paperworkers, AFL-

[11] 16 AAA 6.

CIO),[12] but this time with a decision different from that in the *Electric Storage Battery* case.

On a Saturday, the employer had assigned five first-shift employees to what was to be five hours of inventory work, but which actually took eight to nine hours. This, according to the union, was a violation of a clause providing that "when operations are scheduled for Saturday, the first and second shifts will each be five hour shifts. . . ." Under this clause, the union contended, the first-shift crew should have been permitted to work only five hours, the remainder going to a similar crew from the second shift.

Management's answer was that the quoted language applied to machine operations only and governed procedures not applicable where only one shift was scheduled on inventory. Furthermore, it was said, the union's position would make any misjudgment of the estimated time for the work unreasonably costly.

John Perry Horlacher found this defense weak. First of all, if the overtime distribution provision did not apply to non-machine operating employees, there was no clause that did cover their conditions of work. "It seems a little odd that there could have been a deliberate mutual intent to produce such a result." The language of the overtime clause is "inclusive," not "restrictive." There would have to be "rather compelling reasons" for excluding some employees from coverage of this clause. It was probably true, as management representatives asserted at the arbitration hearing, that the five-hours-on-Saturday provision came about because the parties wanted to avoid longer shifts in the machine operations. "It does not automatically follow, however, as the company argument implies, that the provision must be limited in its application to the principal occasion which brought it into being." He went on to say:

A rule or principle stated in the general form carries with it a presumption of general applicability. This of course can be rebutted but it is not sufficient for rebutting the presumption to prove that the rule grew out of situation X and thereby infer that it applies only to X. This *may* be the case. But if the rule is inclusively framed, the evidence that it does not apply also to Y or Z ought to be pretty clear and convincing.

Furthermore, to uphold the company's interpretation would be to

[12] 4 AAA 17.

rob other provisions of the agreement, dealing with "time allocation for shifts other than the first," of meaning. "The principle that the construction of one clause of a contract should give the fullest effect to the entire agreement and not nullify or impair some other provision would in this instance favor the broad construction." While upholding the union's view that second-shift employees should have been called in for the three to four additional hours it took to complete inventory, Mr. Horlacher made it clear that the decision would have been different if fewer hours had been needed.

Tasks Incidental to Inventory

The assignment of employees to inventory work on overtime was not in itself an issue at the *American Bosch Arma Mississippi Corporation* (International Union of Electrical, Radio and Machine Workers, AFL-CIO),[13] But certain "clean-up" tasks given the employees to fill in time while awaiting a check of auditors was protested. The type of clean-up work that was performed could not be regarded as "available overtime" within the meaning of the overtime distribution clause, Arbitrator Paul H. Sanders ruled. Furthermore, the fact that the work was performed when inventory was taken made the "normal rules inapplicable." If the aggrieved employees had complained about improper distribution of the inventory work itself, including the incidental clean-up work, a different question would have been presented. As that was not the issue here, the grievance was denied.

Experimental Work

The contract at *Teer, Wickwire & Company* (International Association of Machinists, AFL-CIO)[14] required that overtime work be distributed "as equitably as possible among all employees as their skills will permit within their respective classifications"; but management thought the usual procedures did not apply when the work to be done was experimental, or "preproduction." Consequently, when it became necessary to do a small amount of such work on a Saturday, it was assigned to a leadman alone. A production worker, who had been operating the machines set up by the leadman on the

[13] 10 AAA 2.
[14] 4 AAA 8.

same work during straight time hours, was not offered this overtime work. The union filed a grievance in his behalf.

The critical question, in the view of Charles A. Rogers, was whether running the machine was within the leadman's job classification. A reading of the job description convinced him that it was not; the leadman was to operate machines only to the extent necessary for "instructing and training operators." With no production worker in attendance, there was no one to "instruct" during overtime. Furthermore, leadmen had not performed machine operation in the past, except on one occasion when the union's concurrence was obtained. The award directed that the machine operator be paid for the overtime assignment he missed.[15]

Latitude for Management

However, at the *Wayne Pump Company* (United Automobile Workers, AFL-CIO),[16] experimental work, it was found by Herman Lazarus, need not be governed by the usual overtime distribution rules. But here there were at least two important elements not present in the *Teer, Wickwire & Company* case.

The first point of differentiation was that the employees who performed the work during straight time hours were permitted to continue on overtime. While this resulted in an imbalance of overtime within an "overtime group," the assignment was proper, because the union had not objected to those employees doing the experimental work during the day.

The practical effect of the Union's position would have been to require the company, at the close of the regular eight hour day, to release employees who were not in [certain overtime groups] and substitute employees in [other] groups.

The second difference was that the overtime equalization pro-

[15] Nor was Mr. Rogers convinced that the work performed on the Saturday in question was "minimal," as the employer had asserted, or that very few pieces of good quality were manufactured. The evidence showed that about 300 pieces were produced, as against 180 on a weekday, and that half of them were of good quality. The arbitrator also found it "of interest to note" that after the Saturday when the violation took place, the grievant worked on the next 4 to 6 Saturdays along with the leadman, until the experimental job was released for production.
[16] 20 AAA 5.

vision of the contract was phrased so as to give management considerable latitude. It read:

The company agrees that, to the best of its ability, it will endeavor to
equalize the hours of overtime work among the employees in an "overtime group" who are capable of doing the overtime job.

The arbitrator found that this language did not impose "a fixed and
absolute obligation to equalize overtime" on management. Especially did the use of the word "endeavor" imply that exceptions
could be made under "special and abnormal" conditions.

I believe that such a situation confronted the company. The company
was behind in its schedule of production and it was clear that prompt
completion was important if the company was to obtain new business.
In view of the many production problems and the special nature of the
work required, it would have been unreasonable to expect [management]
to change its work crew at the end of the working day and to bring new
men to work on a project which was dissimilar from that normally done
in connection with the company's standard items.

While holding this award appropriate because of the "unusual
problems involved," Mr. Lazarus cautioned that under more commonly met circumstances "the equalization rule must normally
apply."

SENIORITY STATUS AND OVERTIME

Since many benefits and privileges of the collective bargaining
agreement accrue to employees in accordance with their length of
service, it is understandable that the question of granting preference
to senior employees in the distribution of overtime should arise.
Where the contract makes length of service one of the determining
factors, the problem is no more complicated than any other; that is,
standards of practicality, ability, and convenience may have to be
faced, as in most equalization-of-overtime cases. But where the contract does not specifically indicate whether senior employees are to
get preference, new problems of contract interpretation may arise.

A case in point arose at *Vickers, Inc.* (Allied Industrial Workers
of America, AFL-CIO),[17] where the union objected to the assign-

[17] 8 AAA 3.

ment of overtime to probationary employees in one department at a time when senior employees in another department were not given overtime. The contract provided only that overtime be divided "as equally as possible among employees on the basis of rotation within their line and/or department." On the basis of this provision alone, which specified departmental seniority, there did not seem to be any ground for the union's contention. But the union also cited the probationary clause, which read, in part:

Any newly hired employee employed for less than thirty (30) consecutive days is a probationary employee, and his employment status during such period shall be considered temporary. He shall have no seniority during that period, nor be entitled to any of the other privileges available to those employees who have completed their probationary periods.

Thus, the question before Wilber C. Bothwell was whether overtime was one of the "privileges" of seniority. He answered that it was not. The "privileges" referred to in the clause the union relied upon were those growing out of the seniority provision, not the overtime clause, which made no reference to seniority:

If the agreement between the parties had included a clear provision that overtime work was not to be assigned to probationary employees, or that it was not to be assigned until all seniority employees in the classification were requested to work, then the practice as established here would not have been controlling. In that case, the arbitrator would have ruled in favor of the union.

The contract at the *Gorham Manufacturing Company* (International Jewelry Workers Union, AFL-CIO)[18] was similar to that at *Vickers, Inc.* in that it did not specifically state that seniority would be a governing factor in the distribution of overtime. Under this contract, Lloyd H. Bailer held that it was not wrong for the employer to send a senior employee home three hours before the end of a scheduled overtime period, while permitting juniors to perform work the former could have done. Although it might have been preferable as a matter of "good labor relations" to have permitted the senior to work to the end of the scheduled period, "the contract affords no basis for holding that management was required to take this step."

[18] 5 AAA 5.

REMEDIES FOR IMPROPER DISTRIBUTION
OF OVERTIME

When a dispute arises over assignment of overtime, the sharpest battle often relates not so much to the fact of improper distribution, but to the remedy. The employer may seek to correct the balance by offering a grievant the next overtime opportunity. He may even want to "create" overtime for the employee. But the union's request is usually for monetary relief. Which remedy is more appropriate is a question that has come before dozens of arbitrators in reported cases. In some of these, the issue was not only whether the next work opportunity is an appropriate remedy, but the time limit within which that opportunity must be forthcoming.[19]

"Make-up" Overtime

One case, clearer than most because the employer conceded an "unintentional error," came before Archibald Cox at *The Electric Storage Battery Company* (International Union of Electrical, Radio and Machine Workers, AFL-CIO).[20]

The facts were typical. On Saturday, October 17, 1959, the company required overtime on a certain operation. Two men on the overtime roster to whom the work should have been offered were overlooked by the supervisor, resulting in an admitted imbalance. To the union's demand that the error be corrected by back pay, management offered the two low overtime men involved the oppor-

---

[19] Not every violation, of course, results in an awarded remedy. At the *American Can Company* (United Papermakers and Paperworkers, AFL-CIO), 10 AAA 3, a junior employee was offered a temporary transfer on an overtime basis, thus disregarding a senior who should have been given the work. Arbitrator John W. Seybold denied the union's request for a monetary remedy, because management "corrected the complained-of condition with reasonable promptness after it was called to its attention." There was still another reason for not burdening management with a monetary remedy. The grievant had refused to do the work in question in the past, giving management reason to believe he still preferred not to do it. Under the circumstances, the foreman's "oversight" was "not only understandable, but perfectly natural." It was also relevant that the company had "gone to some lengths" to accommodate employees who had strong objection to operating certain machines. "It does not seem appropriate to penalize the company in this instance, when the 'wrong' was so promptly rectified, and when [the grievant] has not gone out of his way to consider the company's problems," Mr. Seybold concluded.

[20] 19 AAA 22.

tunity to make up the time lost, but refused to pay for time not worked.

Several weeks later, these two grievants were, in fact, offered overtime. They accepted the work, but without acknowledging that it represented a proper disposition of the grievance.[21]

Here the union was upheld because an offer of make-up work "merely shifts the burden to others." In fashioning a remedy,

we are forced to choose between denying the employee an adequate remedy or forcing the employer to pay twice for the same work. When the employer causes the loss, however innocently, it is more just that he should bear the cost of making the employee whole than that the employee should be forced to suffer a denial of contract rights without remedy.

Two Hypothetical Cases

Mr. Cox pointed out that there are circumstances when "justice can be done without a monetary payment." Those circumstances were not present in this case, he said, but he thought it would clarify his award to describe a hypothetical case where make-up work would be appropriate.

Suppose that a contract provided that the overtime work in any department should be shared equally and that, in order to accomplish an equitable division, the overtime work on any particular day should be given to the man who had previously received the least overtime. Suppose now that there were five employees in Department 123 who, before March 15, 1960, had accumulated the following overtime hours:

Employee A	18 hours
Employee B	18 hours
Employee C	16 hours
Employee D	8 hours
Employee E	6 hours

Suppose that the company called Employee D for eight hours overtime on February 20. This would violate the contract if Employee E were

---

[21] Mr. Cox wrote that the acceptance of the overtime under the circumstances did not bar the claim to monetary relief. "If the chance to work was a remedy that would in fact make the men whole, they cannot obtain additional relief. On the other hand, if it was insufficient, as the men and the union claim, its acceptance under protest should not bar further recovery. There was no willing election. The men made their position clear. The company received eight hours work for the eight hours pay which it expended. Since the company was not prejudiced, the men are not barred by their conduct."

available, but the violation could easily be corrected by giving the work to E the next time overtime employment was available. If E got eight hours on the second occasion, the mistake would be completely corrected. Employee D would then have sixteen hours overtime and Employee E would have fourteen hours overtime exactly as would have happened if there had been no violation. To require the company to pay Employee E for eighteen hours without working would penalize the company unnecessarily. It would also give Employee E an undeserved bonus. Such a ruling would be warranted only if the evidence showed that the violation was intentional or grossly negligent.

On the other hand, he said there are bound to be some cases in which it is impossible to equalize "general overtime" opportunities after a mistake because the prior right of some other employees to "special" overtime may stand in the way. Again, he posed a hypothetical case:

Suppose that there were a small department of five employees who had accumulated overtime by August 1 as follows:

Employee L	80 hours
Employee M	56 hours
Employee N	16 hours
Employee O	16 hours
Employee P	8 hours

If Employees L and M regularly performed jobs which required substantial overtime, they might be expected to accumulate overtime more rapidly than Employees N, O and P. Suppose that Employee L was given eight hours of general overtime on August 6. Obviously this work should have gone to Employee P. If Employee N or Employee O had been called in by mistake, the wrong could perhaps be remedied by giving Employee P the first opportunity to do general overtime until he caught up with Employees N and O. But the general overtime which Employee L received could never be given back to Employees N, O and P. Employees L and M would always retain the eight-hour improper advantage over the others, partly because of their priority on special overtime and partly because the established practice would call for wiping the books clear at the end of a year. Employee P would therefore be in the same position as a worker who had been discharged without just cause, or who had been laid off in violation of the applicable seniority rule. The only way in which to make Employee P whole would be to give him eight hours pay or to assign him general overtime in preference to Employees N and O. To do the latter would simply shift the burden of the supervisor's mistake onto Employees N and O. The error would not be corrected. Its effects would not be cancelled out.

Returning to the facts of the case before him, Mr. Cox observed that the circumstances of the two grievants were similar to the by-passed employees in the second hypothetical case, in that the sixteen hours of general overtime which should have been given the grievants "could never be restored to the pool." For that reason, they were entitled to monetary relief; the work done by them on October 17 "did not cancel out the effects of the company's error."[22]

[22] In addition to his own analysis of the instant case, Mr. Cox said that "the precedents squarely sustain the union's position" on the justification for monetary relief. "Other arbitration rulings sustain this view. One group of cases deals with situations in which redistribution of future overtime opportunities would result in the equality which the contract sought to achieve. In some cases damages were awarded, despite the opportunity for subsequent equalization, upon the theory that the opportunity to work overtime upon a later occasion is different from the opportunity to work overtime on the day the right was denied. E.g. *U.S. Rubber Co.*, 13 LA 839 (1949); *Bridgeport Brass Co.*, 19 LA 690 (1952); *American Machine & Metals, Inc.*, 20 LA 369 (1953); *Phillips Chemical Co.*, 17 LA 721 (1951); *Ingersoll Rand Co.*, 7 LA 564 (1947); *Monsanto Chemical Co.*, 15 LA 589 (1950); cf. *Standard Oil Co.*, 28 LA 100 (1957). Other arbitrators held that no monetary compensation was due where subsequent equalization had been, or could be, achieved, either upon the theory that the promise to distribute overtime equally required only equal treatment over a substantial period of time or else upon the ground that an opportunity to make up the time lost is an adequate remedy. E.g. *Goodyear Tire & Rubber Co.*, 5 LA 30 (1946); *B. F. Goodrich Co.*, 8 LA 883 (1947); *Borg-Warner Corp.*, 16 LA 237 (1950); *North American Aviation Co.*, 17 LA 320 (1951); *Robertshaw Fulton Controls Co.*, 21 LA 622 (1953); *A. O. Smith Corp.*, 33 LA 365 (1959). Where the consequences of the mistake could not be corrected by a subsequent redistribution of overtime opportunities without invading the rights of other employees, the decisions uniformly award monetary compensation. Thus, in *Firestone Tire & Rubber Co.*, 9 LA 518, 522–24 (1948), the grievant was awarded back pay for the loss of earnings resulting from failure to allow him to work a double shift. In *International Harvester Co.*, 14 LA 430 (1950), a shop steward was given compensation after he had been denied his prior claim on overtime opportunities because the time lost by him could never be made up by giving him the first chance at subsequent overtime; he was entitled to the first chance regardless of the violation. Back pay is also awarded if overtime work is assigned to employees outside a classification in violation of a contract calling for the sharing of all overtime opportunities among employees within the classification. E.g. *Maytag Co.*, 18 LA 190 (1952); *Standard Lime & Cement Co.*, 26 LA 468 (1956); *Bendix Aviation Corp.*, 26 LA 540 (1956). See also *Tenny Engineering Co.*, 16 LA 826 (1950), where foremen had been given an undue share of the overtime work. In *Walworth Co.*, 5 LA 551 (1946) Benjamin Selekman held that mistakes in overtime assignments should be remedied by the redistribution of overtime if the consequences of the mistake could be corrected within three months without violating the rights of other employees, but that the grievants should otherwise be awarded monetary compensation."

The Fallacy of "Created" Work

In the course of the dispute over a remedy for the "unintentional breach of contract" in this case, the suggestion was also made that the grievants might be given overtime work which would otherwise not be scheduled. But this suggestion, too, was inadequate in that it did not really restore the proper balance. It would be appropriate to remedy the grievance in this way, Mr. Cox wrote, only if one could be certain that the work would not otherwise be performed.

But there is no certainty . . . The truth is that the amount of work "required" in an industrial plant involves human judgments concerning different degrees of necessity. Management and supervision can always schedule work which is not absolutely essential. They can always cut out some work which could easily be called necessary. It is not unlikely that the "unnecessary" work done on any one day will be offset by reducing the volume of work judged "necessary" on later occasions.

Monetary Relief Favored

Among other cases in which arbitrators have awarded similarly on the question of monetary relief versus make-up work were:

Downingtown Paper Company (United Papermakers and Paper-workers, AFL-CIO).[23] Arbitrator John Perry Horlacher held that the assignment of millwright work to a laborer on overtime could never be restored to the millwrights by subsequent assignment of overtime, because the contract required equal division of overtime *"within* the millwright department."

American Brass Company (Mine, Mill and Smelter Workers Union).[24] The employer had offered to correct an admitted error by giving the grievant the next overtime opportunity, or pay in lieu of it, if that opportunity should not arise within thirty days. A. Howard Myers said that the offer might be "fair and reasonable," but that he could not make it his award, because it was not the issue before him. "The arbitrator is obliged to rule on the claim of a contract breach [as of the date the breach occurs], not as of a later date." The employer also stated, in support of his offer of a work opportunity, that the grievant had declined overtime on a previous occasion and, being in poor health, was presumed not to want overtime

[23] 1 AAA 2.
[24] 12 AAA 6.

on the day in question. This was the reason he was not offered the overtime. As to this, Mr. Myers said: "I have not been authorized to pass judgment in equity on the reasonableness of the company's offer but on employee rights. Under the stipulated question of the submission, I am obliged to sustain the union position."

Janney Cylinder Company (United Steelworkers of America, AFL-CIO).[25] Some of the facts of this case were discussed earlier in this chapter. Here, the contract itself recognized that "strict adherence to seniority may not always be possible" and permitted an employee denied his turn for "unforeseen reasons" to be given "the opportunity to make up such overtime at the earliest feasible time." Even this, Wayne E. Howard said, did not bar a claim for monetary relief. The company had not exhausted the "reasonable possibilities at its disposal for locating the grievant and offering him the overtime he was entitled to." For that reason, the company could not rely upon "its contractual authority to give by-passed employees future overtime work opportunities."

Leader Iron Works, Inc. (Allied Industrial Workers of America, AFL-CIO).[26] This case, too, was discussed earlier in this chapter. Addressing himself to the remedy, John F. Sembower said that the employer's offer of the next overtime opportunity to a by-passed employee seemed "eminently reasonable on the surface," but the parties had themselves settled grievances of the same kind in the past on the basis of cash payment. Furthermore, the contract did not call for rotation of overtime. Consequently, an opportunity missed by an employee is "lost to him forever." Finally, the grievant's employment might terminate before another opportunity to work overtime might arise. Not wanting to direct the "repugnant" remedy of "made work," Mr. Sembower sustained the grievance and directed back pay for the lost time.

Appropriate Remedy for Incentive Employees

A problem of a different kind, involving the appropriate remedy for employees paid incentive rates, arose at *Landers, Frary & Clark* (United Electrical, Radio and Machine Workers).[27] The issue was

[25] 18 AAA 4.
[26] 18 AAA 14.
[27] 20 AAA 12.

whether their "compensatory payments" should be at the "special hourly rate" they would have earned or at the lower "standard hourly rate," which was generally applicable to situations where employees were paid for time not worked. The company relied largely on a clause calling for payment at the special rate, "provided employees perform such work with skill and effort reasonably commensurate with their special hourly rates." As the "compensatory" payment was for time not worked, it was argued, the higher rate did not apply.

On reading the contract as a whole, Lewis M. Gill found the employer's contentions "unpersuasive." It was true that the clause cited by the company "contemplates situations where actual work in the plant is performed." But the list contains "at least one instance where this is not the case—time spent by union stewards and committeemen on grievances." Even apart from this defect, however, Mr. Gill was not persuaded by the employer's argument:

The problem here is to fashion an appropriate *remedy,* and contracts are usually silent, as this one is, as to the precise remedy to be applied for violation of each of its provisions. The generally accepted principle is that the remedy should be designed to restore to the grievant what he has lost as a result of the violation.

Discharge or other disciplinary cases may involve special problems in this field, in cases where some penalty less than that imposed seems in order, and the back pay is accordingly modified or withheld. Nothing of that sort is involved here, where there is no suggestion of any misconduct by the grievants; the proper remedy here would clearly seem to be an award compensating the grievants for what they would have earned (special hourly rates) had they been called in for the overtime work in question.

SHIFT PROBLEMS AND OVERTIME

Whether certain hours worked constituted overtime or a change in shift became an issue at the *Cities Service Oil Company* (Oil, Chemical and Atomic Workers, AFL-CIO).[28] To fill a vacancy on a four-man night-shift crew, management, relying on a contract provision dealing with changes in shift assignments, directed a laborer

[28] 18 AAA 12.

on the day shift to do the work. The union protested that performance of the work was really overtime, requiring the assignment of an employee in accordance with an overtime roster.

"The plain provision and apparent clear intent of the contract is that time worked outside the listed hours is overtime," wrote Arbitrator W. Willard Wirtz. Furthermore, "any possible question about this must yield to the controlling consideration that the parties had consistently, prior to the case disputed here, recognized assignments such as this one as the contract right of the departmental employees. This practice has been so invariable as to require its recognition as a reflection of the parties' intention that these assignments are necessarily to be considered overtime assignments."

RIGHT OF EMPLOYER TO ELIMINATE OVERTIME

When a sizeable amount of overtime is scheduled every week, employees tend to regard the extra income as a normal part of wages. Efforts to reduce or abolish overtime may then be resisted by unions. By and large, however, barring a contractual guarantee of overtime, arbitrators have generally upheld the right of employers to plan the flow of work in such a way as to make overtime unnecessary.

An interesting illustration of customary overtime becoming an expected part of earnings and an issue in collective bargaining is to be found at *Anheuser-Busch, Inc.* (International Union of Operating Engineers, AFL-CIO).[29]

It had been a long-standing practice here for certain shifts of employees in the unit covered by this union to work on Sundays. During negotiations of the 1955 contract, however, two important changes were decided upon. First, the employer agreed that "whenever possible, the work week shall be Monday through Friday, inclusive." The second change was a provision for double time for work on Sunday. Despite these changes, however, Sunday work continued as in the past, the only difference being that employees now received a higher premium pay.

But shortly after the negotiation of a new contract in 1957, man-

[29] 4 AAA 3.

agement decided to abolish Sunday work. The union objected on several grounds, the chief of which was that the employer had obligated himself to continue week-end work when, in reply to a demand for a wage increase, he had reminded them that they were receiving premium pay on a regular basis for Sundays. To abolish Sunday work now, the union said, was evidence of "bad faith" in bargaining, and warranted an award either restoring Sunday work or rescinding the contract altogether.

The evidence was "quite persuasive" to James C. Hill that the company negotiators had indeed "consciously withheld knowledge of the probability, if not the certainty, that Sunday work could be eliminated in the future, while using the factor of double time and the union's expectation of continued Sunday work." But despite this, he concluded that the union's requested remedies had to be denied.

Despite the absence of the usual "management's rights" clause, the employer had the right to discontinue Sunday work. "The scheduling of work is a normal and customary function of management which would not ordinarily be deemed limited or waived except by some express provision of the agreement," he said. Furthermore, the use of the words "whenever possible" in the workweek clause, together with the newly agreed-upon premium rate in 1955, which was in the nature of a "penalty payment," implied that the company would eliminate week-end work whenever it became feasible:

The elimination or reduction of Sunday work does not alter the basic wage provisions of the agreement. We are not dealing with the removal of a benefit, outside the written agreement, which has become a part of the normal expectation of employees through long practice. While Sunday work is of long duration, the provision of double time was first introduced in the prior agreement of 1955–1957. It serves, and is presumably intended, as a penalty payment from the standpoint of the employer, and as extra compensation to the employees for the inconvenience and disruption of customary social patterns which are involved in working Sundays. Presumably, therefore, when the onerous hours are withdrawn the basis for the extra compensation is also removed. In any event, the contract provisions governing wages and hours merely establish the rate of pay *when* and if the men work a Sunday shift.

In denying the union's request for alternative remedies, Mr. Hill said he could find no "clear or precise way" of equating the "Sunday pay factor" with the wage rates that were established in the 1957 contract. "I find no basis on which one could reconstruct these negotiations for the purpose of assessing what would have happened if the reduction of Sunday work had been accomplished or was known to both parties." Nor could the union's request to rescind the 1957 contract be granted, in view of the provision that "the arbitrator shall have no power to add to or subtract from or modify the terms of the agreement." As the arbitrator is a creature of the agreement, he said, any remedy such as the union sought would have to come from some other forum, such as the courts or the National Labor Relations Board.

Cutting Premium Pay Costs

A most interesting and difficult question of contract interpretation, which arose in two cases, may be stated in generalized form as follows: Given the employer's obligation to distribute overtime in a certain manner, must he follow the procedure inflexibly, modifying it only to the extent necessary to achieve the equality of overtime opportunities required by the contract, or may he modify it in other ways, to reduce the total amount of premium pay, provided no substantial inequality results?

At the *Westingouse Electric Corporation* (International Union of Electrical, Radio and Machine Workers, AFL-CIO),[30] the contract required that "all overtime hours shall be equalized by seniority." It also provided for maintenance of a chart showing the assignment of overtime hours, without a cut-off point and with monthly totals carried forward to the next month.

On a particular occasion, the employer had eight hours of overtime available. Under other circumstances, he might have offered all of it to the man next in line for overtime. But management found some monetary advantage in dividing the work equally among employees from two shifts. The employee who thought he should have been given eight hours filed a grievance.

Robert G. McIntosh said the company had the right to act as it did, since absolute equality in overtime opportunities is not always possible. With only a five- or six-hours difference between the top man and the low man on the overtime roster at the end of the

[30] 15 AAA 2.

month, as was the case here, it could not be said that management had violated the agreement.

Directly affirming the company's right to modify overtime assignments with a view to reducing labor costs, he concluded:

> Some comment was indulged that the company made the assignment as it did because it thus saved money in not having to pay double time for four hours on the several days. If the company's motive was one of saving money, there is nothing wrong in this. As we view motives in labor, the company may conduct itself for any motive in complying with the contract so long as it does not discriminate against employees or the union. This being the opinion, the decision is that the company did not violate the contract.

Deliberate Cutting of Hours Held in Violation

An award by Benjamin C. Roberts suggested a different answer in a case involving *Personal Products Corporation* (United Papermakers and Paperworkers, AFL-CIO).[31] It will be seen, however, that the contract language and many of the facts were different from those in the *Westinghouse* case. For that reason, no inference should be drawn that either arbitrator would have decided differently if he had had the other's case.

In the case before Mr. Roberts, the contract called for time-and-a-half for "all hours worked" when an employee was required to work in excess of two continuous shifts (sixteen hours). Another provision, also relevant to the dispute, required that when an employee is expected to be absent, an employee in his classification on the previous shift be given the first opportunity to work the additional hours.

The dispute arose when a mechanic on one shift was asked to continue into the next shift because the regularly scheduled mechanic on that shift was to be involved in contract negotiation conferences. As mechanics customarily worked eight and one-half hours per day (arriving a half-hour early to get machines ready for production workers), a double shift in this case would have meant seventeen hours, requiring time-and-a-half for all the hours, not just for hours after the eighth. Management, therefore, told the first-shift mechanic to stop work at the end of the sixteenth hour, limit-

---

[31] 21 AAA 3.

ing him to only seven-and-a-half hours of the normal second shift and to straight time rates.

The union asserted that, by shortening the second shift, the company had attempted to "subvert" the agreement. As the grievant had been asked to cover the job of the second-shift mechanic in addition to his own, he should have been permitted to work the normal total of seventeen hours. Management answered that scheduling of overtime was a management right, the contract requiring only that a certain rate be paid "in the event" more than sixteen hours were scheduled.

Mr. Roberts ruled that the deliberate shortening of a shift to avoid premium pay in this case was a violation of the contract. "The testimony is convincing," he wrote, "that the grievant was told he would have to work a double shift in the first instance and that this was reduced solely because of the premium pay provisions that would become applicable. This can be the only acceptable explanation for the subsequent limitation in the hours." Furthermore, he added, the company had failed to rebut union testimony that the shortened schedule had not been dictated by lack of work. "The fact is that the shutdown work still had to be done and from the available testimony . . . this bargaining unit work was performed by supervision apparently in violation of the contract."

Effect of Transfers on Overtime Opportunities

An employee's expectation of overtime may be affected not only by management's deliberate effort to limit premium pay but also by such circumstances as transfers, promotions, demotions, reclassifications, and rotating shifts. Where these changes in status are themselves proper under the contract, loss of overtime opportunities that may result are not generally held to warrant any remedy. A case in point was that at *Yale & Towne Manufacturing Company* (International Association of Machinists, AFL-CIO),[32] where an employee, who was to be transferred to another department, was directed to delay the transfer until his successor could be "broken in." While he waited for the change of assignment to become effective, he was unable to share in the twelve hours of overtime his prospective department worked. This, Eli Rock pointed out, did

[32] 18 AAA 1.

not give him a justifiable grievance, since there was no "specific time limit" in the contract for putting transfers into effect. There did not seem to be any question but that "the decision to fill or not to fill a vacancy must remain in the hands of the company." Furthermore, even if the union's contentions were accepted, it would not follow that immediate transfer would always favor the employee. There could be situations where overtime opportunities were greater in the old department.

Filling of Vacancy Delayed for Sole Purpose of Avoiding Overtime

In the *Yale & Towne* case, there was a sound business reason for delaying the transfer. The loss of overtime opportunities was, therefore, held to be an incidental consequence of a proper management action. The situation was different at the *Celanese Corporation of America* (United Mine Workers, District 50).[33] Here, the company delayed assigning the successful bidder to a new job only because directing the change immediately would have involved premium pay for some hours. The contract required that the employer "endeavor" to fill vacancies within a week, but Saul Wallen ruled that the latitude implied by that word did not extend to purposeful delays. "The parties use the word 'endeavor' apparently because they recognize that there would be circumstances wherein it would not be possible to select and permanently assign in one week," he wrote. "But where no such impediment exists, it does not seem logical to withhold from the bidder the benefit of [the contract] solely because overtime might result."

A secondary argument was put forward by the employer to the effect that the time limit of one week begins not with the beginning, but with the end, of the three-day posting period. In view of all the language of the contract, the arbitrator said, the company "must try to both select a candidate and make a permanent assignment within one week of the time the job is posted."

WORK SCHEDULE CHANGES AND OVERTIME

It is well established in American industrial relations that management has the right to direct the scheduling of work, except to

[33] 23 AAA 20.

the extent that such right has been restricted by the collective bargaining agreement. But changes in work schedules often affect the amount of overtime available, and may even be motivated by a deliberate effort to eliminate premium pay hours. What happens when such issues reach arbitration is illustrated in three cases.

Four-Day Week to Avoid Overtime Pay

At the *Armco Steel Corporation* (United Steelworkers of America, AFL-CIO),[34] July 4, 1958, was a paid holiday, for which employees were due compensation without working. But in view of a provision which required scheduling "on the basis of the normal work pattern," employees were looking forward to work on the holiday and to receiving premium pay under the overtime clause of the agreement. Management, however, scheduled only four days' work that week, relying on a further provision that the workweek clause was not to be construed "as a guarantee of hours of work per day or per week." Peter Seitz found the loss of overtime pay, under the circumstances, not a violation of the agreement:

Despite the requirement that the company adhere to a normal work pattern, where a holiday occurs and such adherence would obligate the company to make overtime payments for work either on the holiday or on succeeding days, the company is privileged to schedule these employees for four days of work as they have in this case.

The union was frankly skeptical of the company's assertion that lack of work was the reason for the unscheduled holiday, but Mr. Seitz saw support for management's position in the fact that no overtime was scheduled during the following week. He added, however, that he was not expressing an opinion as to what his decision would have been if the union had demonstrated as a fact that the shortening of the workweek had been directed "despite the presence of enough work on hand to schedule a five day week."

The union also contended that another provision of the agreement, outlining three circumstances under which the normal workweek could be departed from, barred the company's action in this case. To this Mr. Seitz replied:

If candor is to govern, it must be frankly faced that [the provision the

[34] 6 AAA 14.

union referred to] is not so drawn as to point the way clearly to an an-swer. Here, the normal work pattern in ordinary week by week schedul-ing, concededly, would not regularly require overtime payments; but it is equally clear that it *would* require overtime payments 'regularly' when-ever a holiday occurs in the course of the work week. This circumstance, combined with a broad permission to deviate from a five day work pat-tern and the injunction that the entire section shall not be construed as a *guarantee* of hours of work per week conduce to a conclusion favorable to the company.

Regular Week-End Schedule Instituted

A work schedule problem of another kind arose at the *Cleveland Electric Illuminating Company* (Utility Workers Union of America, AFL-CIO).[35] When the commercial consumers began to outweigh residential users, management concluded that the assignment of a group of employees to week-end overtime, customary in the past, was no longer economical. Instead, it was decided to change the workweek for certain employees so that Saturdays and Sundays would be part of their regular schedules. They would, of course, have two days off during the week.

The employer cited, as authority for the change, the following language in a contract amendment negotiated several years earlier:

The company will base such changes upon need for revision, such as new or changed work requirements of a regular or recurring nature.

Facing a loss of premium pay for working on week ends, the union objected to the change in work schedules on the grounds that no "new or changed work" was involved. Management could, conse-quently, not change work schedules without common consent.

Patrick J. Fisher agreed with management that the quoted lan-guage did not limit schedule changes only to those situations where work requirements had undergone change; the phrase relied upon by the union was illustrative, rather than inclusive.

To hold that the company can make a schedule change only when there are new or changed work requirements would force us to ignore the words "such as." The union offers no explanation regarding their mean-ing. In construing these words the Board of Arbitration is compelled to give them their common, ordinary and usual meaning. The words "such

[35] 3 AAA 1.

as" are merely illustrative. They mean "like" or "similar to." They do not exclude the possibility of making schedule changes for other reasons.

The history of bargaining was also an element in Mr. Fisher's conclusion. The union had tried unsuccessfully to amend the two most recent contracts to require "mutuality" before shift schedules could be changed. This tended to support the employer's view that the union's consent was not required now. On the other hand, the employer's failure to get the union's consent to a counterproposal, which would permit management to change schedules "from time to time," did not mean, as the union asserted, that the right was lacking to management without the proposed clause. "The [arbitrator] cannot interpret this proposal as an admission by the company that it had no right to make changes in group schedules in the absence of the language of the counter-proposal," he wrote.

Daily Schedule Changed

A similar problem arose at another public utility, *The Detroit Edison Company* (Utility Workers Union of America, AFL-CIO).[36] In a frank attempt to eliminate a half-hour of overtime daily, management decided to change the work schedule of an employee from 7:30 A.M. to 4:30 P.M., with a half-hour for lunch, to 7:30 A.M. to 4:30 P.M., with a full hour for lunch. The contract said only that the standard workday was to be eight hours, "consecutive except as interrupted by lunch periods," and that no changes would be made without prior discussion with the union.

The change was discussed with the union, the latter objecting that a long-standing practice could not be altered without common consent. Management directed the change despite the union's opposition, which brought the matter to arbitration before Russell A. Smith. At the hearing, the union put forward the additional argument that a contract clause prohibiting the company from requiring employees to take compensating time off to avoid premium pay barred the change of schedule in this case.

Mr. Smith rejected the union's views on both counts. First of all, he said, the contract gives the employer the right to change schedules after discussions with the union as long as the changes are not

[36] 22 AAA 21.

"arbitrary," provided further that the requirement for eight consecutive hours is observed. Secondly, the clause relied upon by the union prevented "tampering" with a regular schedule; it did not prevent the change of a regular schedule within contractual limits. It "presupposes the existence of a regular work week and schedule, and cannot, of itself, properly be interpreted to prevent changes in such regular work week and schedule so long as the change is not confined within a given work week."[37]

In his discussion of the *Westinghouse Electric Corporation* case, appearing above, the arbitrator reminded the union that the motive of "saving money" through elimination of overtime was not in itself wrong. Mr. Smith wrote similarly in answer to the union's view that the change in schedule was "arbitrary":

In the opinion of the Arbitrator, the union has not shown that the company's decision to change grievant's work schedule was arbitrary. The term "arbitrary," as used in connection with the decision-making process, means "capricious" or "unreasoned." The decision in this instance was based on the desire to reduce costs through the elimination or reduction of the amount of overtime worked by grievant, while still maintaining a schedule which would permit the necessary servicing of the trucks operating out of that warehouse. There were, therefore, sound business reasons for the company's decision to continue a schedule of 7:30 a.m. to 4:30 p.m. for the warehouse, but to specify a one-hour lunch period in order to reduce overtime costs.[38]

COMPULSORY OVERTIME

The frequency of grievances protesting missed overtime opportunities suggests that employees prize highly the right to work extra

[37] Mr. Smith noted that "other arbitrators" have interpreted offsetting overtime provisions the same way. He cited *Western Automatic Machine Screw Company*, 12 LA 38 (1949), and *Olin-Mathieson Chemical Corporation*, 25 LA 619 (1955).

[38] Apparently, one of the reasons for the grievance in this case was the fear that the employer might introduce "split shifts" by varying the length of lunch periods. Mr. Smith said his decision in this case could not support changes of that kind. The contract ". . . requires a standard work day for all employees of eight consecutive hours worked, except for lunch periods. While a one-hour period for lunch at some appropriate time during the work day is certainly comprehended by the term 'lunch period,' it does not follow that more extended periods could properly be denominated lunch periods under the contract. The term 'lunch period' implies its own limitations."

hours and earn premium pay. Nevertheless, situations also arise where the opposite problem is presented; that is, where management seeks to impose penalties on employees who refuse to work overtime and where the very right of management to compel overtime is challenged.

"Employees know that refusal of a supervisor's instruction is insubordination and brings disciplinary action as a consequence," wrote Donald A. Crawford, in a case involving the *Warner Company* (United Steelworkers of America, AFL-CIO).[39] "But there is not nearly the same acceptance by employees, unions, or for that matter, by supervision, of the position that an employee must obey an order to work overtime at the risk of being insubordinate." In this case, he refused to uphold a week's suspension of an employee who had refused to work overtime. It was "by no means clear whether overtime work was voluntary or mandatory," the employer having "condoned" refusal of such work in the past.[40]

Reasonable Overtime May Be Required

Other arbitrators have held more or less to the same effect, that the employer has the right to require a reasonable amount of overtime where custom or the contract does not make overtime voluntary and a reasonable amount of notice is given. What is "reasonable" may vary, of course, from one establishment to another. At the *Gorham Manufacturing Company* (International Jewelry Workers Union, AFL-CIO),[41] the union thought that a phrase in the contract reading, ". . . employees who are asked to work on Saturday . . . ," precluded compulsory overtime. The arbitrator, Saul Wallen, read this clause in conjunction with another which referred to notice of overtime during an employee's preceding work shift, and ruled:

[39] 21 AAA 17.

[40] That the right of management to compel overtime in this establishment was a "cloudy area" was further seen in the fact that it became a "major problem" in the contract renewal talks. "It is not without significance that [the instant] grievance became a matter for discussion in connection with bargaining on the company's proposal for a contract provision requiring mandatory overtime. It would appear that in the case of [the grievant's] refusal to work overtime the company had decided to take a stand on its right to demand overtime work on a mandatory basis and continued this stand in the contract renegotiations."

[41] 5 AAA 14.

If after a schedule is posted it develops that overtime not previously scheduled is needed, an employee is *required* to work it if notice is given during the employee's preceding work shift. If such notice is not given, the employee can only be *requested* to work such overtime.

Definition of "Reasonable" Overtime

An unusual case, in which the claimant was the employer, rather than the union, was arbitrated by Samuel H. Jaffee at the *Celanese Corporation of America* (United Mine Workers, District 50.)[42] The grievance, filed by the company, named 6 employees who had refused a direct order to work overtime. Previously, all 160 employees in the plant had ignored a notice posted on the bulletin board asking for volunteers for extra hours. The company sought a ruling to the effect that, in the absence of volunteers, management could discipline those who refuse to obey orders to work overtime. The union's counter-argument was that overtime could not be compelled under any circumstances.

Mr. Jaffee said that "a flat affirmative or negative" could be given only on a "case-by-case" basis. Nevertheless, he stated some principles. In the absence of contract language to the contrary, he continued, management starts with an "inherent" right to require overtime work. However, he added, "insofar as a general rule may be stated in a case of this kind, reasonableness is required on both sides." Among the factors to be considered are:

the length of the overtime requirement; the frequency of overtime occasions; whether the overtime is time added to the workday, or whether it is to be done on a non-regular day; whether the work is consistent with the health and safety of the employees; whether the overtime is for an emergency situation (or to avoid an emergency); the temporary nature of the overtime; the needs of production; the question of the ability to secure replacements or volunteers . . . So too, on the employee side, the reason for his refusal may be of significance, and this may include the question whether the refusal is individual or concerted . . . Refusals to work overtime may be justified by considerations peculiarly applicable to overtime as distinguished from normally scheduled hours.

Returning to the employer's complaint, Mr. Jaffee said he could not make a finding that the refusal of 160 employees to work overtime was in fact concerted. He did say, however, that whether overtime

[42] 23 AAA 23.

was voluntary or compulsory, "*concerted* refusals are unreasonable and unjustified." He concluded:

Speaking generally, the Company has the right to assign overtime when sufficient volunteers therefor cannot be obtained. Whether particular employees may properly refuse such assignment, however, cannot be answered in the abstract but must be determined upon a case-by-case basis . . . Correspondingly, the matter of whether disciplinary action may be taken against employees refusing such assignments, and if it may, that appropriateness of particular penalties against particular employees, again can be determined only on a case-by-case basis.[43]

Overtime May Be Required in Accordance with Past Practice

The contract at *Whitney Blake Company* (United Electrical, Radio and Machine Workers)[44] said nothing about the employer's right to compel overtime, but it did have a clause reserving to the employer "the right to determine the schedule of hours of work." That, said Saul Wallen, gave the company the right to compel employees to work Saturday overtime. However, that right could be exercised only in accordance with past practice; that is, only

where made necessary by production requirements, if the work involved could not be postponed, after attempts to secure qualified volunteers proved fruitless [and] if reasonable notice is given under the circumstances involved.

Applying this rule to the case before him, Mr. Wallen said that employees who were told of Saturday overtime only one hour before quitting time on Friday had not been given reasonable notice in accordance with past practice, particularly where some had already made commitments for "outside earnings" on that day.

Notice Must Be Adequate

Somewhat similar was the award of Lewis M. Gill in a case involving *Lancaster Malleable Castings Co.* (International Molders

---

[43] Although the employer named six employees who disobeyed a direct order and whom he apparently wanted to discipline, the official demand for arbitration did not state precisely that the arbitrator was requested to indicate an appropriate penalty. Mr. Jaffee was, of course, careful not to do so. For a case in which an arbitrator similarly refused to permit anyone but the employer to take the initiative in assigning disciplinary penalties, see the award of James J. Healy in Chapter 10, note 1.

[44] 16 AAA 9.

and Foundry Workers Union, AFL-CIO).[45] He reversed the discipline of two men who refused a Saturday overtime assignment of which they were not notified until Friday afternoon. The most important weakness in management's case, however, was not that notice was short, but that "no real consideration" had been given to whether the employees had valid excuses:

Men may be required to work overtime, but they should get reasonable advance notice and reasonable consideration of requests to be excused when they have made other plans. It is not in my province to enunciate any specific policy for the parties concerning what constitutes reasonable advance notice, or what constitutes a good excuse for not working—those are matters for the parties to work out themselves in a practical manner, and both sides indicated at the hearing that they were willing to sit down together and discuss the problem, so as to avoid future disputes of this sort.

Order Must Be More than "Perfunctory"

Whether employees who were "notified" of overtime were "ordered" to work was dealt with by Peter Seitz in *American Bosch Arma Corporation* (International Union of Electrical, Radio and Machine Workers, AFL-CIO).[46] The contract gave management the right to compel overtime, but that right had never been invoked in the past. Extra-hours assignments were generally filled by volunteers. Under those circumstances, Mr. Seitz held, it was an error to suspend employees for refusing to work overtime after having been informed, in a "perfunctory" manner, that they were expected to do so. The manner of notification did not constitute adequate warning that "they were not privileged to rely upon the unvarying practice of the past."

The customary method of doing things required the company to do more than it had done to "notify" the employees before noon of their contract obligations to work overtime. The company seemed to have been content to take the technical steps seemingly called for with respect to notification without consideration of the reasonable expectations of the employees, based upon procedures which it had used in the past but which it did not take the trouble to abrogate.

George Savage King found a similar problem at the *West Virginia*

[45] 9 AAA 10.
[46] 10 AAA 14.

Pulp and Paper Company (International Association of Machinists, AFL-CIO).[47] It had been the custom to obtain employees for unscheduled overtime by "requesting" them to work in the order in which their names appeared on a bulletin board and "directing" them to work only where the number of volunteers was insufficient. Under these circumstances, employees who had just completed an overtime assignment ten minutes earlier could not be disciplined for refusing to resume. The fact that the foreman had to call some twenty employees before he found three who were willing to work tended to support the impression of the grievants that they were being "requested," not "directed," to work. "Neither the supervisor nor the foreman seemed to recognize any duty to make sure that it was unmistakably understood by each of the grievants that he was being directed to work," Mr. King said.

The Option Is the Employee's, not the Union's

The right of the *Wolverine Carbon Company* (International Printing Pressmen and Assistants, AFL-CIO)[48] to compel overtime was affirmed by Dudley E. Whiting through interpretation of a clause permitting the employer to "extend the shift hours," during the busy season, by starting the day shift at 6 A.M., two hours earlier than normal. Mr. Whiting did not find that the provision for early starting implied early quitting at the option of the employees. Furthermore, the contention that overtime had always been regarded as optional was upheld only insofar as it applied to "casual daily and Saturday overtime," not to situations where whole departments worked overtime during the busy season. Finally, even where overtime is optional, he said, the option is with individuals, not the union. "Concerted exercise of [the option] at the direction of the union is a violation of the contract."[49]

---

[47] 7 AAA 4.

[48] 14 AAA 17.

[49] There had been a concerted refusal to work to the normal quitting time, for which employees were suspended. The grievance before the arbitrator also concerned the appropriateness of the penalty, but his findings are not relevant to the discussion in this chapter.

10

DISCHARGE AND OTHER FORMS OF DISCIPLINE

No issue comes to arbitration more frequently than discharge for cause and lesser forms of discipline. It might seem paradoxical that this is so in the United States, where the work force is the most reliable in the world. But the paradox is more apparent than real, for the high incidence of discharge cases in arbitration has less to do with personal work characteristics than with the nature of American industrial relations.

Discharge has been called the capital punishment of employer-employee relations. This analogy is perhaps glib; in an open society, where no law bars re-employment of a worker discharged for misconduct and the work force is naturally mobile, dismissal seldom puts an end to one's working life. Nevertheless, termination of employment is the most severe punishment management can inflict, and it does create hardship. Even for a younger man, who will find new employment without great delay, there is loss of income and an embarrassing episode in his work history to conceal or account for. Furthermore, his new job may provide smaller vacation, holiday, and welfare benefits, for these often accrue with seniority. Having much to lose, therefore, he will be inclined to use every avenue of appeal.

The large number of discipline cases in arbitration is also explained in part by the institutional role of the union. Freedom from favoritism on the part of foremen and protection against arbitrary or discriminatory dismissals were among the earliest objectives of organized labor. These objectives have now been largely achieved, at least with respect to the worst excesses of the past. But the tradition lives on; it still exerts an influence. When a worker is discharged, it often carries with it emotional and practical consequences. The union may see it as a challenge to its standing as representative of the employees; for that reason alone, it may be thought necessary to carry the matter to arbitration even where there seems to be little merit to the worker's defense.

Management, too, is subject to pressures. When a worker becomes insubordinate or careless in his work, appropriate action must be taken; and only management can exercise the initiative.[1] For all these reasons, disciplinary issues often seem to be matters of principle, difficult to compromise during grievance procedure.

Arbitration is an avenue of appeal. Awards can uphold disciplinary action taken by management, or reverse it in whole or in part. But arbitrators can neither initiate discipline nor add to penalties. Inevitably, therefore, a study of published awards always shows a significant number of cases which management lost. On the other hand, arbitrators will seldom point out that management was too lenient or that more severe penalties, if imposed, would have been upheld. For this reason alone, it would be pointless to try to compose from published awards a fixed schedule of penalties for given violations. In truth, almost any type of offense might result in any degree of penalty, depending upon circumstances. In one case, disobedience of a work order might be just cause for discharge. In another, there might be some reason why theft of company property —usually regarded as grounds for immediate discharge—would be punishable only by suspension. In this chapter, therefore, we are

---

[1] For an interesting case in which the union tried to initiate discipline by demanding the discharge of a worker whose use of obscene language allegedly created an "intolerable working condition," see *Royal McBee Corporation* (United Automobile Workers, AFL-CIO), 16 AAA 7. "It is easy to succumb to the notion that it is unfair and unreasonable to allow employees to be subjected to obscene language by any fellow employee and not to have available to them any redress," James J. Healy wrote in his award. But it would not be wise to permit an employee to demand discipline of another and then permit an "outsider" to rule on that demand. "The management rights clause foreclosed arbitration of the grievance. The clause reserves to management the right to discipline except as modified by the agreement. A broad allusion to 'working conditions' in the grievance Article does not constitute an effective modification of this reserved right. The concept of union or employee having the right to insist upon discipline of someone is so unorthodox that a specific authorization is needed to establish such right. None is present in this agreement." In short, he concluded, "insofar as discipline of employees is concerned, the action can be initiated by management alone, with the union having the right to challenge the action."

not interested primarily in specific offenses and punishments. No penalty can be assigned to an offense without an appraisal of all the facts, including extenuating circumstances, if any. And these facts are seldom duplicated exactly. We are, rather, concerned with the general rules arbitrators have followed in determining whether the disciplinary *policy*, as distinct from the particular penalties, was arbitrary or discriminatory. In examining all reported cases involving discharge and other forms of discipline, it was found that those in which management's policies were defective, in whole or in part, lent themselves better to the educational purpose of this volume than those in which companies were fully sustained. For that reason, this chapter relies more heavily on the former than the latter. No inference should be drawn that the proportion of "victories" and "losses" here shown reflects the total experience either in arbitration or in the administration of disciplinary policy generally.

EQUAL TREATMENT

Perhaps the first rule of a successful disciplinary policy is that all employees must be treated alike. This does not mean that all must be given exactly the same penalties for the same offenses at all times, regardless of extenuating circumstances. It does mean, however, that all must be judged by the same standards and that rules must apply equally to all. It also means that similar efforts must be made to rehabilitate erring employees.

For instance, Gerald A. Barrett, in arbitrating a discharge case at *Sayles Biltmore Bleacheries* (United Textile Workers, AFL-CIO),[2] reinstated an employee with a record of fifty-four absences in two years, simply because three other employees with worse attendance records had not been discharged. It was up to the company to explain or to justify its action in retaining those three under the circumstances, he wrote, "but the company produced no explanatory evidence at the hearing." The conclusion was "unavoidable" that management was administering its disciplinary policy "in an arbitrary manner." It is the essence of good policy "that it be admin-

[2] 4 AAA 9.

istered evenly and impartially, and that all employees similarly situated may expect to receive similar treatment from the company."

On the other hand, a union's showing of a list of similar offenders at *Socony Mobil Oil Company* (Petroleum Union of Buffalo Refinery Employees)[3] was not persuasive to Jacob D. Hyman, because management had apparently been trying to correct erring employees. It was, therefore, not fatal to management's case that one employee, who apparently did not respond to correction as well as the others, was discharged even though he was absent fewer times than some who were retained.

Dishonesty and Fighting

Surprisingly, unequal and inconsistent administration of discipline has been found, even in matters of dishonesty. At the *Valley Metal Products Company* (United Steelworkers of America, AFL-CIO),[4] for instance, the arbitrator, Jack Stieber, reduced a discharge to a two-week layoff in the case of an employee who had falsified production records, thereby accepting payment for work not done. Mr. Stieber was convinced by the evidence that the grievant had deliberately inflated his work records. But the discharge could not be sustained, he said, in view of testimony by a management witness who admitted that others, who were not punished, were guilty of similar offenses.

A different result came about at *The Buxbaum Company* (United Rubber, Cork, Linoleum and Plastic Workers, AFL-CIO)[5] precisely because, according to George F. Hayes, who decided the case, offending workers were always punished when caught. There was no evidence that management was out to "get" anyone. The grievant's production figures were checked, as were those of other employees; and the discharge followed in accordance with a well established policy of discharging those who falsified work records. "The arbitrator is fully aware of the consequences resulting from a discharge of this type," Mr. Hayes wrote, but the grievant's guilt was clear. "The discharge was for just and sufficient cause."

When two employees come to blows at work, a comparison of

[3] 11 AAA 12.
[4] 9 AAA 18.
[5] 15 AAA 8.

penalties is almost inevitable. If both are punished alike, it may be asserted that the guilt of one was greater than that of the other. On the other hand, if the aggressor is disciplined more severely, management may be accused of discrimination or of having placed the heaviest burden on the wrong employee.

At the *Gorham Manufacturing Company* (Amalgamated Silver, Allied Metals and Craft Workers)[6] two employees engaged in a fight, leading to the discharge of one, while no penalty was imposed on the other. As often happens in such cases, testimony was contradictory as to what had occurred. But his appraisal of the evidence convinced John A. Hogan that one employee had actually started the argument by knocking a casting out of the grievant's hand. "A fair evaluation of all this evidence indicates clearly that both employees were guilty of misconduct and were subject to penalty," Mr. Hogan wrote. "[The grievant] alone was penalized. This constitutes unequal treatment, and the inequity is made worse by the fact that one employee was given the supreme penalty—discharge—and the other employee, though clearly culpable, was given no penalty at all." Reinstatement was directed. But in view of the gravity of the grievant's fault, no back pay was awarded.[7]

Another incident of unequal penalties imposed on two employees who exchanged a few blows occurred at the *Hekman Furniture Company* (United Furniture Workers, AFL-CIO).[8] The grievant was a union steward whose ouster was being sought by other employees. He seized a petition from one of the workers and refused to return it. This led to grappling, followed by a brief fight on the railroad tracks outside the plant. The steward was discharged, and the other employee was given a three-day suspension. To the arbitrator, John A. Piercey, this was unfair. The discharge was reduced to a three-day suspension, putting both employees on a basis of equality.[9]

[6] 5 AAA 28.

[7] The arbitrator noted that the grievant's loss of pay was "substantially reduced" by his having worked at a higher rate of pay elsewhere during most of the period of unjust discharge. It is not possible to know from the award whether this fact influenced the decision.

[8] 20 AAA 16.

[9] For another case which involved both inequality of penalties and the disciplining of the employee who had not provoked the fight, see *Whitney Blake*

Disregard of Instructions

Fighting is not the only occasion when two or more employees are involved in the same incident of misconduct. At *AVCO Manufacturing Company* (United Automobile Workers, AFL-CIO),[10] for instance, two employees balked at obeying new instructions about the starting time for shifts. A second-shift employee was given a two-day suspension for refusing to delay his starting time. The same penalty was given to a first-shift employee who walked off the job early. The second-shift worker filed a grievance, which eventually came before G. Allan Dash. There is no way of knowing what his decision might have been if there had been no comparisons to make. But in his view, the first-shift employee had committed the much more serious offense.

Technically, the grievant's actions did constitute a disregard of supervisory instructions but did not extend to the point of insubordination in the same fashion as did those of the first-shift employee. Since the actions of the first-shift employee were judged by the company as sufficient to sustain a two-day disciplinary layoff against that employee, by contrast the actions of the grievant were improper to the extent of sustaining no more than a written reprimand against him.

Another case in which wrongdoing by two employees involved in the same incident compelled comparison of penalties occurred at *J. Chein and Company* (United Steelworkers of America, AFL-CIO).[11] Irving K. Kessler held that an employee who left his work place without permission to inquire about a shortage in his pay envelope (getting an employee from another department to cover his job while he was away) deserved to be warned. However, he wrote, there was insufficient justification for declaring it to be a "final warning," since (1) the previous warning for leaving work without

---

Company (International Union of Electrical, Radio and Machine Workers, AFL-CIO), 3 AAA 10. Robert L. Stutz ruled that it was improper to discharge a striking employee for assaulting a non-striker where the latter admitted he precipitated the incident by making a remark to the grievant which, "under all the circumstances, amounted to provocation." The grievant's conduct, the arbitrator concluded, was "serious," but not deserving of discharge in view of the "emotionally charged" atmosphere of the strike. Reinstatement without back pay was directed.

[10] 13 AAA 2.
[11] 19 AAA 2.

permission was "unrelated" to this incident and occurred about three years before, and (2) no action was taken against the other employee, who left work in his own department without permission to cover for the grievant.

Unauthorized Strikes

Unequal treatment is often charged when an employer disciplines only one or a few of many wildcat strikers, imposing no penalty on the others. This was exemplified after an illegal work stoppage in one department of the *Studebaker-Packard Corporation* (United Automobile Workers, AFL-CIO).[12] One of the employees was suspended for twelve days for running through the shop, shouting: "Labor dispute, everybody out!" No other employee was given any penalty. The first contention of the union was that the walkout was a spontaneous protest against working conditions. Anything the grievant had said was therefore irrelevant, because it could not be shown that he had actually influenced anyone to leave. Furthermore, it was argued, in failing to discipline others, the company was guilty of discrimination.

"Whether the employees left because of the statements [the grievant] made, or whether they left of their own initiative, is not the important issue in this matter," wrote the arbitrator, Harry Abrahams. "The fact that [the grievant], by his acts, did participate in, did attempt to provoke and did attempt to induce others to take part in the work stoppage that took place is important." Nor did it constitute discrimination against the grievant, as the union asserted, that other employees, who were "of the same opinion" as the grievant, were not disciplined. "The evidence was that [the grievant] did the acts complained of by the company. If there was proof that other employees did the same things and made the same statements as were made by [the grievant], they would also have been subject to disciplinary action by the company. The fact that there was no such evidence against any specific employee did not indicate that [the grievant] was discriminated against."[13]

[12] 13 AAA 22.
[13] For other cases in which the same issue appeared, see *Hudson Pulp and Paper Corporation* (United Papermakers and Paperworkers, AFL-CIO), 14 AAA 4, and *International Smelting and Refining Company* (United Steelworkers of America, AFL-CIO), 18 AAA 7. Both are discussed in Chapter 4.

Discipline as "an Example" to Others

When management tries to solve a problem of general misconduct by punishing one employee as "an example," the defense of unequal treatment and discrimination is almost inevitable.

At the *American Chain and Cable Company* (Allison Employees' Independent Union)[14] a number of employees resisted new work standards, under which greater output was expected. Finally, management advised the two employees of greatest seniority that they would be disciplined if they failed to produce at the required level. When they subsequently failed to do so, each was suspended for two days. This, said Lloyd H. Bailer, was an error.

It appears that the company was confronted with a rather general opposition to the new standard. But since this standard was designed for and made applicable to the department as a whole, it was not proper to require output at a higher level by only two employees, even though they were the most senior, while others in the department were permitted to produce at a slower pace without penalty. It is apparent that the new standard was not being applied to the grievants on a "trial run" basis. If a trial were intended, no penalty would have been invoked for failure to achieve the standard.

The management of *Bonafide Plastics, Inc.* (United Rubber, Cork, Linoleum and Plastic Workers, AFL-CIO),[15] wanting to set an example to other employees, discharged a union officer for stealing half a can of paint. Again, the arbitrator—this time Wayne E. Howard—reinstated the grievant, although without back pay. He wrote: "Were it not for the manner in which the grievant surreptitiously removed the paint and were it not for the serious proportions which the problem of theft and pilfering had reached at this time, there is reason to believe that the offense would have been treated more leniently. In part then, [the grievant] was not only a victim of his own actions, but of the surrounding circumstances which made his action suspiciously close to pilfering, a matter of great concern. Thus, the company, by its own admission, wanted to make an example of him."

The admission that employees other than the grievant were guilty of dishonesty and that the latter was singled out for punishment as

[14] 7 AAA 22.
[15] 10 AAA 12.

an example resulted in an award by Joseph F. Wildebush reinstating an employee of *Royal McBee Corporation* (Business Machines and Office Appliance Mechanics Board).[16]

The grievant had admitted at the arbitration hearing that his carfare reports were false. But, said the arbitrator, the company had long known of the practice of padding reports, and had not taken action. Finally, in January 1959, it was announced that management would no longer take a tolerant view of false reports. But by that time, the grievant had already been discharged to set the example for the others. "If [the grievant] had been discharged *after* January 1, 1959, as a result of the new company policy, the discharge would have been sustained," Mr. Wildebush wrote. But it could not be upheld under the circumstances.

Mr. Wildebush found it "particularly significant" that a union witness at the arbitration had testified: "We all make a little on it but people do abuse it at times." There was also evidence that the company had cautioned union representatives not to proceed with this grievance, "because everybody would suffer as a result of the new company policy of instituting daily reports." In view of the general conditions prevailing among this group of employees, the example made of one of them prior to the change in policy was "discriminatory."

Management at the *General Telephone Company of California* (Communications Workers of America, AFL-CIO)[17] also had a problem with dishonest employees, but procedures for catching them were applied in a non-discriminatory way. The fact that one employee was caught, and not others, did not give the unlucky one a basis for reinstatement.

The facts were interesting. Suspecting that a certain pay station repairman was not turning in all the coins found in telephones he repaired, company auditors contrived a "trap." Marked coins were left in a certain public phone booth, which was reported "out of order." It was intended that the suspected employee be assigned to that repair task. As things turned out, however, another employee, who had not been suspected, went out on the job. He did not turn in the marked coins. Two tests were then set for him. On the first,

16 7 AAA 20.
17 7 AAA 19.

he again failed to turn in the marked coins. By the time he took the last test, however, another employee had been discharged for dishonesty; and everyone was alerted to the danger. Consequently, all coins were properly turned in by him from the third contrived repair job. But, having succumbed to temptation, the employee was discharged for "failure to adhere to company policy in handling company funds."

The union's defense was that the auditors, who had contrived the tests, had not arranged to keep the telephones under constant surveillance. Nor had the grievant been searched to see whether the coins were in his possession, a relevant omission because other employees had keys which could have opened the coin boxes. These and other facts, the union said, cast a "reasonable doubt" on the grievant's guilt.

"Granted that a professional sleuth might have shown greater skills," wrote the arbitrator, Lawrence R. Guild, "it appears that the techniques used and the care exhibited were adequate here. Nor is there the least basis for thinking that the auditors would benefit in any way by finding an employee out of line." Furthermore, the fact that the grievant turned in marked coins in the third test did not prove his reliability, as the union urged, because this test took place after the discharge of another employee for the same offense, which may have "spread the word that [the company] intended to enforce [the rule on turning in coins]." Finally, there was no evidence of discrimination against the grievant. "It cannot be said that the company was 'out to get him.' [He] was one of a number of repairmen to whom no particular suspicion was attached" until after he inadvertently took the first test which had been set up for another repairman. "Simultaneously with [the grievant's] separation, another man was discharged. All of this indicates equality of treatment, not discrimination."

Inconsistency in Acceptance of Excuse

Indulgence with some employees who asked to be excused from work and a less tolerant attitude toward others may be regarded as evidence of unequal treatment in the administration of disciplinary policy. At the *Bridgeport Brass Company* (United Steelworkers of

America, AFL-CIO),[18] for instance, management was found by Robert G. McIntosh to have committed the error of suspending one employee who refused to work overtime after others, who also urged personal business, were excused.

The problem arose when the grievant had asked for and obtained permission to skip his overtime turn if it should fall on the Saturday when he was scheduled to participate in the company's golf tournament. Two days before the event, however, after other qualified employees had declined to work, the permission for this employee to be absent was revoked. He nevertheless refused to work overtime that day, and was given a three-day layoff. Mr. McIntosh said the company had the right to compel overtime, but compulsion must be applied equally to all. "In this instance," he wrote, "the company is exercising its authority only as to [the grievant] and not as to other employees."

Union Employees vs. Non-Union Employees

An apparent difference in treatment of union and non-union employees tends to support the assertion that unequal penalties have been levied unlawfully. Management at the *Columbus and Southern Ohio Electric Company* (International Brotherhood of Electrical Workers, AFL-CIO)[19] may not have intended to discriminate, but Martin Wagner ruled that inequality of discipline had been proved. There was "ample cause" for discharge of a union member who worked only the first two days after the end of a strike, ignoring messages that he would be discharged if he continued to absent himself from work. However, Mr. Wagner ordered him reinstated with back pay because a non-union employee (who had worked during the strike), with a similar record of absenteeism, was given only a warning letter.

If rules are to be persuasive they must be fairly applied. This demands that they be carried out in the same way in all situations that are basically the same. In the light of the evidence, the Arbitration Board finds that the company did not apply the same standards in procedure and consequently in penalty, in [the grievant's] case that it did in other cases of absenteeism that were basically of the same kind.[20]

[18] 5 AAA 23.
[19] 15 AAA 7.
[20] Mr. Wagner had a second reason for reversing the discharge. Evidence

THE RULE OF REASON

Management's traditional right "to direct the work forces" includes the right to promulgate rules of conduct and to punish those who violate them. But, like other management rights, this one is not unlimited; it may be exercised only to the extent that it does not conflict with other provisions of the collective bargaining agreement. The contractual bar against discharge, except for just cause, is particularly relevant here. But even in the rare case of a contract which does not contain a provision protecting employees against unjust discipline, the contract as a whole may be held to afford that protection. The rule of reason may be invoked to challenge any rule that threatens to deprive employees of rights and privileges contained in the contract as a whole.

Policy against Marriage

When a disciplinary penalty is protested, the rule under which it was imposed may be called into question. A case of the *Chief Pontiac Federal Credit Union* (Office Employees International Union, AFL-CIO)[21] illustrates the point. In January 1950, this small financial institution had suffered an unfavorable experience at the hands of a husband, working as a treasurer, and his wife, working as assistant treasurer at the same time. To avoid further collusion and financial irregularity, the board of directors decided it would no longer employ two members of the same immediate family. About eight years later, a young man came to work for the credit union in a minor clerical position. There he met a young lady, also in a nonsupervisory position, and within a short time, they decided to wed. Knowing that a policy question was involved, he asked management to waive the rule against a husband and wife working together. His request was denied, whereupon he married his fiancée anyway and was discharged.

---

showed that, although there was nothing in the contract requiring written warnings before discharges, the company had generally prefaced discharges for absenteeism with such written warnings. "Since absenteeism is an offense that most easily lends itself to corrective rather than punitive action in the first instance, the use of written warnings is understandable. At all events, this seems to have been the course of action which the company has generally followed," he concluded.

[21] 19 AAA 9.

Bringing the matter to arbitration, union representatives called attention to a clause in the contract which read:

There shall be no discrimination under any circumstances because of race, creed, sex, political beliefs, union activity, marital status, age, or national origin.

There was to be no discrimination "under any circumstances," the union representative argued. Since the rule against the marriage of employees was itself in violation of the contract, no penalty could be levied under it.

The company answered that the inclusion of "marital status" in the quoted clause was intended to forbid discrimination on account of the status of marriage as such, but was not intended to nullify a previously established rule. Furthermore, the employer relied on a management rights clause which said, in part: "The adoption of policy and the methods of business operation are solely and exclusively the responsibility of the management." The disputed rule, it was said, came within the purview of that clause.

Meyer S. Ryder decided in favor of the union. "The family membership restriction imposed by the Board of Directors is clearly a condition of employment and work," he said. As such, it is bargainable, and subject to other provisions of the agreement. In short, although policy and methods of business operation are "solely the responsibility of the management," it does not follow "that the management can freely use its creativity to set a condition covering the retention of employment where a bargaining unit employee is thereby deprived of the protection of another part of the agreement."

Coffee-Break Rules

At the *Denver Post, Inc.* (American Newspaper Guild, AFL-CIO),[22] management apparently had a problem with students working part-time, who would try to do some studying on company time, especially during evening hours. This led to the announcement of a rule forbidding studying "while on the job."

Shortly thereafter, this rule was invoked to discharge an employee

[22] 11 AAA 5.

who was caught doing calculus homework during a coffee break.[23] This raised the question as to whether coffee-break time was time "on the job." The employer's view was that, since it was time paid for, all working rules applied. Furthermore, it was said, the fifteen-minute break was intended to permit the employee to refresh himself, so that he might return to work with more energy. It was, therefore, proper to forbid activities, such as studying, which might frustrate that result.

John E. Gorsuch saw no merit in the company's argument. "Each individual finds diversion in his own way," he wrote. "What would be relaxation for one person might well be exertion for another. The arbitrator is not prepared to say that studying calculus would not provide [the grievant] with the type of diversion and relaxation he needed to return to the job with renewed vigor."

Absenteeism

It would seem that a rule requiring employees either to present reasonable excuses in justification of absences or to report back to work within a reasonable time after recall meets the test of fairness. But the application of a reasonable rule may be unreasonable. That was the case at *General Refractories Company* (Brick and Clay Workers, AFL-CIO).[24] The dispute originated with the death, one Saturday night, of one of the employees. On the following Monday, a scheduled work day, nine employees failed to report. They were the deceased's son, a son-in-law, a brother-in-law, a first cousin, four second cousins, and one employee who was not related to the dead man. The company excused the absence of the son, brother-in-law, and son-in-law; but five of the others were warned, and the sixth, a second cousin, was given a three-day suspension.[25] This suspension was appealed to Arbitrator Fred Witney.

Management's case was that the grievant was not closely enough related to the deceased. As it was within the employer's "sole discre-

[23] The employer also had other complaints against this employee, which were brought out in the arbitration; but for the present discussion we are concerned only with the reasonableness of the rule against studying as applied in this instance.

[24] 10 AAA 17.

[25] The difference in penalties was explained by differences in the disciplinary histories of the individuals.

tion" to accept or reject an excuse, the company's decision to reject this one should not be overturned. Furthermore, it was said, management's decision was not arbitrary; drawing the line at second cousins was consistent with another provision of the contract which excused absences that might otherwise disqualify employees from holiday pay only where the absence was caused by death in the immediate family.

The union's answer was that the case should be judged "in the light of the customs and mores of the locality," a small town in Kentucky. It had been a long-standing custom for the members of the deceased's family to dig the grave; failure to participate could lead to "criticism, loss of face, and even personal animosity." Furthermore, in a small, tightly knit community, a second cousin was declared to be a closer relationship than it is in a large city.

Mr. Witney first disposed of the company's argument that it was the sole judge of what was reasonable. "If the company and the union had intended to confer upon the company the unilateral right to judge the reasonableness of an employee's excuse for an absence," he wrote, "they would have adopted unambiguous and unequivocal language to accomplish this result."

In the matter of the reasonableness of the second cousin's excuse, Mr. Witney again upheld the union. In the light of community standards, there could be no more justifiable excuse for absence than the need to perform "this doleful task." Morever, there was an apparent inconsistency in management's regarding the grievant's absence to attend the funeral as reasonably motivated, but not his absence to dig the grave. "It can hardly be argued successfully that [the grievant] should be disciplined for engaging in a task which is clearly a prerequisite for the funeral."

Finally, the company's reference to death in the immediate family, in the clause stating eligibility for holiday pay, was not relevant. In this case not the forfeiture of holiday pay but discipline, the placing of an employee's job "in jeopardy," was the issue. "It is one thing for an employee to lose holiday pay, but an entirely different problem exists when discipline is involved."

An unreasonable interpretation of a reasonable absenteeism rule was discovered at *R. T. French Company* (United Packinghouse

Workers, AFL-CIO).[26] The issue was whether an employee who was absent for five successive days without notifying the company was guilty of five infractions or one. Acting on the assumption that the former was the correct interpretation, the employee was discharged. This was in accordance with an established schedule, calling for a reprimand after the first three offenses, a two-week suspension after the fourth, and discharge after the fifth. The penalty was reduced to a one-week suspension, but the matter was nevertheless appealed to Robert R. France.

Mr. France found that the company had failed to notify the grievant of any penalty until after the end of the fifth day. Consequently, the five consecutive absences had to be regarded as a single offense, for which the penalty was merely a reprimand.

Failure to Return from Layoff

Most collective bargaining agreements require employees on layoff to report back to work within a stated number of days after being notified to do so. If they fail, they may be discharged or be deemed to have abandoned their jobs, which amounts to the same thing. But again, whether the rule can be applied in particular cases depends upon whether there was a reasonable excuse for absence.

At *Borg-Warner Corporation* (Allied Industrial Workers, AFL-CIO),[27] the arbitrator, John F. Sullivan, ruled that an employee who went on a fishing trip during a period of layoff, and who did not report for work within three days of the day his wife received the recall telegram from the company, could not be discharged. Normally, the company would have accepted that excuse for absence as "reasonable." But in this case, the employee had been given a return-to-work date when the layoff occurred, and had been told at the same time that an earlier recall was possible. By going on a fishing trip, the company said, the grievant "deliberately placed himself outside the reach of a notice." Furthermore, he had not notified the company that he would be away.

There was nothing in the agreement, Mr. Sullivan wrote, that

[26] 16 AAA 23.
[27] 16 AAA 14.

imposed on an employee the obligation to notify the company of his whereabouts.[28]

Non-receipt of a letter of recall was also an issue at *Blocksom & Company* (Upholsterers' International Union, AFL-CIO),[29] but here it was agreed that the grievant was not personally at fault. He had recently moved to a new boarding house, and was not yet known. When the registered letter of recall arrived, someone told the postman that the addressee was unknown. Having failed to report within three days, management discharged him.

The authority for this action, according to the employer, was a provision of the agreement which read:

An employee shall lose all seniority rights in the event:
1) He is discharged for just cause or quits.
2) He is absent from work for a period of One (1) year.
3) If after having been laid off temporarily, he does not report for work within three (3) work days after being notified to do so, such notice to be sent by registered mail to the last known address of the employee, unless his failure to not [*sic*] report is beyond the employee's control.

The company's position was that the three-day time limit takes effect with the giving of notice, and that the "beyond the employee's control" exception applies only where the employee *did* receive notice. Mark J. Fitzgerald, S.J., read the clause differently. "Upon examination of the recall clause it appears to this arbitrator that the three work days allowed for the reporting period begin to run the day after the employee has been notified by registered letter. However, in the case of [the grievant], the registered letter was never in his possession for him to read. In effect, [he] was never notified of his recall." Furthermore, he added, "the phrase dealing with failure to report because of circumstances 'beyond the employee's control' logically seems to cover both failure to receive a notice of recall in

---

[28] Although the grievant was reinstated, no back pay was awarded because his wife had not notified the company that her husband could not be reached within three days. Management representatives at the arbitration indicated that if she had done so, the discharge would not have occurred. The grievant's wife had notified the union, but this did not satisfy the obligations of an employee to the company, Mr. Sullivan said.

[29] 7 AAA 18.

the first place, and failure to report within three work days, though the notice of recall has actually been received. According to the company's interpretation of this clause, if the registered letter of recall is returned to the sender for any reason, termination of the laid-off employee is in order. In effect a statement of an uninformed person at the grievant's address that he was 'unknown' there, could deprive [him] of his employment by such interpretation."

Failure to Report Absence

The fact that an employee has a poor record of attendance, and is under notice that his next unexcused absence will result in discharge, does not by itself preclude the possibility that he may be saved from discharge by a reasonable excuse. That was the finding of arbitrator Joseph Lazar in a case at *Green River Steel Corporation* (United Steelworkers of America, AFL-CIO).[30] The grievant was reinstated (but without back pay) because (1) his absence was caused by his wife's illness and the need to care for nine children, (2) a message notifying the company of the reason for the absence was given to a fellow employee early enough before the start of the grievant's shift, (3) the fellow employee forgot to report the message to a foreman until forty-five minutes after the start of the shift, and (4) it was "common practice" for employees to "report off" in advance of absences through fellow employees.

The critical fact, in management's decision to discharge the grievant, was that the company had not been notified of the reason for the absence. This failure of communication, Mr. Lazar wrote, could not be held against the grievant alone:

In view of the past practice and custom of a fellow-employee reporting off for an absent employee, I do not feel that it is completely fair and equitable to place the entire risk and full peril of failure of communication on the shoulders of the absent employee.

On the other hand, it was not reasonable to make the employer bear the entire burden of responsibility for failure of communication when messages are carried by fellow workers. The telephone might be a more reasonable means of "reporting off" under the circumstances. In this case, the grievant said he had tried to use the phone, but found it out of order. Although there was "reasonable doubt" as

[30] 17 AAA 19.

to the truth of this statement, the arbitrator saw "no evidence of fabrication" by the fellow employee who had been given the message. Taken all together, there was no basis for accusing the grievant of "irresponsibility."

Absence in Jail

When an employee is kept in jail for antisocial conduct, he endangers his job. Absence for such a reason is seldom regarded as "reasonable" within the meaning of collective bargaining agreements.[31] But did it make a difference if an employee was imprisoned only for want of bail and was eventually acquitted of the charge for which he was arrested? In a case of the *American Chain and Cable Corporation* (United Steelworkers of America, AFL-CIO),[32] the arbitrator, William N. Loucks, said this was a saving factor. The company was wrong in its dual assertion that (1) discharge was justified because the grievant remained away from work longer than the period of time permitted, without reporting the reason for his absence; and (2) discharge was justified because imprisonment did not constitute "just cause" for absence.

[The grievant's] entire period of absence was due solely to being imprisoned on charges ultimately found by a proper court to be without merit. The Arbitrator regards this cause of absence to be just cause. If [the grievant] had been found guilty of some or all of these charges, one might argue that he brought this period of imprisonment on himself and that, therefore, his imprisonment was not a just cause for absence within the meaning of [the contract]. However, this cannot be validly argued in the face of [the grievant's] acquittal.

Falsification of Employment Application

Willful falsification of an employment application on a matter which, if disclosed, would have barred employment, is generally regarded as just cause for discharge. But when a long period of time elapses before the erroneous information is discovered, a number of questions may be asked about the reasonableness of the company's application of the rule. One such question is whether management

---

[31] For a case involving refusal of an employer to give a leave of absence to an employee in jail for drunken driving, see *Hudson Pulp and Paper Company* (United Papermakers and Paperworkers, AFL-CIO), 20 AAA 9, in the next chapter.

[32] 16 AAA 22.

did all it reasonably could to investigate facts stated in the employment forms.[33] Another is whether the passing of time has given the employee immunity from punishment. "Statutes of limitations" are occasionally found in collective bargaining contracts. But even where a contract does not place a time limitation on punishment for falsification of an employment application, it may be asserted by the union that such a limitation is implied by the rule of reason which presumably governs all contract interpretation.[34]

That was the defense at *The General Electric Company* (International Union of Electrical, Radio and Machine Workers, AFL-CIO),[35] where an employee of three years' standing was discharged for having concealed a history of epilepsy when he had filled out his employment application.[36] There was no doubt that the employee knew his epileptic condition was a material fact, for his employment application form included a medical history questionnaire which asked, "Did you ever have a fit or convulsion (epilepsy)?" His answer was, "No."

Despite the purposeful falsification, the union appealed the dis-

---

[33] Some matters, of course, lend themselves to easier investigation than others. A job applicant's previous employer can be telephoned or written to for verification of facts. On the other hand, an applicant's assertion that he was never arrested is more difficult to substantiate.

[34] Robert A. Leflar came upon a situation at the *General Electric Company* (International Union of Electrical, Radio and Machine Workers, AFL-CIO), 16 AAA 10, where he believed there should be a reasonable time limit on the use of previous offenses against an employee, although the contract contained no such limitation. The issue was just cause for the two-week suspension the company had given two employees for horseplay on the company parking lot. Both grievants had been disciplined before for similar offenses. In one case, the previous penalty was administered three months earlier and was, in Mr. Leflar's judgment, clearly relevant to the severity of the present suspension. The other employee had been disciplined eighteen months earlier. The arbitrator left it open as to whether an incident that far in the past should still be used against an employee. He wrote: "The arbitrator does not undertake to lay down a rule for the parties' future disputes, but he suggests that the employer announce a policy under which an employee's disciplinary slate be wiped clean after a year, or at the most two years, of conduct without cause for discipline."

[35] 5 AAA 22.

[36] The employment application contained this statement, to which the applicant signed his name: "I certify that the above answers are true and complete and am aware that any material falsification of fact on the above is grounds for discharge."

charge to Leo C. Brown, S.J., urging that three years of satisfactory work should be a bar to discipline.

Father Brown upheld management. He said he might agree with the union's "statute of limitations" view if the grievant had concealed some defect that was subject to correction. But in a case of this kind, where a permanent handicap is involved, the company has the same right to discharge the employee now as it had to bar him from employment in the first place.

This Arbitrator agrees with the union's general position but would distinguish on the basis of the kind of facts which the applicant failed to disclose. Where the condition, which the questions are designed to bring to light, is itself subject to change—for example, an employee's dependability and moral responsibility—it may well be that the record of years of responsible conduct as an employee becomes a better indicator of the employee's reliability than some undisclosed incident in the past. But, where the undisclosed fact relates to a permanent handicap, the situation is considerably different.

Although denying the grievance, Father Brown indicated that if the grievant had had very long service, his decision might have been different, for it would have created a doubt as to whether the disability had, in fact, been permanent.

Inadvertent Falsification

The feeling that an employee's wrongdoing was purely formal was expressed by Arthur Stark, in a case involving *P. R. Mallory & Company* (International Union of Electrical, Radio and Machine Workers, AFL-CIO).[37] The grievant was an employee who was discharged for failing to disclose a three-year-old back injury during a pre-employment medical examination. Management learned of the injury two months after the girl was hired, when she asked for treatment of a backache. Although pre-employment examinations are important to management, and job applicants must be "honest and responsive," Mr. Stark wrote, the company must bear "a certain degree of responsibility" for the way it asks questions. He noted that the doctor had asked about such symptoms as insomnia, allergies, nervousness, and frequent colds. But there was not a single question concerning the back.

[37] 19 AAA 23.

Two of three employees of *Westinghouse Electric Corporation* (International Union of Electrical, Radio and Machine Workers, AFL-CIO),[38] who were discharged after invoking the First and Fifth Amendments before a Congressional committee,[39] were also accused of having falsified employment applications. Although James C. Hill, who rendered the award in this case, dealt fully with this charge, it was a secondary issue in the case. Whether his decision would have been exactly the same if it had been the sole issue for discharge cannot be known.

At any rate, Mr. Hill ruled that the failure of one of the grievants to state on his employment application that he was a member of the Communist party did not constitute just cause for discharge, where the evidence presented before the Congressional committee by two of the Federal Bureau of Investigation agents related only to time *after* he was hired.

The evidence of wrongdoing by the second employee was clearer. It was "certainly not to be condoned," the arbitrator wrote, that the grievant had concealed previous employment when filling out his application for a job. But this falsification became known to the employer eight years after the employee was hired and three years before the discharge. "I do not believe [management] may harbor a specific offense over so long a period without notice to the employee or the union and then bring it forth as a basis for discharge," Mr. Hill wrote.

Hazardous Work

The rule that an employee must obey work orders, using the grievance procedure to protest them later, if he so desires, is generally accepted, with one limitation: no employee can be disciplined for refusing to do work he believes to be unsafe or injurious to his health. It may not matter that a particular assignment was not, in fact, unsafe. If the employee honestly believed it was, that usually constitutes an adequate defense against punishment for refusing a work order.[40]

---

[38] 22 AAA 12.

[39] That aspect of the case is discussed elsewhere in this chapter.

[40] On the other hand, if the arbitrator is persuaded that the employee's assertion that he feared a health hazard was not bona fide, his refusal to do the

For instance, at the *Stubnitz-Green Corporation* (United Automobile Workers, AFL-CIO),[41] management thought an employee was insubordinate when he refused to perform certain tasks on a platform three feet off the ground. For this he was discharged. During the grievance discussions that followed, it developed that the employee had a "deep-seated fear of height," which accounted for his truculent attitude.

The arbitrator, G. Allan Dash, concluded that the grievant had acted in such a way as to give management reason to believe the discharge was warranted. When the company was made aware of the grievant's fear of height, however, the discharge should have been rescinded.[42] But he stated as a rule that "an employee who is insubordinate to the degree of refusing outright to perform a work assignment is properly subject to severe discipline unless such performance exposes the employee to a significant danger to his health or safety."

work will be held just cause for discipline. For instance, at the *John Oster Manufacturing Company* (International Brotherhood of Electrical Workers, AFL-CIO), 17 AAA 20, an employee who repeatedly refused to invert certain objects after dipping them in an acid bath was held by H. Herman Rauch to have merited discharge. The defense that (1) inverting these objects was not part of the "standards" used in setting a rate for the job, and (2) the acid would hurt the grievant's hands and damage his clothing was rejected. Mr. Rauch wrote: "First, in respect to the matter of the 'standards': Whatever justification this excuse might have would revolve around the question of whether or not, as the 'standards' were then established, he was being paid for turning the 'caps' upside down. The answer to that is a question of fact which this panel need not determine. The contract between the company and the union which establishes [the grievant's] rights provides a method for finding out whether or not he was being paid for doing the work as requested under the then existing 'standards.' The grievance procedure was put into the contract for the purpose of settling any question of that kind. In respect to the matter of getting what he called 'acid' on his hands and clothes, the [arbitrator] concludes that, from the evidence, this was more of an excuse than a reason. The fact is that others have done the job and did not find it unreasonably hazardous or injurious. There is nothing in the evidence which gives the panel reason to believe that [the grievant] was justified in refusing to do the job as assigned because it was so injurious and painful to his hands that he would suffer damage to his health or safety by complying."

[41] 18 AAA 16.

[42] Full back pay was not awarded to the grievant because of some faults committed not only by himself but also by the union. The remedy aspect of the case is not relevant to the present discussion.

Inadvertent Sleeping at Work

Sleeping on the job is usually regarded as an offense warranting a heavy penalty. But even here, reasonable excuses and extenuating circumstances must be taken into account. At *Ex-Cell-O Corporation* (United Automobile Workers, AFL-CIO),[43] a two-week suspension was held by Dallas L. Jones to be excessive in the case of an employee who was found asleep in the locker room. The arbitrator had found the evidence "credible" that the grievant had fallen asleep inadvertently after having lain down to relieve a headache. Although he had not been an exemplary employee, there had not been occasion for the company to do more than warn him in the past four years. This was one point in the grievant's favor. Another fact tending to support the union's position was that the two-week suspension seemed "so much greater than that assessed in the recent past" in cases of serious violations of rules. Mr. Jones thought some penalty was warranted; but he reversed management completely, giving the grievant his two weeks' pay because of a provision in the agreement barring the arbitrator from modifying penalties.[44]

Quality Control and Discipline

Discipline is clearly a management function, and so is quality control. Normally, the right of the company to exercise initiative in both respects is unchallenged. But in one case, *Walben, Inc.* (Northeast Independent Aircraft Products Association),[45] the union objected to the obvious implications for discipline of a new quality control system established by the company. The arbitrator was John Perry Horlacher.

His decision was that the company had the right to establish a quality review board whose function, in part, would be to identify

---

[43] 14 AAA 5.

[44] Mr. Jones wrote: "It is the Arbitrator's opinion that the preponderance of evidence does support the union's position that the disciplinary layoff assessed the grievant was unjust. At the hearing, the company specifically denied the Arbitrator the power to modify penalties on the basis that the labor agreement between the parties does not allow for modification. Therefore, although the Arbitrator believes that some discipline is warranted, he must fully sustain the grievance and reverse the penalty. He does order, however, that these proceedings shall be made a part of the grievant's record."

[45] 23 AAA 19.

employees responsible for "discrepant" work. Although the system has an impact on discipline, he said, it must be regarded as "a device for improving quality." Nor was the company required to permit the union to participate in the decisions of the board. Moreover, the company had the right to institute a reprimand system based on the findings of the quality review board, despite the absence of any contractual provision specifically authorizing such a system of reprimands. This was not to say that the system established by management was without faults. One valid criticism was that it did not provide time limitations on use of previous offenses.[46] The union's remedy, however, lies in grievance procedure if any injustice results, Mr. Horlacher wrote.

So far, management was upheld at every point. When, however, management applied the new system to discharge an employee for discrepant work, the outcome was reversed. The method used to detect poor work was "to a significant extent ineffective," Mr. Horlacher wrote. The company was trying to be fair, but "substantial fairness was not achieved." What had happened here was that the grievant had himself reported defective work, and this was the only evidence against him. Thus, the quality review board's actions favored employees who "beat the system" by not reporting defective work, while it penalized others for their honesty. If the company gave the matter "sufficient attention," the arbitrator added, it could devise a system that would identify virtually all instances of bad work. "Its failure to do so, with the subsequent discrimination worked against [the grievant], who was honest enough to report all his discrepancies, requires setting aside his discharge."

THE TEST OF INTERNAL CONSISTENCY

No universally recognized formula guides management in establishing disciplinary policy. One employer may prefer to improvise, assigning penalties for violations on a case-by-case basis. His aim will be to maintain a logical relationship between offense and punishment, without announcing specific penalties in advance. Another employer may compile a virtual code of standard violations and a

[46] See the discussion of "statutes of limitations" elsewhere in this chapter.

range of penalties which depend upon how often the violations occur.

Nor is the lack of uniformity limited to procedures and penalties alone. What constitutes a violation also varies from one establishment to another. Drinking on the job, for instance—a cardinal offense in most companies—may be a minor indiscretion in a few. Similarly, insubordination and abusive language directed at management, a serious violation of rules in one company, may be mere "shop talk" in a more permissive environment.

Recognition and acceptance of the disciplinary system to which the parties adhere as the frame of reference for judging the suitability of penalties is a characteristic of the experienced arbitrator. In general, arbitrators see their function as a limited one; penalties that are inconsistent with established standards in the plant will be modified only to the extent necessary to bring those penalties into line.[47] The fact that the arbitrator would have imposed a different

[47] Occasionally, contracts bar an arbitrator from substituting "his discretion for that of the company or the union." That was the case at *Gouverneur Talc Company* (United Steelworkers of America, AFL-CIO), 20 AAA 2. Here, the issue before Robert F. Koretz was the discharge of an employee who, in a fit of anger over loss of a coin in a vending machine, upset the machine, causing personal injury and property damage. The union's request for a reduced penalty was rejected, partly because of the hazardous nature of the operation (mining). Referring to the contract's limitation of his function, Mr. Koretz wrote: "It seems to me that the agreement thus recognizes a view taken by many arbitrators in reviewing penalties imposed in discipline cases: in substance, that the penalty to be imposed for an offense rests primarily in the sound discretion of management, which cannot be set aside by an arbitrator unless there has been an abuse of that discretion. Considering all the evidence, including the conduct precipitating the discharge, the prior conduct leading to disciplinary action, the absence of any showing that other employees have been treated differently, the nature of the employment, and the adherence of management to the procedural rules in connection with discharge, I cannot conscientiously find that management has abused its discretion, whatever might my judgment be, were I in management's position. And I wish to emphasize that my holding does not mean that I necessarily agree completely with management's characterization of [the grievant]; it only reflects my opinion that I find no warrant in the evidence for setting aside management's exercise of its discretion, for which the agreement forbids me to substitute my discretion."

See also *General Electric Company* (International Union of Electrical, Radio and Machine Workers, AFL-CIO), 23 AAA 17, where Elmer E. Hilpert wrote: "It may be that, in the circumstances appearing in this matter, *some* companies would have imposed a penalty less than discharge, or that *some other* members of management, at this, or at another works of this Company, would have

penalty in the first place, if it were his decision to make, is insufficient reason by itself to modify a penalty.[48] In short, the test is not whether the punishment imposed was ideal, but whether the company's action was so out of line as to be "arbitrary" or "discriminatory." That is why commutation of discharges to suspensions (often in the form of reinstatement without back pay)[49] is common, while

---

imposed a lesser penalty, or that the Arbitrator, or some other arbitrator—had he the *initial* responsibility of making the managerial decision—might have imposed a lesser penalty. But that is not the basis for arriving at a determination that a given penalty is 'too severe.'"

See also *John Oster Manufacturing Company* (International Brotherhood of Electrical Workers, AFL-CIO), 17 AAA 20, where, in reply to a union's request that a discharged employee be treated with leniency, the arbitrator, H. Herman Rauch, said: "The union made certain pleas for consideration of [the grievant's] situation which reach beyond the bounds of justice due under the contract. The [arbitrator] must recognize that, under the contract, [his] functions are limited to giving everybody what is due. Anything beyond that must come voluntarily from the good will of the parties—it cannot be imposed upon either of them without their consent."

See also *Royal McBee Corporation* (United Automobile Workers, AFL-CIO), 1 AAA 13, where, in response to a union's request for downgrading, rather than discharge, of an employee who did unsatisfactory work, arbitrator Benjaman C. Roberts wrote: "Grievant was not lacking in the ability to perform the work [in his own classification]. It was the failure of the application of his capabilities to his work that led to his severance from the company. While the parties may by agreement seek to rehabilitate such an employee, it would be an abuse of his authority for the arbitrator to impose it as an equitable remedy."

See also *The Atlantic Refining Company* (Atlantic Independent Union), 3 AAA 20. Following an accident in which he was held negligent, a tractor driver was discharged. This was a second "major offense" within the meaning of a negotiated definition, and discharge was within a negotiated "table of standard penalties." To the union's request that the discharge be reduced to a lighter penalty, Benjamin F. Boyer replied: "It is true that a lighter penalty than discharge *could* have been imposed by the company. Under all the circumstances of this case, I am unwilling to find that [the grievant's] superiors abused their discretion when they decided to fix the penalty at discharge."

[48] Arbitrators are sometimes barred by contract from modifying penalties. For one such case, see *Ex-Cell-O Corporation*, 14 AAA 5, discussed earlier in this chapter.

[49] Barring a contractual restriction, arbitrators are generally free to award back pay to employees who were unjustly discharged or suspended. The object of such back pay awards, however, is not to impose a penalty on the employer, but to "make the employee whole" for his losses. For this reason, and also to avoid unjust enrichment by grievants who may not have been entirely guiltless, arbitrators generally offset against the back pay obligations of the employer moneys the grievants may have earned in other employment during the period they were barred from their regular jobs. Occasionally, equitable considerations

reduction of a three-day suspension to a layoff of one or two days, for instance, is seen less often. When punishment is reduced in this way, the reason usually is found in some internal standard.[50]

---

impel an arbitrator to limit the employee's back pay bill still further. Several illustrative cases may be cited.

At the *Magnavox Company of Tennessee* (International Union of Electrical, Radio and Machine Workers, AFL-CIO), 10 AAA 19, arbitrator William M. Hepburn found that an employee who should have been given a two-week suspension was discharged. He therefore awarded reinstatement for the employee, who would normally have been awarded back pay for the period from the end of the two-week suspension to the date of the award. But in this case, the grievant had chosen to sit idly by, waiting for the arbitrator to reinstate him. If he had made the effort, Mr. Hepburn wrote, the grievant could have found another job within the next four weeks. He was therefore entitled to back pay only for this four-week period, not for any time subsequent to that. "[The grievant] is not entitled to remain idle longer and permit his losses to accumulate," the arbitrator wrote. "This is not a case where an employee who was without fault was discharged due to a mistaken belief concerning the fault. Nor is it governed by the principles (involving public policy) of the Taft-Hartley Act."

Another case illustrating application of equitable principles in fashioning the remedy occurred at *Stubnitz-Green Corporation* (United Automobile Workers, AFL-CIO), 18 AAA 16. Here, too, an employee discharged (for reasons not relevant to this discussion) was reinstated with what would have been two weeks' loss of pay. G. Allan Dash, the arbitrator, withheld back pay for additional time lost because of "(1) The employee's failure to present a doctor's certificate indicating treatment for a nervous condition prior to the date of the incident; (2) the union's delay in pressing the grievance to arbitration; (3) the major doubt that the grievant, because of his nervous condition, would have been able to do much work during a significant part of the period since his improper discharge; (4) the fact that layoffs during the interim period would have caused the grievant to have lost some of the work time; (5) the employee's failure to appeal the findings of the Unemployment Compensation Board of Review which permitted the company to conclude that the employee and/or the union had accepted the conclusion that the employee was responsible for 'wilful misconduct'; and (6) the probability that part of the extended period which the grievant has not worked since May 27, 1957 has enabled him to get his nerves under control so as to become a satisfactory employee after his return to work."

See also *Jetronic Industries, Inc.* (United Steelworkers of America, AFL-CIO), 9 AAA 11. John Perry Horlacher reinstated an employee unjustly discharged for overstaying a medical leave, but without full back pay, because "both [the grievant] and the union were at fault" in not raising the question at issue (the right of the company to deny the employee another week of leave) until after that week had passed. The arbitrator reduced the employer's back pay obligation by two weeks.

[50] Before undertaking a detailed analysis of discipline imposed by the management of the *General Electric Company* (International Union of Electrical,

Inconsistent Enforcement

When management's imposition of discipline fails to meet the tests arbitrators subject it to, more often than not the reason lies in the erratic or inconsistent enforcement of the rules. This lapse comes about in many ways, not the least of which is a desire to be lenient with employees. Leniency by itself is not regarded as a fault, provided it is practiced without loss of internal consistency. The case of *P. R. Mallory & Co., Inc.* (International Union of Electrical, Radio and Machine Workers, AFL-CIO)[51] illustrates a reason why discharges are sometimes not sustained.

The grievant was a man who had been retained for thirteen years despite a "generally unsatisfactory record" of attendance and work performance. A year before his discharge, he was warned that continued absence without permission or notice to the company would result in dismissal. Nevertheless, that warning was followed by seven offenses of the same kind, with nothing said to him about them. The employer finally discharged him. But following the long period of inaction by management, the discharge was "unduly abrupt," said the arbitrator, Theodore W. Kheel.

The grievant was reinstated without back pay. This amounted to a very long suspension which, the arbitrator said, should be a warning that the company "will be fully within its rights in finally imposing the penalty of discharge now that he has been appropriately and emphatically warned."

Erratic administration of discipline was also commented upon by David Dolnick, arbitrator in a case of *A. E. Staley Manufacturing Company* (Allied Industrial Workers of America, AFL-CIO).[52] In thirteen years of employment, the grievant had received fourteen warnings of poor work, some of which were "final warnings," and

---

Radio and Machine Workers, AFL-CIO), 17 AAA 1, against thirteen employees accused of misconduct during a legal strike, arbitrator William E. Simkin established the "general framework for appraisal." Eight suspensions of five days or less would either be upheld entirely or reversed, depending upon whether there was "just cause" for discipline. It would be "picayune," he said, to scale down such discipline to suspensions of shorter duration. On the other hand, five suspensions of ten to twenty days present situations where "more discretion may be exercised." They may be upheld, reversed, or scaled down.

[51] 22 AAA 7.
[52] 24 AAA 24.

had been suspended twice. The trouble with this record, Mr. Dolnick said, was that the final warnings were disregarded and led to no immediate punishment. On the other hand, penalties were imposed while the grievant's work was improving. Management finally discharged him, but Mr. Dolnick ordered him back on the job. "An employee has the right to know how and under what circumstances he is liable to penalty and discharge," the arbitrator wrote. "The company has no right to permit unreasonable time to elapse between incidents, waive penalties, and assess them at its pleasure. Certainly an employee who is permitted to accumulate tenure in the face of warnings is entitled to reasonable notice before discharge." Mr. Dolnick's decision in this case was also based in part on the fact that the offense for which the grievant was discharged was not a "serious violation of company instructions." It was more in the nature of an act of thoughtlessness which "any reasonable person" might have committed and which, moreover, caused no serious damage.

On the other hand, withholding of punishment for some offenses is not necessarily evidence of erratic or inconsistent disciplinary policy. The decisive question is whether management's action was part of a conscious, deliberate effort to rehabilitate problem employees. At *Olin Mathieson Chemical Corporation* (Oil, Chemical and Atomic Workers, AFL-CIO),[53] William J. Kridel upheld a three-day suspension for an employee who, for the fifth time in the previous eighteen months, had refused to obey work instructions. The union pointed out at the arbitration hearing that some of the past incidents should not be used against him, because they did not result in penalties. The implication was that they were not serious transgressions or were, in any event, forgiven by the company.

Mr. Kridel was convinced by the employer's evidence that the facts were not quite as the union had portrayed them. It was true that on a number of occasions no discipline had been imposed, because management had thought that withholding punishment at that time would help the grievant correct her ways and "permit union officials to assist her in this regard." It was also significant, he said, that none of the written reprimands preceding the final suspension was protested by the union.

[53] 6 AAA 3.

Range of Penalties

A case at the *Holley Carburetor Company* (United Automobile Workers, AFL-CIO)[54] affords a clear example of disciplinary penalties modified to make them consistent with standards the employer himself prescribed. The grievant in this case was discharged for deliberately stealing a used cabinet, contriving to involve another employee in the means used for getting it out of the plant, without the latter's knowledge. There was no question about the employee's guilt. In fact, the union sought only to get the penalty reduced, so that the man, with eighteen years of unblemished service, would at least get his job back. A two-day suspension was the union's recommendation.

After hearing evidence, Meyer S. Ryder observed that the company had had a range of penalties to choose from, with the object of "correction of employee behavior" and that "the company itself forthrightly states that seniority and employment records must be considered in the choice of penalty." This being so, he said, it was not inappropriate to see whether mitigating circumstances were present in this case. He found at least four:

1. The grievant's eighteen-year employment record was "entirely devoid of any acts justifying the imposition of discipline."

2. The "possible long term social and economic impact" of a discharge must be considered in the case of a man "who has given his entire working life thus far" to one employer. This must be taken into account as well as "the loss of employment benefits built up over eighteen years of service," which would "dissolve as a result of one rash act."

3. The nature of the grievant's record and offense did not support a conclusion that there was "no reasonable hope of personal correction." Although there was "premeditation," the theft represented "some lapse of rational behavior." Except for this lapse, the grievant would have realized that, having asked for the cabinet (which he thought was surplus), suspicion would be directed at him when it was missed. "In the face of all that happened, the Arbitrator believes [the grievant] did have the emotional conflict he testified to after he took the cabinet and that his uncertainty concerning its return was caught short by the discovery of his guilt."

[54] 21 AAA 8.

4. Reduction of the penalty will not have an adverse impact on the behavior of other employees.

Reinstatement without back pay was directed.[55]

Conflict of Rules and Penalties

Employers who establish in advance carefully worded schedules of offenses and penalties do not necessarily avoid disputes over disciplinary actions. The reason is that particular acts of wrongdoing do not always lend themselves to easy classification. When an employer punishes, under one rule, a violation more properly dealt with by another rule, a lack of internal consistency may be found.

That was the situation at *Nosco Plastics, Inc.* (Rubber, Cork, Linoleum and Plastic Workers, AFL-CIO).[56] Company regulations distinguished between offenses which may result in immediate discharge ("gross negligence while at work or on company property" and "insubordination," among others) and "minor offenses," which may result in lesser forms of discipline ("failure to carry out instructions," "inattention to duties," and "excessive profanity," among others). The grievant in this case was discharged for leaving a machine idle while drinking a beverage at a soft-drink dispensing machine, using profane language when chided by the foreman, and declaring that he wouldn't work under such oppressive conditions. Was this a "major" violation or a "minor" one? Management said it all added up to a gross violation, justifying discharge.

Harold M. Somers added up the offenses differently. For a finding of "gross negligence," he said, there must be something "much more

[55] Mr. Ryder emphasized that his decision was based on the special circumstances of this case. Among the other facts taken into account was the four-month interval between the discharge and the date of the award, during which the grievant had done some work elsewhere at lower wages. He wrote: "Under all of the circumstances obtaining in the matter involving a serious breach of plant behavior but where substantial extenuating conditions are present the undersigned believes and hereby holds that the penalty of discharge levied in this matter was excessive. He believes the amount of time that has elapsed since the grievant's suspension and the reason for the suspension is sufficient penalty. He does not see where any back pay is justifiable under these circumstances considering the nature of the violation, the means used in executing the violation and the involvement of another employee in the means used without that other employee's consent or knowledge."

[56] 20 AAA 21.

grossly willful" than drinking at a dispensing machine which the company provides for that purpose. True, the grievant had exercised poor judgment in leaving his machine idle when he did, but gross negligence implies an act which may damage persons or property, elements not present in this case. Nor did the loss of production, valued at approximately the grievant's daily pay, make the offense a major one. In view of the minor offenses committed, including use of "excessive profanity," the discharge was commuted to a one-month suspension.

The contract at the *Continental Can Company* (United Papermakers and Paperworkers, AFL-CIO),[57] established two lists of offenses. One was a "corrective discipline" list, which included eight violations, such as "leaving the premises while on duty without permission." The other was a dischargeable offense list, with four items, one of them being "wilful disorderly conduct."

When an employee, having become disturbed at the unexpected and unexplained appearance of a time study man at his place of work, stopped his machine and went home (after finding the foreman and telling him he was leaving), it became necessary to determine what classification of offense he had committed. Management decided the dischargeable offense list covered the situation and dismissed him.[58] Arbitrator Mark L. Kahn thought otherwise.

It is the Arbitrator's judgment that [his] misconduct definitely fell within the first category of offenses listed under Article X, Section 7, as calling for corrective discipline. Although none of the acts listed under this first category precisely describes [the grievant's] offense, it falls more under "Leaving the premises while on duty without permission . . ." than under any other heading. The fact that [he] also interfered with production and thus might be charged also with "Neglect of duty"—likewise a first category act under Article X, Section 7—tends to aggravate the offense. On the other hand, the fact that [he] sought out his foreman tends, under all the circumstances, to mitigate his offense. [The grievant] did not behave in a disorderly manner—in fact, he left the scene so quietly that, so far as [the plant industrial engineer] was concerned, [he] "disappeared"—and the Arbitrator finds that [the grievant] did not commit the "Wilful disorderly conduct" listed as a cause for immediate dis-

[57] 15 AAA 20.
[58] Apart from the two lists, management believed the grievant's actions came under the heading of a "quit" or "strike," dischargeable under other provisions of the agreement.

charge under the second category of Article X, Section 7. It is also the Arbitrator's judgment that [the grievant] did not "quit" (per Article I (h)), nor did he "strike" (per Article XII, Section 3).[59]

A union's attempt at the *United Wood Products Company* (Upholsterers' International Union, AFL-CIO)[60] to make an act of unreasonable violence appear to be subject to a rule covering "horseplay" did not succeed with Carl A. Warns. The grievant was a twenty-two-year-old employee who, in a spirit of "vigorous youthful unrestrained enthusiasm," squeezed an elderly fellow-employee so hard that several of the latter's ribs were broken. Admittedly, there was no malice in this action. Nevertheless, management thought discharge was justified. Mr. Warns agreed.

The union had argued that the offense came under "Rule 15— Horseplay," the penalty for which was warning in the first two instances and discharge only after a third offense. Mr. Warns pointed out in reply that the rule's definition of horseplay referred to actions involving "potential" danger to others. Here, the injury was not potential but present and substantial.

GUILT IS PERSONAL

The fact that two or more employees seem to be involved in the

[59] Having determined that the grievant was subject to "corrective discipline," Mr. Kahn had to resolve a collateral issue concerning use against an employee of previous offenses. The difficulty was that the contract provided for a sequence of penalties for offenses, but provided also that no violation occurring more than a year earlier was to be held against an employee. The grievant in this case had been punished as a "second offender" 7 months earlier, but his "first offense" took place more than a year before his unauthorized leaving of the plant. Did that make the current offense another "second violation" (because it was the second in a 12 month period) or did it make the current offense a third violation (because it followed the second within twelve months)? Mr. Kahn's answer: "The intent of the agreement will best be effectuated by holding that under these circumstances the penalty for a second 'second offense' within the year—one which has occurred more than one year after the 'first' offense— should be less than discharge but considerably more substantial than 7 days. (A 7 day suspension would have been the penalty for a second offense in 12 months. A third offense, also occurring in 12 months, would have resulted in discharge. The grievant was given a 30 day suspension by award of the arbitrator). A discussion of other statute-of-limitations problems will be found earlier in this chapter.

[60] 19 AAA 13.

same act of misconduct does not necessarily justify the same penalty for all. In arbitration, as in other forums for the administration of justice, guilt is personal, and may not be established by association alone. Two cases will illustrate this maxim.

The first occurred at *L. F. Grammes & Sons, Inc.* (United Steelworkers of America, AFL-CIO).[61] An employee in this establishment overstayed his lunch period by a half-hour, during which time he drank intoxicating liquors, and was thereafter caught loitering in the men's room. When told by the foreman to go home, he became abusive and disorderly. For this he was discharged. With him the employer discharged another worker who had gone to lunch with the first employee, and who was thought to be equally guilty. Management's assumption that the second employee had similarly misconducted himself was based only on the fact that the two were friends who "shared many things." Rolf Valtin upheld the discharge of the first employee, but reinstated the second with the loss of only one week's pay. The case of the second employee differed from the first in four ways: (1) he was "*not* caught in a drunken condition" and hence *not* told to go home; (2) he was seen walking about instead of working, but management apparently took no action against him for this: (3) he was contacted, not in response to anything he did, but on the assumption that he shared the guilt of his friend; and (4) although the second employee became argumentative when told to go home, he did not become as insubordinate as the other employee had.

The second case, at *Arvin Industries, Inc.* (International Association of Machinists, AFL-CIO),[62] was in some ways similar to the first. One Saturday morning, a superintendent, making a routine check of production under way, found a large number of employees missing from a certain area. After waiting a few minutes to see whether they would return, he went to the men's room and found them loafing there. All the employees who were standing around at that moment were marched into the personnel office and suspended for the rest of that day and the following Monday. Carl A. Warns was the arbitrator in the case of one employee who filed a grievance.

Mr. Warns found that (1) the grievant was not a member of the

[61] 12 AAA 5.
[62] 12 AAA 19.

group that was loafing; his work station was elsewhere in the plant; (2) there was no evidence that he was absent from his work station an "unreasonable" length of time; and (3) there was "nothing in the evidence or argument" to suggest that an employee, taking a mid-morning rest period, should not lean for a moment or two against a wall and chat with fellow employees.[63]

Strong Suspicion Is No Substitute for Proof

A reasonable certainty that an employee is violating the company rules may be sufficient for disciplinary action only if no protest is entered. If a grievance should be filed, however, and the case goes to arbitration, direct proof may be necessary if management's action is to be sustained.

At *De Luxe Die Works, Inc.* (United Automobile Workers, AFL-CIO),[64] for instance, management thought it was reasonable to believe that an employee was taking an excessive time away from his job on a certain day. The supervisor had looked his way on twelve occasions and found him at work only three times. As the employee's work history and general behavior had not been of the best, to say the least, it seemed appropriate to impose a three-day disciplinary suspension.

But when the matter came to arbitration, Howard A. Cole found many questions unanswered. The employer's case "fell short" because the supervisor had made no "real attempt" to find out exactly where the grievant was, what he was doing, or how long he had been away from his place of work.

Had [the supervisor] done more by way of checking, than merely observing from the main aisleway the approximate number of times when [the grievant] was not at his press, the company might well have been able to make the kind of showing necessary in order to support a sufficiently certain finding of guilt. However, such a finding cannot be reasonably premised on the minimal information provided by the extremely limited investigation which [the supervisor] chose to make.

[63] Mr. Warns found some inaccuracy in the grievant's statement about the length of time he was away from his work station, but his thirty years of employment, with "a clear record as far as this proceeding is concerned," entitled him to the "presumption" that he was telling the truth when he denied loitering. This presumption, the arbitrator added, deserves equal weight with the company's argument that the superintendent must be believed because "he has nothing to gain by improper discipline of employees."

[64] 21 AAA 10.

Conceding that the supervisor "had other things to do" than compile data on one employee, Mr. Cole nevertheless could not conclude on the record before him that the company had proved its case.

"Actions Speak Louder than Words"

If an accusation of wrongdoing by an employee is to be upheld, it may be necessary for management to show that its own actions were based on a belief that the charge against him was true. For instance, at *Merrill-Stevens Dry Dock & Repair Company* (Industrial Union of Marine and Shipbuilding Workers, AFL-CIO),[65] Paul W. Hardy refused to uphold a discharge for intoxication where the company's actions at the time of the violations were not consistent with a belief that the grievant was, in fact, drunk. Evidence was "contradictory," he said, as to whether the grievant was escorted to the gate, a precaution that would normally be taken when a worker was found intoxicated. Nor was he sent to the medical department, another common measure in such cases. The sole evidence of drunkenness was the grievant's reply to the foreman when asked whether he was drunk. He had answered: "Yes, I am drunk and I have been drunk for years." This was undoubtedly an insubordinate and insolent reply, Mr. Hardy said, deserving of discipline; but the charge of drunkenness was not proved where management did none of the things at the time that would prove it believed the man was intoxicated.[66]

The same defect in management's case was discovered by arbitrator Israel Ben Scheiber at *Helena Rubinstein, Inc.* (Oil, Chemical and Atomic Workers, AFL-CIO),[67] where an employee was discharged for drinking and sleeping on the job. Reinstatement without back pay was directed because the guards, who testified at the arbitration that they observed the grievant asleep with a bottle of whiskey beside him, neither reported the incident promptly nor confiscated the liquor. Both actions were required by company rules. "From this it would appear," wrote Mr. Scheiber, "either that the

[65] 12 AAA 3.
[66] The grievant was also accused of inefficiency. That aspect of the case is not relevant to this discussion. The outcome of the case was reinstatement without back pay.
[67] 23 AAA 7.

incident did not occur or that such an offense is not deemed to be of a very serious nature, and in any event is regarded as a rather casual occurrence by the guards, who are presumed to reflect the company's attitude."

The reason the guards said nothing about the grievant's drinking and sleeping on the job until some time after the incident, when they were asked a direct question about it, was stated to be that they wanted to be "nice guys" and give the employee "a break." This was not an adequate defense, the arbitrator said, particularly in view of the testimony of the company's director of plant safety that guards always made notations in their books when they came upon such incidents.

The "strange testimony" of the guards, Mr. Scheiber concluded, created a reasonable doubt which had to be resolved in favor of the grievant. This did not mean, however, that the grievant was necessarily innocent of the charge. "Rather, it is a Scotch verdict of 'not found' which merely is a finding, that on all the proof submitted, it has not been proven beyond a reasonable doubt that the grievant is guilty of 'possessing liquor while on duty'."[68]

Retroactive Discipline

It is a rule both of law and of common sense that no person can be punished for something he did prior to the enactment of the law or rule making the act a punishable offense. In no reported arbitration case has it been found that management tried to invoke retroactively a rule of conduct or a new disciplinary policy. There were two cases, however, in which the combination of circumstances were such as to lead arbitrators to believe the "no retroactivity" principle was violated unintentionally.

The first was at the *American Machine and Foundry Company* (United Automobile Workers, AFL-CIO).[69] A new rule was established by the company, directed against employees who conduct their personal financial affairs in so disorderly a manner as to result in the garnishing of their pay. The new rule called for written warn-

---

[68] The arbitrator found other mitigating circumstances justifying reinstatement; however, the grievant was not only denied back pay, but his seniority was reduced by the amount of time he was not permitted to work.
[69] 17 AAA 6.

ings, suspensions, and finally discharges for future incidents of pay deductions through action of creditors.

Some months later, several employees, who were already deeply in debt when the new policy was announced, got into further financial trouble, resulting in garnishees. One was discharged, and the others were suspended. "In a sense," wrote Arthur Stark, "management applied an *ex post facto* policy, since the major events leading to [a grievant's] garnishments were the result—not the cause—of his problems. It was unjust to discharge him, since (1) he could not be expected to achieve the impossible; and (2) the punishment can in no way be interpreted as a disciplinary act designed to improve his behavior. The other grievants, too, were caught in a web which, by pure happenstance, was cast out at a time they were vulnerable. It was unjust to suspend them for actions which, basically, preceded adoption of a new company policy." In this case, the union questioned the right of the company to discipline for garnishments at all. Mr. Stark acknowledged that garnishments were "on the periphery of employer-employee relations," but as there was nothing in the contract to prevent management from forbidding future garnishments, the schedule of penalties for future violations was not in itself improper.

A grievance involving retroactive application of a rule also occurred at the *American Bosch Arma Mississippi Corporation* (International Union of Electrical, Radio and Machine Workers, AFL-CIO).[70] An employee, who became emotionally upset and absented herself from work for three days, after having been discovered by her husband in the company of a foreman, was discharged. Among the reasons given for the dismissal was violation of a rule forbidding fraternization with supervisors. Jay Murphy agreed that the company could have a rule of this kind, but since no such rule had been announced until after this incident, the grievant was reinstated.[71]

THE CONSCIOUSNESS OF GUILT

Even in an establishment where disciplinary rules are spelled out

[70] 8 AAA 15.

[71] There were additional reasons for the reinstatement, which are not pertinent to the discussion in this chapter.

in employee handbooks, where notices are posted at time clocks, letters placed in pay envelopes, and other usual means of communication between management and employees are utilized, it is not possible to formulate expressly every possible type of offense against industrial discipline. This accounts in part for the relatively large number of cases in which arbitrators found that the grievants had somehow been unaware that they were, by their actions, inviting penalties.

"Perfunctory" and Misunderstood Work Orders

In a case of the *American Bosch Arma Corporation* (International Union of Electrical, Radio and Machine Workers, AFL-CIO),[72] for instance, seventeen employees were suspended for three days after refusing to work overtime. As management had the right under the contract to compel overtime, it did not appear that there could be ground for a reversal. But Peter Seitz did reverse the action on a showing, first, that the employer had never invoked his contractual right on such matters in the past and, second, that the work order had been given by the foreman in a "perfunctory" manner, leading the employees to believe this was just another one of those requests they were free to accept or refuse.[73]

Routine work ordered during straight time hours may also provide occasions for misunderstanding. In *Mohasco Industries, Inc.* (Textile Workers Union of America, AFL-CIO),[74] Milton Rubin said that discharge was too severe a penalty for an employee who refused to wash windows (a once-a-year task generally performed

[72] 10 AAA 14. This case was discussed more fully in the preceding chapter.

[73] On the other hand, a soft-spoken manner does not necessarily detract from the effectiveness of a foreman's work order. At *Kalasign of America* (United Papermakers and Paperworkers, AFL-CIO), 21 AAA 12, for instance, an employee was suspended for refusing to obey a work order. His defense was that he thought the foreman was asking him to do the work, not telling him. Louis A. Crane was not convinced the grievant was not conscious of wrongdoing. "It is true that the foreman did not give him a 'direct' order," he wrote. But that was because the foreman does not usually talk in those terms. "He was described by union witnesses as an even-tempered, mild-mannered man who phrases his directions in the form of requests or even favors. The witnesses candidly acknowledge that 'everyone' is aware of [the foreman's] method of assigning work."

[74] 15 AAA 22.

by all employees in one department) where there was no evidence
that the grievant had reason to know that discharge would be imposed. On the contrary, when told by the foreman that if he did
not perform that task he "might as well punch the card and go
home," he asked whether he was being discharged. "Not necessarily," was the reply. Furthermore, said Mr. Rubin, other employees
had similarly declined to wash windows several days earlier without
incurring more than an "incident report." He concluded:

> Certain standards have developed for the determination of the propriety
> of a discharge for alleged insubordination or refusal to obey instructions.
> The severity and finality of this discipline, a form of "employment death,"
> warrants the strict application of standards, as safeguards for consistent,
> discriminate and deserved application, that (1) the instructions be clear
> and reasonable, (2) that the ordered task be feasible of performance
> without danger to health and safety of the employee, and (3) that the
> employee has been made aware, or that he be made aware, of the dis-
> charge consequence prior to its imposition. [The grievant's] discharge
> fails under the third test.

Reinstatement without back pay was directed, with the admoni-
tion to the grievant that "if, in the future, this penalty should prove
to be insufficiently corrective, the severest discipline would then be
warranted."[75]

Refusal to Cross Picket Lines

The failure by management to enforce a contractual right is not
always a matter of neglect or oversight. Sometimes it is a question
of policy. During a strike of hospital workers in New York, employees of *Thomas A. Edison Company* (International Union of Electrical, Radio and Machine Workers, AFL-CIO),[76] whose task it was

---

[75] For another case in which management's action was not upheld because
of the misunderstanding by employees of a work order, see *West Virginia Pulp
and Paper Company* (International Association of Machinists, AFL-CIO), 7
AAA 4, discussed earlier in this chapter. George Savage King wrote: "The
company must establish that it has in fact directed the employee to do something, or it must establish his knowledge of a situation which imposes on him
a duty to act. Neither the supervisor nor the foreman seemed to recognize any
duty to make sure that it was understood by each of the grievants that he
was being directed to work and that a refusal would expose him to at least
the possibility of disciplinary action."
[76] 15 AAA 24.

to service certain electronic equipment, refused to cross the picket lines of the hospital workers' union. Management directed members of supervision to do the work and took no action against the servicemen. But as the strike wore on, it became inconvenient to service the equipment with supervisors alone. At that point, the company directed its servicemen to perform those tasks. When several refused to cross the picket lines, they were suspended. The grievance eventually came before Carl Rachlin.

The suspensions were not proper, he said. "Where the employer has led the employees to believe that a certain condition prevails, it would appear to be improper to change the condition while the strike continued.[77]

Awareness of Work Requirements

Failure to do "a fair day's work" for "a fair day's pay" is generally held to be good cause for discipline, provided the employee knows the productivity expected of him. At *Johnson and Johnson* (Textile Workers of America, AFL-CIO),[78] an employee did not know, with the result that an official reprimand in his file was ordered expunged by the arbitrator, George Moskowitz. "It's one thing for the employer to use planning estimates for scheduling purposes and cost computations," the arbitrator wrote, "but quite another to use such estimates as a basis for warning, reprimand or discipline when neither knowledge of, nor agreement with such estimates is brought home to the employees or their bargaining representatives."

Unclear Denial of Leave

Management's failure to give an employee a clear warning proved to be a decisive weakness at the *Whirlpool Corporation* (International Association of Machinists, AFL-CIO).[79] The grievant in this case was a man whose excessive absenteeism in the past had brought him an official warning that his next absence without just cause

[77] Although upholding the grievance in this case because of management's earlier acquiescence, Mr. Rachlin rejected the union's contention that the grievants had a "natural right" not to cross a picket line. Only an honest fear of violence would have justified refusal to go to work, and the evidence in this case did not support the assertion that the servicemen feared bodily harm.

[78] 16 AAA 5.

[79] 19 AAA 10.

would result in dismissal. Despite this warning, he stayed out for three days in October 1959 to work on a well that had run dry. He had telephoned the company and explained the reason for his absence to one of the girls in the personnel department. Her answer was that the foreman had said that the grievant had a responsibility to his job. But she did not say that the excuse would be unacceptable. "In such circumstances," Ronald W. Haughton wrote, "[the grievant] was justified in assuming that he could stay away from work and take care of his problem at home without fear of discipline. It would have been another matter if he had received a direct communication from the company informing him that in view of all the circumstances, including the possibility of obtaining [a plumber to fix his well], and a consideration of his bad past record he must report to work or take the consequences."

The *Whirlpool* case was typical in that the fault lay with lower echelons of management, not with the policy-making levels. That was also true at the *American Bosch Arma Mississippi Corporation* (International Union of Electrical, Radio and Machine Workers, AFL-CIO).[80] Here, Gerald A. Barrett ruled that although a three-day suspension was the customary penalty for employees who left work without permission during scheduled hours, an employee on the late shift who left at 6 P.M. on a Saturday to keep a social engagement could not be punished. It appeared that the foreman, in discussing her request for permission to leave, had permitted her to believe that if she feigned sickness, she might be discharged, but that if she told the truth about her reason for leaving, no penalty would result. "It is this action which so misrepresented the policy of the company and thereby deluded the grievant, as to require the finding that discipline in this case was lacking in proper cause," he concluded.[81]

[80] 13 AAA 4.

[81] Although upholding the grievance, Mr. Barrett cautioned the parties not to be misled as to its scope. "The scope of this decision should not be the subject of confusion between the parties. Employees have no right to leave their jobs during the course of a shift, in the absence of permission from supervision," he wrote. "The desire to keep a social engagement clearly does not constitute a compelling emergency. When employees elect to leave their jobs during the course of a shift without obtaining permission, they render themselves liable to disciplinary action."

PROCEDURAL DEFECTS

The defendant in a criminal action may win acquittal because of a procedural defect in the case against him. Can the same result be achieved in arbitration? Only an indefinite "it depends" can be given in reply to that question. The five cases that follow—one in which the union prevailed completely, three in which the grievants were reinstated without back pay, and a fifth in which management's view was upheld—illustrate the circumstances that may be decisive.

Suspension Pending Discharge

At the *National-U.S. Radiator Corporation* (United Steelworkers of America, AFL-CIO),[82] the contract provided only one way for management to discharge an employee. It required that he be suspended for five days or less, "preliminary to discharge," during which time grievance committeemen would be notified, so that grievance procedure could be invoked. This was expressed in what the arbitrator, Cyril J. Kavanagh, called "simple and unmistakable language." Nevertheless, management discharged an employee directly, without the preliminary five-day suspension. Mr. Kavanagh held this to be a fatal defect, justifying reinstatement of the employee with back pay (but with deduction of moneys received in other earnings as well as from unemployment compensation, in accordance with a contractual provision) despite the fact that the grievant, an absentee, deserved some punishment.

Taking the role of devil's advocate, the arbitrator asked what difference this procedural error made; a suspension would have "ripened" into discharge, and the dismissal would in any event have been subject to review in arbitration. To this he answered:

The parties must have thought that there was good reason to provide for suspension subject to discharge rather than for outright discharge. It is their contract and the arbitrator has no authority to change it or to substitute his judgment for theirs. They have made their bargain and must stick to it. It is not my province to say that I see no possible harm that befell either [the grievant] or the union by reason of the outright discharge of [the grievant] rather than his suspension subject to discharge. The contracting parties knew what they were trying to accom-

[82] 16 AAA 3.

plish when they so carefully worked out this procedure and they used simple and unmistakable language to describe it. It is our duty to respect and abide by their agreement. Any other approach would do violence to our role as arbitrator.[83]

Notification of Steward

In the second case, *Chicago Rawhide Manufacturing Company* (Amalgamated Meat Cutters and Butcher Workmen, AFL-CIO),[84] the grievant prevailed again, but not as fully as in the *National-U.S. Radiator* case. Here, the contract required the union steward to be notified, "whenever it is possible or practical to do so," prior to the discharge of any employee. Despite this, the company discharged an employee for absenteeism without notifying the steward in advance. Perhaps it was the grievant's record which made management believe the procedural violation would make no difference.[85] At any rate, she was discharged by a telegram addressed to her, with no message to the steward.

It was both "possible and practical" to have followed contractual procedures, wrote Pearce Davis, who arbitrated the dispute. "The problem that the company faced in the case of the grievant was of long standing. There was no emergency involved in the nature of the grievant's offense. The company would not have been handicapped in any way had the discharge action been delayed to permit the contractually required prior notification."

For this reason only, despite her bad record, the grievant was reinstated. But she received no back pay.

[83] Mr. Kavanagh said he believed his decision on this procedural question was consistent with the viewpoint of arbitrators generally. He quoted with approval this statement from an award the union had cited to him: "Arbitrators in general recognize that strict adherence to grievance procedure is necessary to promote good and constructive relationship and its attendant benefits. Arbitration awards are evidence that the parties are expected to comply with its procedure by observing its formal requirements. To disregard procedure in any respect opens the entire instrument to violations and eventually renders it meaningless. It is especially important that there shall be strict compliance with the technical construction of the provisions embodied in grievance procedure." The case was identified only as that of the *Shenango China Company.* The arbitrator was not named, nor was it indicated whether the award was published.

[84] 10 AAA 18.

[85] In eleven years of employment, her absences ranged from 18 per cent of working time during one year to 1.5 per cent during her best year.

Coerced "Quit"

The third case, at *Arvin Industries, Inc.* (United Automobile Workers, AFL-CIO),[86] was unusual. A resourceful employee machined a device for tripping the mechanism of an automatic vending machine, so that it would yield candy bars without coins being deposited. This employee, together with two others who were seen using the device, were thereupon called into the personnel office for a conference. In the presence of two uniformed police officers, they were given an opportunity to sign a "voluntary quit" form and told that unless they did so, they would be discharged for dishonesty. Each of the employees signed. The one who fashioned the contrivance accepted the outcome; no grievance was filed in his behalf. The case of the other two eventually came before Harry J. Dworkin.

The arbitrator said the evidence did not sustain the employer's contention that the two grievants were in conspiracy with the third employee, who had manufactured the device. They merely took advantage of the non-functioning of the machine. True, this was an "improper and illegal act," deserving of "appropriate discipline," but not necessarily the same as for conspiracy. On the other hand, he rejected the union's argument that the grievants were merely enjoying a "free gift, bonus or windfall." Even if they had done no more than take advantage of a "mechanical imperfection," they were guilty of "a form of theft" and "unlawful conversion."

The outcome of the case was determined partly by the way management had dealt with the situation. It was "contrary to the letter and spirit of the grievance procedure," Mr. Dworkin wrote, to coerce employees into quitting by (1) telling them it would be to their advantage to "quit," thereby avoiding discharge for dishonesty; (2) giving the grievants the impression that the union president approved this course; and (3) permitting two uniformed police officers to be present at the meeting where these representations were made.

Delayed Notification of Discharge

The fourth case, at *Jefferson City Cabinet Company* (International

[86] 15 AAA 15.

Union of Electrical, Radio and Machine Workers, AFL-CIO),[87] involved a different kind of procedural violation on management's part. It consisted of discharging an employee on August 8 and, through an oversight, not notifying him of it until October 6, the day before he tried to return to work. (The grievant was out sick. The discharge was for refusing to permit the company doctor to examine him and determine whether his claim for disability compensation was justified.)

The grievant's action was "in defiance of the instructions of management" and "would warrant discharge," wrote Harold T. Dworet in his award. But because of the "confusion" caused by the delay in telling the grievant of the action taken against him, he was reinstated without back pay.[88]

Formal Written Notice

In the fifth case, the grievant's claim of a procedural defect in the case against him availed him nothing at all. The employer, *Minerals and Chemicals Corporation of America* (United Stone and Allied Products Workers, AFL-CIO),[89] discharged an employee for striking another worker with a heavy metal object. The evidence was strong against the grievant; his only defense was that the company had neglected to give the union written notice of the discharge. Arbitrator George Carroll said that this defect made no difference in the circumstances of the case. The purpose of the notice-in-discharge provision was to guarantee that the employee would know exactly what charges he faced. But here there was "uncontroverted testimony" that both the employee and the union understood fully the reason for the discharge. Furthermore, by discussing the discharge during grievance procedure, the union had in effect waived the written notice provision. The arbitration said the discharge was justified despite the grievant's satisfactory work and attendance record over a long period of time.

[87] 14 AAA 9.

[88] Other circumstances in this case, including the fact that the grievant's disability originated with an on-the-job injury, may have contributed to the arbitrator's decision to reinstate him without back pay. It cannot be said with certainty from a reading of the opinion and award that the same decision would have resulted if the delayed notice of discharge were the sole issue.

[89] 13 AAA 23.

The Phrasing of Discharge Notices

It is possible to carry too far the analogy between an employer's discipline for industrial misconduct and public prosecution of law breakers. The union at *Royal McBee Corporation* (United Automobile Workers, AFL-CIO)[90] did that in attacking the phrasing of the discharge notice as if it were, in effect, a defective indictment.

The facts of the case were not complicated. The grievant, according to James J. Healy, to whom the grievance was referred, "was proving himself less and less a desirable or satisfactory employee." He was warned that he was inviting discharge by his proclivity for defying the foreman, trying to undermine his authority, and shirking tasks. Finally, on July 22, 1958, in the presence of another employee, he told the foreman to "shut up" when asked why a job was taking him so long to do. For this, he was dismissed, the discharge slip stating the reason as "willful insubordination."

The union's defense of the grievant turned largely on the meaning of that phrase. The term, it was urged, means intentional disobedience. Whatever the grievant's faults were on the day in question, he had not been intentionally disobedient.

Mr. Healy found no merit in that defense. "It is true," he wrote, "that the proximate cause for discharge probably is described poorly by the term 'willful insubordination,' which connotes deliberate disregard of instructions." But, he added, it would be wrong to judge the merits of the company's action by the wisdom of its choice of words. "The behavior *per se* is the criterion by which the action of discharge is to be judged, not the words used to characterize the behavior."

The arbitrator differentiated this case from others, in which management shifts ground completely, trying to justify discharge in terms never mentioned before:

If a man were discharged for theft, for example, and then the company tried to justify the discharge solely on the basis of poor quality of work, one could invoke the technical point of "improper description" used by the union. But no such obviously disparate statement of cause exists here. In fact, to support this and other technical points advanced by the union in this case could work to the disadvantage of the union in the long run.[91]

[90] 6 AAA 11.

[91] Mr. Healy did, in fact, deal with a situation in which management tried to

Adding to Penalties

In one respect at least, principles of law enforcement are transferable to the field of arbitration. An employer who imposes one discipline on an employee will not be permitted to increase the penalty later. This, in effect, was the decision of Ronald W. Haughton at the *Whirlpool Corporation* (International Association of Machinists, AFL-CIO).[92]

The grievant in this case was an employee who, with the knowledge of the company, maintained a private business as a plasterer. In September 1959, he absented himself from work, reporting sick. Management suspected that his "outside interests" were the real reason for his absence, and imposed a three-day suspension on him. This suspension was not protested. At the same time, management initiated an investigation of the employee's activities. The result was the disclosure of facts tending to justify the suspicion. The employee was thereupon discharged.

"The essential point," Mr. Haughton wrote, "is that the absence was found in the first instance to have been *unexcused*." For that, a three-day suspension was imposed. This was not suspension pending a final determination, but a final determination in itself. Even though the penalty was based only on suspicion, the fact that it was not protested "means to the arbitrator that the penalty and the charge were allowed to stand, and must be regarded as having been accepted." It follows then, he concluded, "that it was improper for the company to reopen the case by discharging [the grievant] on account of the same unexcused absence for which discipline had

support a discharge on grounds never before asserted. In *Metal Hydrides, Inc.* (International Union of Electrical, Radio and Machine Workers, AFL-CIO), 11 AAA 19, discussed earlier in this chapter, the grievant was discharged for a series of offenses. Some time after the incident that provoked the dismissal, the employer investigated his employment application for the first time and discovered purposeful falsifications. This evidence against the grievant was not put forward during grievance procedure. When it was shown to Mr. Healy for the first time at the arbitration hearing, the union objected to admissibility of that material, and the arbitrator sustained the objection. To conceal knowledge of these grave charges, Mr. Healy wrote, shows a disregard of good labor relations. The company had no right to permit the union "to carry the case to a hearing on the assumption that it had to meet an understood set of charges against the aggrieved" and then produce an amended list of charges against which the union had not had an opportunity to prepare.

[92] 18 AAA 13.

already been imposed and accepted." Reinstatement with full back pay was directed.

Management's Obligation to Deter Potential Violators

When it can be shown that management had an opportunity to deter an employee from committing a dischargeable offense and failed to do so, or that an employee was not permitted to correct a course of conduct in time to avoid punishment, arbitrators may judge the defense to be not merely "technical."

One case in point was that of the *American Machine and Foundry Company* (United Automobile Workers, AFL-CIO).[93] An employee who was given a disciplinary suspension thought he had devised a clever way of minimizing the financial loss: he applied for medical benefits, claiming "permanent disability" payments for days when he was idle solely because of the disciplinary suspension. Oddly enough, the employee made no secret of his plans. He even spoke to a representative of the personnel department about it. It is not possible to know from the award of Benjamin C. Roberts whether that management representative deliberately remained silent, so as to let the employee end his career with the company, or whether he was merely negligent. At any rate, he did nothing to deter the erring employee, who, in due course, was discharged for filing a false claim for medical benefits.

Standing by itself, the employee's attempted fraud merited discharge, Mr. Roberts wrote. But that penalty could not be sustained in this case because the company could and should have tried to deter the grievant.

The company at a crucial point in the events had the opportunity to caution [the grievant] concerning the impropriety and consequences of filing for the disability and medical benefits for the period in question, and pursuing to a conclusion a course of conduct directed toward perverting the use of the disability and medical benefits. Nevertheless, it did not, although the immediate occasion to do so presented itself.

The fact that an attempt to dissuade the grievant might not have been effective was held "not material at this juncture." The non-

93 17 AAA 7.

fulfillment of the company's obligation was a mitigating factor in this case, justifying reinstatement with partial back pay.[94]

Recovering Good Standing

The rule that management must deter employees from wrongdoing whenever possible may also be broadened in application. Often, employees impulsively commit some act of insubordination and quickly recover their sense of responsibility. Arbitrators may require that an avenue of retreat be left open to them. At any rate, if an erring employee offers to perform a job he first refused to do, for instance, discharge for that refusal may not be upheld.

That was what happened at *Babcock and Wilcox Company* (International Brotherhood of Boilermakers, AFL-CIO).[95] An employee first refused a work assignment which he thought was outside his classification. Shortly thereafter, while walking toward the personnel office where a disposition of his case was to be made, the grievant discussed the matter with his steward. On the latter's advice, he promptly offered to do the work as directed. But the offer was rejected. Calling attention to the company's published "Guide for Effective Shop Discipline," which provided for immediate discharge in case of "insubordination or willful disobedience of orders," the employer dismissed the worker.

The award, written by S. S. Kates, pointed out that the grievant had no right to refuse immediate performance of the job. He should have "sought out" the union representative "at a convenient time after performing the job." But the fact that he "repented" constituted a mitigating factor, tending to overcome "any impairment of plant morale which normally might result from refusal of supervisory orders." In the "particular circumstances" of this case, Mr. Kates concluded, discharge was not warranted. Reinstatement without back pay was directed.

Almost the identical issue was presented at the *Paper Products Manufacturing Company* (United Papermakers and Paperworkers, AFL-CIO),[96] where an employee refused a work order. She later

[94] Mr. Roberts said that the grievant's fourteen years of seniority was an additional factor favoring reinstatement.

[95] 17 AAA 15.

[96] 4 AAA 14.

thought better of it and offered to do the work, but management insisted that she first apologize to the foreman whose work order she had declined to obey. She refused to apologize and was given a three-day disciplinary layoff, as punishment both for the refusal of the work order and the refusal to apologize. Whether this penalty was just was the question before John Perry Horlacher, who was selected to resolve the dispute.

It appeared clear, the arbitrator wrote, that if the grievant had apologized, there would have been no penalty at all. The question therefore was: "Does adding the recalcitrance about saying she was sorry warrant adding a three-day suspension?" His conclusion:

[The grievant] was clearly wrong in her initial refusal to follow her foreman's instructions. This serious offense, however, was substantially mitigated by her subsequent reversal of her attitude. What remained of her offense, even if this be regarded as augmented by a refusal to comply with a not improper request for an apology, does not, it seems to me, justify a three-day suspension although some discipline seems warranted. I think this should not go beyond loss of pay for the remainder of the day. This is sufficient punishment for an insubordination which was soon retracted but not regretted.

TECHNICAL DEFENSES

Since arbitration is an avenue of appeal through which the innocent employees (or those who cannot be proven guilty) may preserve their jobs, technical and procedural defenses are often put forward, as they are in courts of law and other forums of adjudication.[97] One of these defenses, based upon an express or implied "statute of limitations," is discussed elsewhere in this chapter. An-

[97] For a case in which the union asserted that "flaws" in management's case during grievance-processing required acquittal of the employee in arbitration, see *Hudson Pulp and Paper Company* (United Papermakers and Paperworkers, AFL-CIO), 20 AAA 9. The discussion of this question by Arbitrator James C. Hill will be found in the next chapter.

See also *J. W. Rex Company* (United Steelworkers of America, AFL-CIO), 7 AAA 13, discussed elsewhere in this chapter. Lewis M. Gill said the employer violated the contract when he refused to recall an employee in his turn. The company's reason was that the grievant had been doing careless work. What the company should have done, he said, was to recall the employee in accordance with his seniority and *then* take whatever action was deemed appropriate. It may be argued that the result would be the same, but the method used by management to accomplish results is often decisive.

other such defense is "double jeopardy." This issue arises when an employee is discharged or otherwise disciplined for an act which also brought him before a criminal court of justice. Does acquittal in court necessarily bar discharge on the same grounds? And does conviction in court automatically justify discharge without any further showing of just cause? It was the first, rather than the second, question that came before Benjamin C. Roberts at *The New York Times Company* (American Newspaper Guild, AFL-CIO),[98] but his discussion sheds light on both questions.

Double Jeopardy

In July 1957, management learned that a supervisor in the composing room of the newspaper was taking bets on horse races. He was discharged. In the course of the investigation, however, it became apparent that extensive gambling and loan shark activities were centered in that department. Arrangements were made with the Police Department for an operative to assume employment there and investigate. As a result of observations extending over a month, several employees were arrested and discharged the same day. They were tried in court and acquitted, whereupon the union filed a grievance protesting the discharge.[99]

The union's first contention was that the employer should not be permitted to accomplish in arbitration what it could not get in a criminal court.

To this, Mr. Roberts replied:

The Court of Special Sessions made its findings under the criminal code. The Arbitrator must make his findings under the contract and within the rules of the forum over which he presides. He cannot be limited to the acceptance of the court's holding or acquittal as dispositive of the issues before him. It can well be that one may not be guilty of a crime and yet have conducted himself in a manner that has given sufficient cause for discharge under the collective bargaining agreement. There can be situations of conviction of criminal conduct which may not be sufficient

[98] 2 AAA 1.

[99] The union demanded reinstatement with back pay, but urged, as an alternative, that if the discharge be sustained, the arbitrator find that no "gross insubordination" was involved. The reason for this request was that, under the collective bargaining agreement, discharged employees were entitled to severance pay unless the discharge was for "gross" misconduct. The severance pay aspect of the case is not relevant to the discussion here.

to justify sustaining a dismissal under a collective contract. The company in the former and the collective bargaining representative in the latter cannot be denied the opportunity to present its own case in arbitration and as a matter of contract application under the criteria agreed upon by the parties.

One of the interesting facts of the case was that the employer had evidence proving the two grievants were conducting gambling activities in the plant, but somehow this had not been put before the jury by the public prosecutor. Without speculating on why the prosecutor had not done so, Mr. Roberts said the failure in the other forum could not foreclose the employer from using the evidence in arbitration.

A second technical issue arose from the refusal of the grievants to take a lie detector test. No adverse inference could be drawn from that refusal. Mr. Roberts said that the fact that the usual rules of evidence do not apply in arbitration "does not mean that the refusal to take a lie detector test in that forum should permit an inference that is not acceptable in other proceedings."

In view of the evidence against the grievants, and in view also of the fact that both had been warned in general (and one personally) against gambling, they were held by the arbitrator to have been "grossly insubordinate," giving them no right to severance pay.

Off-Property Crimes

When an employee is convicted of a crime committed off company property, does that give the employer the right to dismiss him? That issue was presented to Dudley E. Whiting at the *Gear Grinding Machine Company* (United Automobile Workers, AFL-CIO),[100] resulting in a decision in management's favor. One of the facts of the case was that the grievants, who were found guilty of extortion, had preyed on customers of the employer. As these employees could carry out their crimes only because they were employees and union officers, Mr. Whiting said, the company had a clear right to take action against them.[101]

[100] 16 AAA 13.

[101] It should not be inferred that Mr. Whiting would have decided the employees could not be discharged if the crime were in no way connected with the employment relationship. Whether employees convicted of major crimes could be discharged as morally unfit under *any* circumstances was not the precise issue in this case.

The union's chief contention was that the alleged extortion occurred off the premises of the company and outside working hours.
"It is generally recognized," Mr. Whiting wrote, "that an employer
may not exercise his power of discipline to control the private lives
of his employees. However, it is equally well recognized that misconduct, off the employer's premises and outside working hours,
which is attributable to the employment relationship or deleterious
to the interests of the employer is a proper basis for the exercise of
that disciplinary power."

Non-Work-Connected Crimes

The connection between the off-premises crime and the employment relationship which was present in the *Gear Grinding Machine*
case was lacking at *Congoleum-Nairn, Inc.* (United Rubber, Cork,
Linoleum and Plastic Workers, AFL-CIO),[102] which accounts, in
part, for the different outcome. Here, a laid-off employee's recall
rights were terminated following his arrest (off company premises)
and conviction for possessing policy slips. Holding this to be a violation of the agreement, Howard M. Teaf reinstated the employee
with back pay, for five reasons:

1. There was no evidence that he had engaged in gambling activities in the plant
2. His work in the plant was not unsatisfactory, except "on the
   matter of absences"
3. No connection had been established between the grievant's
   absenteeism and his gambling
4. No fellow employees had found it objectionable to work with
   the grievant
5. A newspaper account of the arrest did not identify the grievant as an employee of the company

Mr. Teaf attempted no generalizations as to whether other crimes
committed off company property would be just cause for discharge.[103] In the circumstances of this case, he found the employer's

---

[102] 21 AAA 4.

[103] See also *Federal Bearings Company* (United Automobile Workers, AFL-
CIO), 20 AAA 10, where the employer gave an employee a leave of absence
in advance of his trial for second-degree manslaughter, but refused to extend
the leave after his conviction. This had the effect of discharge. Lloyd H. Bailer
said the refusal to extend the leave was not a violation of the contract under

assertion that continued employment of the grievant would be harm-
ful to the company was merely a "guess," not a "judgment based on
observation." Awards by other arbitrators in cases of other parties
were held not relevant; nor were two incidents of discharge by
management in the instant case of value as "direct precedent." One
of those discharges had been of an employee who went on a "mur-
derous shooting spree." In the other, the employee had made false
claims for unemployment compensation, partly at the company's
expense.

A much more direct precedent[104] was found in a case where it
was held that conviction resulting from "domestic difficulties" did
not warrant discharge when the employee was otherwise satisfactory. Another "pertinent reference"[105] was a case in which it was
held that the right to discharge employees "on sight for intoxication"
did not extend the employer's control to conduct during their own
time and away from the employer's premises.

Finally, Mr. Teaf gave no weight to evidence produced by the
company that the grievant had been convicted of stealing a car

---

the circumstances of the case. He added, however, that his decision was not
to be taken to mean that "any jail sentence, regardless of the duration and
irrespective of the reasons for the sentence" would be sufficient grounds for
discharge.

See also *Baltimore Transit Company* (Amalgamated Association of Street,
Electric Railway and Motor Coach Employees, AFL-CIO), 15 AAA 21, where
a bus driver was discharged after being found guilty of assaulting a police
officer. Arbitrator David H. Stowe upheld the discharge, but said it was "doubtful" that the company had the policy it claimed to have of automatically discharging employees after conviction for criminal offenses. If such a policy existed in the minds of management, he said, it had never been communicated
to the employees. But in any event, he added, such a restricted policy could
probably not be accepted in arbitration. "Such a policy, universally applied,
would ignore the specific facts and circumstances of each case. It is conceiva-
ble that a conviction could result from his conduct while an employee was not
on duty, which would be in no way related to the company's business and in
which the company would have no concern. The propriety of a discharge must
be determined on whether it is justifiable under proper rules and regulations
of the company and on the effect of the act committed by the employee on
his responsibilities as an employee or on the general well-being of the company.
It is the circumstances and specifics of the misconduct which are the basis for
just cause for discharge rather than the mere fact of conviction alone. The
Arbitrator, therefore, must reject the company's contention that conviction of a
criminal offense automatically constitutes just cause for discharge."

[104] *Mansfield Tire & Rubber Co.*, 31 LA 775.
[105] *Lamb Glass Co.*, 32 LA 420.

twenty-eight years ago, when he was eighteen years of age. This, the arbitrator said, "should have no bearing on the character and employability of a man now."

Refusal to Testify before Investigating Committees

American citizens have the right under the Fifth Amendment to the Constitution to refuse to answer questions of Congressional investigation committees where they honestly believe that an answer may be self-incriminating. And in the eyes of the law, no adverse inference may be drawn from such refusal.

But does that mean that no adverse inferences may be drawn in the private sphere of employer-employee relations? May an employee be discharged merely for refusing to testify? May the refusal to testify carry with it such implications for the employment relationship as to constitute just cause for discharge?

These and other questions were dealt with by James C. Hill at *Westinghouse Electric Corporation* (International Union of Electrical, Radio and Machine Workers, AFL-CIO).[106] The grievants were three employees who were discharged after invoking the First and Fifth Amendments before a Congressional committee investigating Communist activities. The employer denied that he discharged them for invoking the Fifth Amendment. He asserted the reason for discharge to be the adverse effect their continued employment would have on customer, employee, government, and public relations. Thus, it appeared from management's position that the dismissals were not thought of as disciplinary at all.

But Mr. Hill said that the tests of "just cause" had to be met in any event.

The termination of these three employees, in the circumstances of the case, cannot be removed from the normal usages of a disciplinary measure. They were released because of acts of voluntary behaviour. It does not alter this fact to point out that the company based its case on the effects of their behaviour on the morale of the employees in the plants and the reputation of the firm among its customers and in the community. Under the circumstances, the employees are entitled to challenge the existence of just cause for their release.

And in applying the test of just cause,

[106] 22 AAA 12.

the presumption must be that an employee may not be discharged, under an Agreement which prohibits discharge without just cause, solely because he invokes the privilege of the Fifth Amendment in response to an inquiry of this kind. Secondly, he may not be properly discharged on the grounds that his refusal to testify warrants the inference that he is guilty. Neither of these considerations is compatible with the fundamental concept of just cause for discharge.

Although ruling that an employee could not be discharged solely for invoking the Fifth Amendment, Mr. Hill observed that "the problem does not end here," for the employer's business interests may be affected by the employee's "legitimate refusal" to testify. Where business needs "counterbalance" fundamental guarantees of individual liberties, he said, the former can prevail only on a showing of "convincing evidence beyond speculation" that the position of the employer was affected adversely by the employee's exercise of his constitutional rights.

Applying this premise to the facts and evidence as presented to him in the arbitration, Mr. Hill ordered the grievants reinstated with back pay, largely for three reasons:

1. The weight of evidence "affords little basis for a firm conviction" that retention of the grievants would have constituted "a significant threat" to the business. Nor would it have impaired relations with the government or customers.

2. There was also "very limited evidence" to support the employer's view that employee morale would have been affected, even taking all statements "at face value."

3. The employer's contention that the grievants were security risks raises not only the question of the weight of evidence but the more important issue "as to whether it is appropriate for a determination of this nature to be made by a private employer."

As the national security system operates through government boards designed to safeguard both the national security and the rights of individuals, he said, determinations of security risks should be made through such agencies, except under "extraordinary circumstances." Furthermore, he added, neither the grievants nor a majority of the employees in the plants where they were employed were engaged in "classified" work. Nor was there evidence of a "threat to the acceptability of the company" as a defense contractor. In any event, the government's *Industrial Security Manual* does not require the discharge of employees who cannot be given access to classified material, and specifically states that whether such employees should be assigned to non-sensitive work "should be resolved consistent with normal employer-employee relationships."

Mr. Hill explained that just cause for discharge would have been established if the company had been told by a government agency that retention of the grievants was "prejudicial" to its obtaining defense contracts. But no evidence of this was presented, he said. A "further consideration" relevant to the employer's ability to obtain defense contracts was the fact that "all of the testimony before the House Committee on Un-American Activities concerning [the grievants] related to their activities and affiliations in the period of approximately 1945 to 1949, and possibly extending to 1953." Nor was there testimony which identified any of these employees as members of the Communist party as of the time of the hearings or at any time during the preceding four or five years. In the case of two of the grievants, there "is no real indication in the record that the public hearings brought forth anything which was not already known to the company."

DENIAL OF CONTRACT BENEFITS AS A FORM OF DISCIPLINE

In a non-union establishment, disciplinary penalties can take almost any form that doesn't violate the law. In addition to the conventional forms of discipline—warnings, suspensions, and discharges—the employer may withhold holiday pay, discriminate in assignment of overtime, transfer to less desirable shifts, lay off during slack periods without regard to seniority, and show favor to some and displeasure with others in dozens of other ways.

Where working conditions are governed by collective bargaining agreements, on the other hand, the employer's powers are generally restricted to the measures within the sequence from reprimand to discharge.[107] So well established is this limitation that not a single

[107] For an excepion to the general rule, see *New York Daily Mirror Division of the Hearst Corporation* (American Newspaper Guild, AFL-CIO), 23 AAA 12, where the employer, after futile warnings, docked wages from weekly salaried employees for "repeated and unjustified lateness." Arbitrator George J.

case has been reported in which management frankly sought to withhold a contract benefit from an erring employee. Nevertheless, the issue of withheld benefits did arise by implication in six cases, most of which were not classified as discipline cases at all.

At the *Oil Heat Engineering Company* (International Brotherhood of Teamsters),[108] for instance, the contract said that in order to receive paid vacations, drivers must have worked at least 125 days during the preceding year. One employee worked exactly 125 days, but on 2 of those days, he had left early, without permission. On the basis of this, the employer denied vacation pay to the driver. The question that came before Peter Seitz was one of vacation pay —whether unauthorized partial absence on 2 days was disqualifying. He said it was not,[109] but he also discussed the implications of the employer's position in the area of discipline. "If the grievant did, in fact, fail or refuse to finish out his day," he wrote, "the company had the right not to compensate him for the hours he took off. More importantly, the company had the right to discipline or discharge employees who fail or refuse to perform their work as scheduled. The non-crediting of days for vacation purposes is not a proper method of exercising the disciplinary authority which every employer possesses unless it is expressly negated by the agreement."

A similar attitude was expressed by Ronald W. Haughton in a case of the *Electro-Mechanical Products Company* (United Automobile Workers, AFL-CIO),[110] where the issue was call-in and holiday pay; but, again, the problem of an improper form of discipline was present.[111] The grievance arose when two employees reported for work two hours late on the day after Labor Day. They were denied admittance to the plant under a "general factory rule"

Mintzer wrote: "Repeated and unjustified lateness may be good and sufficient cause for dismissal. Discharge is the maximum penalty an employer might invoke. A pro rata reduction from an employee's salary for repeated and unjustified lateness is a lesser penalty and may be invoked by the employer rather than the extreme penalty of dismissal." The issue here seemed to be disciplinary only because the grievants were weekly salaried employees. If they had been hourly rated employees, it is doubtful that a union would have thought it amiss to deduct wages for time not worked.

[108] 17 AAA 2.
[109] This aspect of the case is also discussed in Chapter 8.
[110] 17 AAA 10.
[111] The holiday-pay aspect of this case is discussed in Chapter 7.

requiring employees who were more than thirty minutes late to get permission from the foreman "through the Personnel Office" before they could enter. Management refused permission in this case, chiefly because work on this day was required as a condition for receiving holiday pay.

Mr. Haughton observed that permission to enter the plant despite lateness had always been given when the "production schedule was tight." It had been "quite routinely" given immediately before and after this incident. This led to the conclusion that the refusal in this case was disciplinary in nature. Analyzing the case from this point of view, he said it was significant that no "serious consideration" had been given to the reasons the employees had for arriving late. As production requirements were no less urgent on this day than on other days when tardy employees were permitted to work, the award directed call-in pay to the grievants.[112] This also established their eligibility for Labor Day pay.

John Perry Horlacher came upon a similar problem at *Charles Lachman Company* (Textile Workers Union, AFL-CIO);[113] but inasmuch as the employees had disqualified themselves from holiday pay by their partial absence the day before Christmas,[114] it was not necessary for him to resolve the conflict between the union's contention that holiday pay could not be withheld as a form of discipline, on the one hand, and, on the other, the employer's contention that denial of holiday pay was proper discipline in this case. Nevertheless, Mr. Horlacher wrote: "I agree with the prevailing opinion that it is improper to take away benefits guaranteed under a labor contract as a form of punishment. Whether under certain circumstances exceptions should be made to this proposition, as the company contends here, is an issue which ought to be determined only if it is clear that the grievants lost holiday pay benefits to which they were manifestly entitled under the Agreement."

---

[112] The remedy of four hours' call-in pay corresponded to the union's demand. In view of the arbitrator's reasoning, however, one might wonder whether the grievants could have received pay for six hours, if the union had demanded pay for all the hours the grievants were prepared to work. For if what happened was, in effect, unjust discipline, the employee had lost six hours' pay, not four.

[113] 7 AAA 21.

[114] The holiday pay aspect of the case is discussed in Chapter 7.

The fourth case involved overtime at the *Hudson Wire Company* (Allied Industrial Workers, AFL-CIO).[115] In February 1959, management announced that the plant would be in continuous operation for twelve days. On learning this, one of the employees asked his foreman for permission to absent himself from the Saturday-night shift. He was told that if he failed to appear that night, he would not be permitted to work on Sunday, a premium pay day. The employee stayed out Saturday and was consequently denied an opportunity to work Sunday, which brought the matter before Joseph E. Kallenbach. If it be assumed that the grievant was an absentee, the arbitrator said, the proper penalty would have to be that prescribed under plant rules, which called for a reprimand on the first offense, not "an involuntary loss of another day's work at premium pay." The grievant was awarded pay for the Sunday's work of which he had been deprived.

The fifth case, at *J. W. Rex Company* (United Steelworkers of America, AFL-CIO),[116] involved recall from layoff. Here, management refused to recall an employee from layoff in accordance with his seniority, asserting that he was not competent to do the work. The employee had, in fact, been given a written warning for poor work on the day after his layoff; but the arbitrator, Lewis M. Gill, said this did not justify departure from clearly expressed contractual requirements that employees be recalled in reverse order of their layoff:

What the company should have done was to recall [the grievant] and *then* to take whatever action it deemed appropriate because of his poor work. It might be argued that this was a mere procedural irregularity, without any actual showing of damages, and that the case should be treated as though [the grievant] was removed from the job for poor work on November 5th. The difficulty with that approach is that the notice given to [him] on the 5th simply is not, in my opinion, open to such a construction. Following the listing of the defects in his work, there appears the word "Warning." I think the only possible construction to place on that notice is that he *would* be removed from the job *if the defects were not corrected.* If, instead of ending with the word "Warning," the notice had said "Removed from job" or words to that effect, the case would, of course, be different.

[115] 13 AAA 6.
[116] 7 AAA 13.

The sixth case involved unjustified absenteeism, but the employer, *Waller Brothers Stone Company* (United Stone and Allied Products Workers, AFL-CIO),[117] was not trying to discipline the employee directly. The dispute came about when the employee was disqualified for a job because of his attendance record. As the contract did not refer to absenteeism as a ground for disqualification, and as another provision of the agreement provided penalties for unjustified absences, Harry J. Dworkin said that to uphold the employer would amount to adding penalties. It was also pertinent to his decision that the contract provided for a trial period of up to thirty days when an employee bumped a junior out of a job. This trial period was sufficient to protect the employer's interests if the applicant's attendance record didn't improve, Mr. Dworkin said.

[117] 22 AAA 2. This case is also discussed in Chapter 3.

11

NON-DISCIPLINARY TERMINATIONS OF EMPLOYMENT

The word "discharge," in labor relations, has come to be associated with disciplinary action by the employer, taken against an employee who offends too seriously or too often against reasonable rules of conduct. Thus, discharge is a penalty for a voluntary act which the employee knew, or should have known, was endangering his job. But not all discharges are disciplinary in nature. Some come about for reasons over which the employee may have no control. Incompetence, as distinct from carelessness or deliberate inattention, is one example. Physical disability is another. In this category may also be included absenteeism cases, where circumstances make it impossible for the worker to improve his record of attendance.[1] There are borderline cases, to be sure; incompetence may look like carelessness, and one may not always be certain that an employee has done all he could to avoid absences. But the distinction between disciplinary and non-disciplinary terminations is, nevertheless, an important one; for in clear cases, at least, the usual standards of "just cause" for discharge and the sequence of warnings and penalties preceding discharge do not apply.

Cases involving termination of employees for reasons other than misconduct were found to involve: probationary employees; workers deemed incompetent or physically unable to work safely; involuntary absentees; employees whose recall rights were cancelled

---

[1] For an example of a non-disciplinary absentee case, see *P. Sorenson Manufacturing Company, Inc.* (United Automobile Workers, AFL-CIO), 1 AAA 14. Thomas A. Knowlton held that the employer had the right to discharge an employee who was absent 111 days in 10 months, despite the fact that the absences, caused by physical disability, were unavoidable. The employer is within his rights in terminating employment of such a worker, he wrote, "not as a disciplinary matter but simply because the employer has a right to expect a reasonable level of productive attendance."

after they had been on layoff beyond a stated period; and employees who, in effect, were discharged by being denied leaves of absence.[2]

PROBATIONARY EMPLOYEE DISPUTES

During the first thirty days of employment, under the typical collective bargaining agreement, an employee has no seniority rights and no job security. As that period is generally intended to give management an opportunity to judge his suitability and make a final decision about keeping him, discharges are usually permitted during this time without a showing of just cause.[3] But this does not necessarily mean that probationary employees have no rights under a collective bargaining agreement. Many provisions of the contract give employees rights that do not depend on seniority, and such provisions may apply to probationary employees no less than to others. This creates an area where management's actions with respect to new employees may be protested and reviewed in arbitration.

Notice in Layoff

For instance, at the *Baker Castor Oil Company* (Oil, Chemical

[2] One case, involving an employee who wanted a leave of absence to cover time he was to spend in prison, was included in this chapter. Although misconduct of the employee was an element in the employer's refusal of the leave, the direct issue before the arbitrator was not "just cause" for discharge as such, but management's right to deny a leave and to regard the absent employee as having abandoned his job.

[3] Although the *Electric Storage Battery Company* (International Union of Electrical, Radio and Machine Workers, AFL-CIO), 17 AAA 13, had the right to discharge probationary employees without a showing of just cause, Bert L. Luskin, who heard the case, held that a dispute over such a discharge was arbitrable. However, he added, as he would have no right to consider "the merits or justification of the discharge," the grievance protesting the discharge was denied without further hearing. After listening to arguments on the arbitrability aspects of the case, he wrote that it "would serve no useful purpose" to conduct further hearings on the merits of the discharge. "Although the grievance is arbitrable since it involves the interpretation and application of specific provisions of the agreement, the grievance must be denied for the reasons hereinbefore set forth, since the contract provisions would not permit the arbitrator to grant the relief sought." For comments on the arbitrability aspect of this decision, see "Do We Need a New Look at Arbitrability?" in *The Arbitration Journal*, Vol. 15, No. 4 (1960), p. 161.

and Atomic Workers, AFL-CIO)[4] there was a provision requiring the employer to give employees five days' notice before layoff. The contract also contained the usual clause requiring employees to complete thirty days of service "in order to have seniority rights." In June 1958, five probationary employees were laid off with only three days of notice. When the union protested, the company answered that notice was not required in this case because probationers are regarded as employees without contractual rights, where layoffs are concerned. Furthermore, it would be unrealistic to have to give five days' notice to employees who could be discharged at will without a moment's notice. To interpret the contract as the union urged, management argued, would change the thirty-day probationary period to a twenty-five day period and guarantee new employees five days of work or pay.

This defense was not persuasive with Monroe Berkowitz, who had been selected to decide the case. True, he said, the employer could have discharged the probationers "for almost any reason," but they were not discharged. They were laid off. That made all the difference.

Notice of Termination

At the *Philadelphia Inquirer* (Newspaper Guild, AFL-CIO),[5] management was faced with a grievance not because notice had not been given, but because it had. The contract called for a three-month probationary period, "during which the employee may be dismissed upon two weeks notice" without a showing of "good and reasonable cause." In February 1959, a copy boy, nearing the end of his probationary period, was given notice of discharge, effective two weeks later. As he was permitted to work to the end of his notice period, it resulted in five days of work beyond the day on which he would have acquired the status of a regular employee.

The union's contention was that, despite the notice, the employee survived his probationary period and could be discharged only for cause. The company answered that it had satisfied the only obligations it had with respect to a probationer. A bona fide decision had

[4] 1 AAA 4.
[5] 11 AAA 22.

been made as to his employability, and two weeks' notice had been given.

Frederick Harbison arbitrated the case. He said that the first part of the critical clause[6] could be interpreted to support the union position; but the last phrase, giving the employer three months "during which a bona fide decision by the Inquirer of the employee's employability shall be final" suggested an opposite answer. Both parts of the clause "begin with the words 'during which' and clearly refer to the three month probationary period. The latter phrase does not conform to the Guild's view that a dismissed employee's last day worked must fall within the period, because it states clearly that the company has this same period 'during which' to make a bona fide decision."

Thus, he said, if the union's interpretation were upheld, it would mean that the company would have had not three months to make the decision about whether to keep an employee but three months less two weeks. "If the company is precluded from making its decision within the final two weeks of the probationary period," he reasoned, "these final two weeks are improperly included under the designation 'probationary period.' "[7]

Calendar Days vs. Days of Work

When a contract gives an employer thirty days within which to make a final decision about a worker's employability, does it mean thirty calendar days or thirty days of work? Must the thirty days be consecutive? What is the effect of partial days of absence on an

[6] The full text of the clause read: "The Inquirer will not discharge any employee except for good and reasonable cause; provided that the first three (3) months of employment shall be a probationary period during which the employee may be dismissed upon two weeks' notice in writing (except that in the case of persons who had been unemployed when coming to the Inquirer the two weeks' notice shall not be required if the person is dismissed within the first two weeks of employment); and during which a bona fide decision by the Inquirer of the employee's employability shall be final."

[7] This decision was in line with past practice. It appeared that in the previous two years there were three cases in which probationary employees were permitted to work out their notice period, thus working eight, six, and twelve days, respectively, beyond the end of the three-month period. Although the Guild had known of these incidents, no objection had been raised, nor did the matter come up in subsequent negotiations.

employee's acquisition of seniority? These are questions that arose in three cases.

The least complicated of the three was that of *Fab-Weld Corporation* (International Union of Electrical, Radio and Machine Workers, AFL-CIO).[8] G. Allan Dash's award was that employees who were laid off before their first thirty days were up and later hired for another period of less than thirty days did not acquire seniority despite the fact that both periods of employment totaled more than thirty days. The employer was therefore not required "to advance any sustainable position" for terminating them. In short, when they were rehired, it was as new employees.

The union had argued that "two pieces of work" occurring within the same year must be added together for purposes of establishing the point at which an employee acquires seniority, but Mr. Dash said he could not agree with that interpretation, for it would amount to an alteration of the agreement. He pointed out that there was nothing in the contract "which recognizes this one-year qualification." And if he were to uphold the grievance without the one-year qualification, he said, it might affect the seniority rights of present and future employees in a way that neither party would like.

The second case was like the first, except that here probationary employees were "released" and rehired more than once, giving rise to a suspicion that the contract was being deliberately evaded. That was the basis of a grievance at *Borg-Warner Corporation* (United Automobile Workers, AFL-CIO).[9] Despite the union's suspicions, however, there was sufficient evidence for a finding by Ronald W. Haughton that no violation had occurred.

The status of three rehired grievants was that of brand new employees, Mr. Haughton ruled. He gave three reasons: (1) the union had been informed of their earlier dismissal, accepting the term "release," which the employer had used, as synonymous with discharge; (2) the apparent reason for using the word "release" was to create a better impression on subsequent employers; and (3) the grievants were consistently given new clock numbers with each new term of employment. "Since the record is clear that the parties understood that released probationary employees, in fact, were dis-

[8] 17 AAA 12.
[9] 22 AAA 11.

charged, for whatever reason, it follows that the employment status, if renewed, would have to be in the nature of a new hire," Mr. Haughton concluded.

The third case, *R. T. French Company* (United Packing House Workers, AFL-CIO),[10] involved a more complicated set of facts. The contract said that employees who have been "in the employ of the company" for less than thirty days may be discharged with or without just cause. But it did not indicate whether thirty days of work or thirty calendar days were meant.

The basic facts were undisputed. An employee was hired on January 25, 1960, and worked continuously, eight hours per day, five days per week, through March 7, 1960, except for the following lost time:

1. She was permitted to leave work one hour early on February 16 because her daughter had suffered an accident in school. She received pay for seven hours that day.

2. She left work one hour early on February 19, when all employees were sent home because of a severe snowstorm. Again, she was paid only for the time worked—seven hours, but the company credited this as a full day of work for purposes of computing the probationary period.

3. She performed no work on February 23 because of a death in the immediate family. She was paid in full for the day under a contractual provision giving employees up to three days' pay for absence due to death in the family.

The grievant was notified a few minutes before the end of her shift on March 7 that she was being discharged, but was permitted to work to the end of the shift. Thus, her employment history included these facts:

Total calendar days worked	43
Total days on which pay was received	31
Total hours for which pay was received	246
Total actual hours worked	238

The union argued that the grievant had survived her probationary period and could therefore not be discharged without a showing of

[10] 21 AAA 21.

just cause. Thus, there was presented this sequence of questions for William E. Simkin, the arbitrator, to answer:

a. Is the "probationary period" 30 calendar days?
b. If the "probationary period" is not 30 calendar days,
    1. Does the employee cease to be a probationary employee when she works and is paid for the entire last day of the "probationary period" and is notified of termination only a few minutes before the end of the shift?
    2. Is a full "day" to be counted if the employee leaves the work place for any reason before completion of 8 paid hours of work?
    3. Is a "day" to be counted when the employee is paid for the day under a labor agreement provision even though no actual work is performed that day?

The more comprehensive question—calendar days vs. days of work—was resolved in the company's favor. The history of bargaining supported the employer's assertion that the current contract language was intended to extend the probationary period by one day for each day of absence. But the kind of absence the negotiators had in mind, Mr. Simkin added, was a voluntary absence "for the usual reasons." This did not include days paid for but not worked, in accordance with some other contractual provision. Thus, February 23 had to be credited as time worked for purposes of determining when the probationary period was completed.

The union was upheld on the matter of a partial day's absence—such a day had to be credited as a full day worked, even though it was not fully paid for.

There is nothing in the agreement or in evidence of intent that supports a definition of thirty days as exactly 240 hours of work, despite the definition of a normal work day as eight hours. A day must be counted as a day whether it be a short day or a day that includes a couple of hours of overtime.

The final question was decided in management's favor. Mr. Simkin was not persuaded by the union's contention that an employee completes her probationary period and acquires seniority at the end of the eighth hour of work on the thirtieth day, even though notice of termination was given earlier. If an employee is to be terminated, he said, it is obvious that not much work can be expected of her after she learns of it. This makes it advisable to notify her as near to quitting time as practicable. Furthermore, it would not necessarily be to the union's advantage to hold otherwise, for that would compel the employer to give new workers less than a thirty-day trial. In "doubtful cases," it might be better for the employee to get all possible time to establish qualifications.

The effect of Mr. Simkin's answers to the four questions was to find that the grievant in this case had already survived her probationary period when she was notified of termination. In accordance with a stipulation of the parties, reinstatement with back pay was directed "without further argument as to whether the company did or did not have proper cause for the termination."

Discriminatory Discharge

Although employers are not usually required by contract to justify discharges of probationary employees, they may be required to do so when the union asserts that discrimination for union activity was the real reason for the termination. When such an assertion is made, however, the burden of proof is heavily upon the union. In this respect, Bert L. Luskin pointed out, in a case involving *The Magnavox Company* (International Union of Electrical, Radio and Machine Workers, AFL-CIO),[11] that the union must be prepared to prove that the grievant was discharged "for that reason and that reason alone." This burden of proof would be similar to that borne by employers who try to establish "just cause" for discharging senior employees.[12]

According to the union, the grievant had been a satisfactory employee, performing her assignments without company criticism until, at a lunch hour meeting of the union one day, she offered to accept the post of department steward upon completion of her probationary period. Following this, she was told that her work was falling short.

---

[11] 20 AAA 8.

[12] The clause which gave the union an opportunity to grieve in behalf of the probationer read: "New employees hired by the Company having less than sixty (60) days of actual work service with the Company shall be considered as probationary employees and have no seniority; however, if retained by the Company beyond their probationary period, their seniority shall date from date of hiring. The discharge of probationary employees shall be subject to the grievance procedure, only if the discharge is discriminatory because of Union membership or activity."

Her discharge soon followed. All this occurred within the probationary period.

As further proof of the causal connection between the grievant's union activity and the criticism of her work, the union pointed out that the employee who replaced her was permitted to produce at "considerably below" the level she had attained.

There was no doubt, Mr. Luskin wrote, that the grievant related her discharge to her willingness to accept union office. But he was not convinced that the connection was more than coincidental. Furthermore, "the fact that other employees may or may not have been able to attain an efficiency rating of 100 percent would have no bearing on the issue," he said. In fact, as "just cause" was no issue where a probationary employee was involved, it would serve no useful purpose to compare the production records of the grievant with those of any other employee. "The company can set any standards that it deems appropriate for probationary employees, and can evaluate the services of a probationary employee using any standards or guides that it may decide to follow."

Finally, the fact that the contract in this establishment provided for a union shop, making it obligatory for new employees to become members after a stated interval, added to the burden the union had to carry if it was to prove discrimination. "Other stewards are elected, and there is no evidence in the record which could support any contention that the election of a steward, as such, would or could lead to discrimination because of an employee's functioning in that capacity."

INCOMPETENCE

It is almost an axiom that an employee who is unable to perform with reasonable competence on a job may be discharged. But what happens when such an employee is retained for many years despite "marginal" work? Does she thereby acquire a contractual right to continue at that level? That was the question put before Burton B. Turkus in a case at the *Royal McBee Corporation* (United Automobile Workers, AFL-CIO).[13]

[13] 21 AAA 16.

The grievant in this case was a factory clerk, described by Mr. Turkus as "a mature, intelligent, well-mannered individual who throughout her long employment has earnestly endeavored to perform her duties as a satisfactory employee." The difficulty was that in eleven years of employment, she had never done satisfactory work. But she was not discharged. Instead, she was "passed from foreman to foreman," until the most recent transfer, in 1957, to a department where her work became "increasingly and inordinately slow, inaccurate and inadequate." Finally, in October 1959, she was discharged for incompetence.

Mr. Turkus upheld the discharge, but not without strong censure of management. It was understandable, he said, that a foreman should try to be a "good Joe" and "pass the buck" to another supervisor, but it was a service neither to the employee nor to the company. All that was accomplished was a "lamentable waste of years" for the employee, leading to a "final and demoralizing humiliation."

The company had a moral obligation to find some other work for the grievant, the arbitrator said. But the company had the right, under the contract, to discharge her. As the task of the arbitrator was to rule on contract rights, he saw no alternative but to deny the grievance "despite the conviction that, in the setting and under the circumstances of this particular case, the exercise of that right in the manner here employed was neither fittingly considerate nor especially conducive to a more harmonious and understanding labor-management relationship."

Demotion for Incompetence

A less drastic way of coping with incompetence is, of course, to demote the employee to a more suitable job, rather than discharge him. Although this more lenient course preserves the employment relationship, it nevertheless raises questions about job security and contractual rights. At the *Union Oil Company* (Oil, Chemical and Atomic Workers, AFL-CIO),[14] for instance, the issue was whether a man who qualified for maintenance helper could be demoted to laborer two years later because of "inadequate" work.

The only reference in the contract to demotion was in a provision calling for application of seniority when employees were to be

[14] 5 AAA 21.

downgraded. As the grievant had more seniority than other maintenance helpers, and as the latter were permitted to continue in that
semiskilled classification, it was on this seniority-in-demotion clause
that the union relied.

That provision was "clearly not applicable," Howard F. LeBaron
wrote. It was intended only for situations where downgrading was
made necessary by reduction in force. The lapse of time since the
grievant qualified, he said, was important. But the importance lay
in the heavy burden of proof it placed on the employer, not in a bar
against downgrading as such. That burden of proof was met in this
case. It was particularly in management's favor that the decision to
demote had not been made "lightly" or "capriciously." By attempts
to help the grievant overcome his deficiencies,[15] supervision had
demonstrated "fairness and equity." Finally, the record contained
no hint of hostility on the part of management either toward the
union or the grievant.

To the same effect was a decision of Sidney Sugerman in the
case of *Peter J. Schweitzer, Inc.* (United Papermakers and Paperworkers, AFL-CIO).[16] Here, too, an employee was downgraded,
after surviving his trial period and working sixteen months on a job.
The employer's action did not purport to be disciplinary; the grievant's low production, which was the cause of the downgrading, was
not alleged to be purposeful.

No formal production standards had ever been established in this
plant, the only contract provision relevant to the dispute being one
which said that "the ability of any employee to perform the type of
work shall be subject to the joint judgment of the company and the
union," with grievance procedure and arbitration as the means of
resolving differences.

To determine whether the evidence justified downgrading in cases
of this kind, Mr. Sugerman wrote, it would be necessary to rely on
one or more of three criteria:

1. The standards the parties would themselves apply, in terms of
   their past practice
2. The "external standards in common industrial experience"

---

[15] The grievant had been urged to attend classes, but he chose not to act
on this suggestion.
[16] 21 AAA 22.

3. The "more fair and reasonable" of the respective contentions of the parties as to the grievant's ability

In view of the nature of the case, he said, he was relying on the third approach. The company's evidence had consisted mostly of production records showing that the grievant had consistently performed below the level of other employees in his classification. This evidence, if it had stood alone, would not have been persuasive, Mr. Sugerman said. "An employee may well be at or near the bottom of productivity showings in his unit and still be adequate to his job." In this case, however, "evidentiary tabulations from production records" were supplemented by testimony about the grievant's "shortcomings" and by efforts by management to help him overcome them. "While it is true that other employees also had low production records and low rates of improvement, there is nothing in the record to demonstrate or even suggest that any of them also had comparable shortcomings in specific details of workmanship."

Although the grievance was denied, Mr. Sugerman was not convinced that management's preliminary measures had been flawless. If a "final warning" had been more timely, the ultimate decision to demote the grievant "might have appeared more correct" to him and to the union. Despite that observation, however, Mr. Sugerman concluded, somewhat as Mr. Turkus did in the *Royal McBee* case, that the task of the arbitrator is not to rule on whether there is "some equitable bar" to the company's assertion of incompetence, but to decide whether the employee is able to perform the work within the meaning of the contract. "The latter question, in all the circumstances, must be answered in the negative."

MEDICAL DISCHARGES, DEMOTIONS, AND LAYOFFS

Determining a worker's competence presents no unusual problems for management, it being generally acknowledged that only the employer is qualified to make that determination in the first instance. But when a decision must be made as to whether a worker is physically fit to work or whether his medical condition constitutes a hazard, difficulties of a different order appear. For here, management must often rely not on its own judgment but on the advice of medical specialists. And medical specialists have been known to differ among themselves. The dilemma of conflicting medical evidence is also one which confronts arbitrators.[17]

Avoiding Choice among Medical Opinions

Faced with such a problem at *E. W. Bliss Company* (United Steelworkers of America, AFL-CIO),[18] Edwin R. Teple, called in to arbitrate the disagreement, resolved it without actually deciding which of the "contrary opinions" of medical authorities was the more accurate. He ruled, in effect, that as long as the management acted on the advice of a reputable physician, qualified to give that advice, it didn't matter that another doctor, not engaged by the company, was of a different opinion.

The issue in this case, briefly stated, was whether the company had the right to discharge an employee on a finding by the company doctor that he was suffering from paresis, in addition to other disorders. During the extended discussions of the grievance that followed the company doctor's report, the employee was examined by other doctors, one of whom pronounced him "physically qualified to perform ordinary duties at work." Despite this advice, the worker was refused reinstatement.

Citing a half-dozen published awards by other arbitrators, Mr. Teple said he agreed, in general, with the prevailing view that "the company retains the inherent right to terminate or discharge

[17] One case, decided by A. Langley Coffey, illustrates the extent of confusion possible for a layman who must resolve contradictory diagnoses. By the time this case reached him, the grievant, who was allegedly suffering from a cardiac disorder, had been examined by six physicians, not counting doctors retained by a workmen's compensation board. Some were general practitioners; others were specialists. One doctor who advised the return of the grievant to his job was shown to have had little understanding of the nature of the work. Furthermore, the examinations occurred over a long period of time, when the patient was in various stages of relapse and recovery. For a layman forced to choose among medical diagnoses, this constituted an additional difficulty; for it was clear that the doctors were not really dealing with exactly the same medical problem. Mr. Coffey's decision was that management had done "no more in the instant case than exercise a sound managerial judgment by refusing to permit the grievant to exercise his seniority at this time and under all the conditions existing." But this did not mean, he added, that the employee could be deprived of his seniority. His seniority "remains unimpaired," to be asserted in the future for a job "if there is a substantial change for the better in grievant's physical and mental condition" [*Kerr-McGee Oil Industries, Inc.* (Oil, Chemical and Atomic Workers, AFL-CIO), 2 AAA 10].

[18] 19 AAA 7.

(in the broader sense of the word) an employee who is no longer capable of regularly performing the duties of whatever job or jobs may be available." The only question to be decided was whether the determination in this instance was "fairly made," based upon "reliable information or advice."

The company was entitled to rely and act upon the judgment and advice of its own doctor, provided there is no substantial evidence that the grievant had been treated in an unfair or discriminatory manner. It is not up to the Arbitrator, even if he were competent to do so, to decide which doctor is right or whose judgment he would be inclined to follow. So long as the grievant has been given a fair opportunity to present contrary evidence or to rebut the opinion of the company's own medical adviser, the company's final determination should not be disturbed in circumstances such as these.[19]

Some of the evidence on the grievant's behalf consisted of a showing that he continued to operate two businesses (a repair shop and a slag-hauling company) on his own time before and after the discharge. This evidence, Mr. Teple said, was "not enough" to alter his conclusion that the grievant was not in fit condition for regular work. At best, it proved that he was capable of working part of the time. But this did not affect the employer's case, because "it was not necessary for the company to determine that he could never physically perform the functions of the job."

[19] Mr. Teple added: "This rule has also been adopted by other arbitrators in similar situations. In *Lone Star Steel Co.*, 20 LA 710, the employee was suffering from a heart condition and sugar diabetes. The employer's refusal to reinstate him after his return from an extended illness was held to be justified on the basis of the recommendation of the company's doctor, notwithstanding the testimony of the employee's own doctor that he could do his job satisfactorily and without danger if he did not overexert himself or become emotionally upset. In *Ideal Cement Co.*, 20 LA 480, the employer was held to be justified in refusing to rehire an employee after an operation for a brain tumor, on the basis of its medical adviser's report that continued employment would endanger the safety of the employee himself and others. This ruling was made in the face of contrary opinions expressed by three other doctors, one of whom testified in person, that the employee could work without danger to himself or others, as well as testimony that the grievant had been operating his own farm. The cases found in which the employer's determination that the employee was not physically capable of doing any work failed to receive support, lacked the medical authority existing in this case and the others cited above, or were fundamentally different in other respects. See *Temco Aircraft Corp.*, 22 LA 826; *Whitney Chain Co.*, 24 LA 385; *Peter Breidt Brewing Co.*, 12 LA 9."

"Preponderance" of Medical Evidence

A conflict of medical testimony was resolved differently by John A. Hogan at *Shahmoon Industries, Inc.* (United Steelworkers of America, AFL-CIO);[20] but there was a "strong preponderance of medical evidence" on one side, in this case, which made it different from that before Mr. Teple.

Two employees were barred from work on a finding by the company doctor that they were suffering from heart disease. The personal physician of these employees found no disabling condition; and the Lahey Clinic, to which they were later sent, supported the conclusion that they were able to work.

Mr. Hogan upheld the grievance. "The company doctor is not a heart specialist," he wrote. "No electrocardiogram was taken. No details of the doctor's findings were submitted in evidence." On the other hand, the private physician was "a specialist in internal medicine" whose report stated that an electrocardiogram was taken, showing no change for several years. A comprehensive examination was also made by the Lahey Clinic, "with emphasis on heart evaluations." Its "impartial report" advised that the employees were able "to return to work on a normal job capacity." In view of the preponderance of medical evidence in favor of the grievants, the employer was directed to reinstate the two employees.

Effect of Findings by Public Agencies

Cases involving conflict of medical evidence are sometimes complicated by decisions of government boards and physicians employed by public agencies as to an employee's condition. Is the arbitrator then bound by such rulings? In the *E. W. Bliss* case, referred to above, for instance, the union had argued that the grievant, having been denied a disability pension under the Social Security Act, had to be presumed to be able to work. The arbitrator, Edwin R. Teple, disagreed. Disqualification in that forum, he said, was not binding on him, because he had to observe a different set of standards. To be eligible for disability payments, the employee would have to be "totally unable to perform any useful service whatever," and it would have to be determined that "this total and

[20] 19 AAA 8.

absolute inability will be permanent." His own frame of reference, on the other hand, was the collective bargaining agreement and the employer-employee relationship. For that reason, he concluded, a man did not have to be completely disabled before an arbitrator could find him unfit for work.

John W. Seybold, arbitrating a case at *Lebanon Steel Foundry* (United Steelworkers of America, AFL-CIO),[21] expressed himself more fully on the reasons why arbitrators need not feel bound by findings of other forums.

The grievant, an employee with a "long and continuous history of physical disability," had been cleared by the company's medical director for light work, but was not permitted to return from layoff to his regular laboring job. He thereupon applied for workmen's compensation, but partly on the findings of his own physician that he was fit to work, no disability payments were awarded.

"Is it possible for a man to be fit enough to be denied workmen's compensation and yet not fit enough to perform the available work?" Mr. Seybold asked. His answer:

It is not our responsibility to judge whether or not the criteria applied by the Workmen's Compensation authorities are or are not reasonable, or whether or not they should be related to the type of work the employee has performed in the past, or the type of work presently available; but it most certainly cannot follow that every employee who is denied Compensation must therefore be considered, by definition, physically fit to perform any and every type of employment. Under all the circumstances, we find that the company has not violated the contract in continuing to consider [the grievant] as available for those types of employment which do not involve heavy labor. The union's grievance is accordingly denied.

ABOLITION OF RECALL RIGHTS AFTER LONG ABSENCE OR LAYOFF

Collective bargaining agreements often contain provisions cutting off seniority and recall rights of employees who have not worked for a stated period of time. Such clauses are usually intended primarily to clear the rolls of laid-off employees who have no practical prospect of being recalled. But those provisions may also apply to

[21] 17 AAA 18.

employees whose physical condition makes a return to work un-likely. In short, termination-of-seniority clauses gives the employer the right to effect non-disciplinary discharges.

The contract at *Bird and Son, Inc.* (United Papermakers and Paperworkers, AFL-CIO)[22] listed sixteen grounds for discharge and six additional reasons for non-disciplinary termination of seniority, but long-term absence was not mentioned in either category. Never-theless, management believed it had the right to terminate an em-ployee who faced a twelve- to eighteen-month period of absence due to physical disability. The employer's asserted ground was a general clause giving management the right to "relieve employees from duty because of legitimate reasons."

Arbitrator A. R. Marshall disagreed with this view. The very fact that the contract described in such detail circumstances for termina-tion of seniority operated to exclude other, unlisted circumstances. He recalled the "general rule" of contract interpretation that "when one or more things of a class are expressly mentioned, others of the same class are excluded."

The union's contentions in this case were also supported by cita-tions of awards by other arbitrators for other parties. Mr. Marshall found the factual situations "somewhat different" from that in the case before him, but at least two were "helpful":

In both cases, as in the instant dispute, there was no long-term sickness or disability clause in the contract. In the *Don Lee Broadcasting System* case (1 LA 571) an employee who had been sick about 10 weeks was ordered reinstated to his job by Arbitrator William Strong, with the finding that he should be regarded as having been on a leave of absence. *The International Harvester Company* case (24 LA 274) involved a permanently-disabled employee, with over 25 years of service and need-ing only three years to retire with disability benefits, who was terminated after having been off his job for three years. Arbitrator W. Willard Wirtz found no contract provision specifically covering the issue of termination but thought that the grievant was entitled to remain on company rolls for an equal length of time as laid-off employees (who under the con-tract could retain seniority for a period equal to length of service).

Although the grievant in the instant case was a young man, with relatively low seniority, the situation was similar to the two cases

[22] 18 AAA 19.

referred to because all turned on contracts which contained no specific provisions covering long-term disability.

LEAVES OF ABSENCE

When an employee must be absent from work for an extended period of time, whether for medical or other reasons, a leave of absence which keeps his job open pending his return becomes an important element in job security. Employees are not, however, automatically entitled to leaves, for this is a right or privilege that exists only to the extent that collective bargaining agreements provide for it. For instance, at the *Belgian Lines, Inc.* (Office Employees International Union, AFL-CIO),[23] after the union won recognition and negotiated its first contract, management decided its policy would be to give the employees all the contract benefits and nothing more. Some time later, one of the employees asked for "a paid leave and/or an advance on his paid vacation," so that he might visit a foster parent who was then critically ill. The company refused the leave, and the union brought the matter to arbitration.

Sidney Sugerman, who heard the case, said that although the company was apparently "determined to deal with personnel as severely as need be within the new set of rights and duties fixed by contract with the union," it was within management's rights to follow that course. "As [the grievant] was not entitled to paid leave as such for this absence, it was no act of discrimination to deny it to him though he and others may have enjoyed that sympathetic consideration before the union came on the scene." In short, it may have been "harsh" to deny the leave, but it was "not necessarily unjust," and it was no violation of contractual rights.

Leaves for Short-Service Employees

When an employee is on leave of absence, his job can be filled by another only on a temporary basis. Because it is not always easy to do so, employers are sometimes understandably reluctant to extend the leave privilege to recently hired workers. It was for such a reason that management of the *Simmons Company* (Upholsterers

[23] 8 AAA 5.

Union, AFL-CIO)[24] decreed that no employee with less than six months of service would be permitted to take a leave of absence. This rule was tested in arbitration when it was invoked to deny a medical leave to an employee who had survived her probationary period but had not yet worked a half-year.[25] The only contractual provisions relevant to the issue were:

Article 7.03. Seniority shall continue and accumulate while the employee is continuously employed by the COMPANY and during the following periods of absence from work, if leave for such absence is approved and granted by the COMPANY in writing:
  (a) A leave of absence for disability or illness . . .

. . . .

Article 7.04. *Termination of Seniority.* Seniority shall be terminated for the following reasons:

. . . .

  (b) When the employee is discharged for just cause. . . ."

It was a violation of this clause, arbitrator A. C. Russell held, both to pronounce the restrictive policy and to apply it in this case. The employer had argued that the quoted clause applied only *when* the company grants a leave and that the granting as such was a matter within management's discretion. This was a misreading of the clause, the arbitrator said:

The contention of the company that the employee is not entitled to a leave of absence on the ground of illness unless it approves and grants the leave in writing is too broad. That argument leads to the conclusion that the company could grant or refuse such leaves in its discretion. Yet, it is clear that Article 7.03 contemplates that leaves of absence will be granted to employees who are ill. Indeed, there would be little or no purpose served by writing the Article if it merely says that an ill employee may have a leave of absence provided the company in its discretion grants it in writing. If the employee is ill, it is the duty of the company to approve and grant a request for a leave of absence provided the request has been made in an appropriate manner.

The company had also tried to show that it was a "long-standing policy" not to grant medical leaves to short-term employees, but the only evidence was instances in which leaves *were* granted to

[24] 20 AAA 23.
[25] The justifiable cause of absence was not in itself an issue, as the employee had to undergo an operation for appendicitis. Nor was there any question about her offer to return to work as soon as she was physically able to do so.

employees with longer service. For a finding of past practice, Mr. Russell said, it would be necessary to show that there were instances where ill employees with less than six months' service had been denied leaves in the past. This had not been done.

Leave to Cover Jail Sentence

In the *Simmons* case, as we have seen, the denial of a leave was based on the employee's short service; there was no allegation of misconduct. The situation was different at the *Hudson Pulp and Paper Company* (United Papermakers and Paperworkers, AFL-CIO).[26] Here, an employee was denied a leave and refused reinstatement after ninety days in jail as a second-offender drunken driver.

The contract provided for leaves of absence when, "in the judgment of the company," there was "justifiable cause." James C. Hill, the arbitrator, agreed with the company that a leave of absence could be denied in this case, but he did not accept all of the employer's arguments and reasoning. The contract did indeed give management wide discretion in granting or refusing to grant leaves, but this did not mean that the company's judgment was necessarily final or that it could not be reviewed to see whether it conformed to reasonable standards.[27]

"There is an implied obligation," Mr. Hill wrote, "that the company will not act in an arbitrary or discriminatory manner." The emphasis in the leave-of-absence clause on the words "shall," "judgment," and "justifiable" means that "the company is called upon to make a judgment based on reason, not whim."[28]

---

[26] 20 AAA 9.

[27] The employer did not contest arbitrability in this case; but according to the arbitrator, if management's contentions were upheld in full, it would mean that the employer's decision in any case would be "substantially" removed from "challenge by the employee or the union."

[28] The full text of the leave-of-absence clause read: "Article 1. Personal Leave. A leave of absence for personal reasons not to exceed 90 days shall be granted employees if, in the judgment of the Company, such leave is for justifiable cause. All requests for leave must be in writing and the Union will be notified of any leaves granted. Leaves for more than ninety days will only be granted by the Company with the agreement of the Local Union. Any employee will be considered as having quit if he fails to return to work at the end of his leave or if he accepts employment elsewhere. Seniority shall accumulate during such leave."

While the language did not place management's decision beyond review, Mr. Hill continued, it did not give an arbitrator the right to subject it to "full review." It would have been readily possible, he said, for the parties not to have used phrases like "in the judgment of the company." The inclusion of that phrase, therefore, "must be presumed to have some meaning and purpose." That meaning, he concluded, was that "a mere difference of viewpoint on the part of the union or the arbitrator as to the wisdom and fairness of the company's decision is wholly insufficient to set it aside."[29]

Leave for "Personal Business"

When a contract gives employees the right to leaves of absence to take care of "personal business," it would seem, at first glance, that it should apply to a leave for the purpose of caring for one's six-year-old child. Nevertheless, management of the *Warwick Manufacturing Company* (International Union of Electrical, Radio and Machine Workers, AFL-CIO)[30] was upheld in its decision not to grant that kind of a leave to a young woman employee who wanted the week off so that her mother, who normally looked after the child, could visit a relative in another state. There was no emergency compelling the visit at that particular time.

Clarence M. Updegraff, the arbitrator in this case, said that if the employee wanted a day or two to find a baby sitter, that would be an acceptable reason for a leave. But to sustain this claim "would

---

[29] An interesting procedural question was presented by the union's showing that the company had, at one point in the grievance procedure, defended the denial of a leave on the basis of alleged needs of production. By itself, this reason would be a "most dubious" one for refusal of a leave, Mr. Hill said, because the contract relates leaves to the justifiability of the employee's reasons, not to "the state of the business." Another defect in management's case was the first impression, based on erroneous information from the police, that the grievant had driven a car while his license was in suspension. Mr. Hill wrote: "The company acknowledged at the outset of the [arbitration] hearing that this was not true. It is important that [the grievant's] personnel record should be set straight. However, I do not believe that the error alters the case fundamentally. The company still stands on the facts, known to all sides from the start, that [the grievant] was jailed for a second offense of driving while intoxicated." In general, therefore, although the arbitrator admitted that the company's position during grievance procedure contained "distinct flaws," the "central factor" remained unaltered. "The company held that the conviction and incarceration of this employee did not establish justifiable cause for a leave of absence."

[30] 24 AAA 26.

be to adopt a position that whenever any young mother in the employment of the company decides arbitrarily that the available baby sitters are unsatisfactory to her, she may take the full leave of absence for business and use it for child care." This, he said, would be "destructive of the possibility of normally and properly scheduling production," particularly where the work force consisted of many young married women. What, then, did the contract mean by "personal business"? Mr. Updegraff answered: "The provisions in labor agreements for leaves of absence to attend to 'personal business' are usually held to refer to important business transactions which ordinarily cannot be satisfactorily terminated by the employee outside the hours of employment. Typical of these are contracts in respect to lease or purchase of real estate, or sale of real estate, matters of litigation, matters of taxation or other transactions with public officials."

Leaves for Union Officers

Leaves of absence are often given to employees, so that they may participate in union activities and, occasionally, serve a term of elected office. But when an officer is re-elected over and over again, it may be inconvenient for the employer to be technically obligated to restore him to a job after the lapse of many years. This may be particularly true when wage rates have gone up with the passing of time, while the absent employee's efficiency probably went down.

It must have been for this reason that a clause at *P. R. Mallory and Company* (International Union of Electrical, Radio and Machine Workers, AFL-CIO)[31] stated that employees elected to union office "shall" be given a one-year leave of absence and that renewals "may" be given. Under this clause, said Pearce Davis, an arbitrator selected by the parties, the company had the right to refuse a further renewal of leave to an officer of the international union who had not worked in the plant for ten years. "The contract is not ambiguous," he wrote. "Its meaning is clear and unmistakable. The entire tenor is permissive and not mandatory."

Although it was not the "governing factor" in his award, Mr. Davis pointed out that his decision in favor of management was in accordance with "customary industry practice." He acknowledged

[31] 24 AAA 14.

that the company was dealing more harshly with international-union officers than with local officials, but he pointed out that management had the right to discriminate in that manner because the former, being removed from the local scene, are not "intimately connected with the problems of the particular plant."

12

CONCLUSION: PRECEDENT, PAST PRACTICE AND PREDICTABILITY

No precedent, not even his own previous decisions, binds the *ad hoc* arbitrator of grievances. His frame of reference is the agreement of the parties and their bargaining relationship, and his award represents his own judgment of what the agreement means and where the equities lie.[1] True, parties sometimes cite awards by other arbitrators in apparently similar cases. And arbitrators, too, occasionally conduct research among published awards. But the object, in both instances, is to use decisions of other arbitrators for their persuasive value, as supporting data, not as the controlling factor in the case.[2]

Thus, the doctrine of *stare decisis, et non quieta movere*—adhere

---

[1] Although arbitrators are not bound by decisions of others, they will be most reluctant to upset an award of an arbitrator who decided a case for the same parties. See, for example, the decision by W. Willard Wirtz for *Cities Service Oil Company* (Oil, Chemical and Atomic Workers, AFL-CIO), 13 AAA 13, in which management was upheld in its view that there was no contractual obligation to send a messenger to the home of an employee who had no telephone to tell him of an overtime opportunity. The grievant in that case lived five-and-a-half miles from the plant. There had been a previous case in which an arbitrator upheld management's refusal to send a messenger twenty-two miles on the same kind of an errand. Mr. Wirtz said that the earlier decision "does not in itself control the present case." But it is plain, he added, that there is a connection between the two. "The previous decision is a material *fact* in this situation as it presently exists, and must be recognized as such. Given this fact, it would be irresponsible to uphold the present grievance claim unless it should be felt that the prior award was clearly and significantly wrong. This is not my feeling."

[2] See, for instance, the decision of Archibald Cox in *Electric Storage Battery Company* (International Union of Electrical, Radio and Machine Workers, AFL-CIO), 19 AAA 22. After explaining in considerable detail why money, not another overtime work opportunity, was the proper remedy for management's error in distributing overtime under the circumstances of the case, he cited about twenty published awards, in most of which the arbitrators came to similar conclusions. This case is discussed in Chapter 9.

to precedents; do not unsettle established things—does not apply in arbitration as it does in courts of law. Nevertheless, the predictability of decisions and the reluctance to unsettle established things which, in courts, are a consequence of *stare decisis,* are also found in arbitration. The difference is, however, that judges follow precedents set by other judges, while arbitrators look to the past practice of the parties.

Past practice is, of course, most influential in arbitration awards where the contract is either silent on a matter at issue or ambiguous, or where some internal inconsistency appears among the provisions.

"If one of the parties has long applied in practice one of the two or more possible interpretations of an ambiguous provision," wrote Paul R. Hays, in *Royal McBee Corporation* (United Automobile Workers, AFL-CIO),[3] "the other party may be justified in asserting that it would be wronged by a change in that practice." Furthermore, the other party may have an "equitable claim" in that, relying on an expectation that the practice would continue, it did not seek to change the ambiguous provision during negotiations.[4]

---

[3] 5 AAA 6. This case is also discussed in Chapter 8.

[4] Other examples of cases in which arbitrators relied on custom and usage for resolving controversies over unclear contract language were:

Socony Mobil Oil Company (Independent Oil Workers), 7 AAA 5. Charles T. Douds ruled that no extra pay was due employees whose shift extended a half-hour past midnight into a holiday. For several years in the past, it had been the practice of the company not to grant such extra pay, and the union had not protested before. "Where there is a question about the intention of the parties as to the meaning of a provision of a contract," he wrote, "one of the best ways to resolve the problem is to examine the practice of the parties in applying the disputed provision in similar situations in the past." It seemed unlikely to the arbitrator that the union "would overlook so many opportunities to protest or grieve a failure to pay what the contract required over such an extended period of time." This case is also discussed in Chapter 7.

Chesapeake Corporation of Virginia (United Papermakers and Paperworkers, AFL-CIO), 6 AAA 12. Paul N. Guthrie dismissed an overtime-pay grievance on a showing that such pay had not been given in the past and that the union had sought unsuccessfully in negotiations to get contract language granting what it asked for in the grievance. "The history of negotiations on the subject, and the actual payment practices" support management's position, he concluded.

Iowa Manufacturing Company (International Association of Machinists, AFL-CIO), 17 AAA 16. Walter L. Daykin found that jobs were "intentionally described only in a limited manner." Under the circumstances, the fact that towmotor operators had in the past "voluntarily assisted in the loading and unloading" of their vehicles meant that the employer had the right to require

PAST PRACTICE IN CONFLICT WITH
CONTRACT LANGUAGE

Arbitrators often express the view that where the language of the contract is clear, a past practice in apparent violation of its terms cannot alter the meaning of the written instrument. Many examples will be found in the preceding chapters.[5] There are times, however, when past practice is so purposeful that arbitrators are compelled to conclude it was the practice, not the language of the contract, which expressed the agreement of the parties.

Such a situation came before Peter Seitz at the *Great Atlantic & Pacific Tea Company* (Amalgamated Meat Cutters, AFL-CIO).[6] The overtime provision of the contract stated clearly that full-time

---

them to do so to the same extent in the future. Furthermore, the arbitrator said, this was also the custom in other establishments.

Erwin Mills, Inc. (United Textile Workers of America), 2 AAA 2. James A. Morris ruled that an employee who sought a promotion from learner in the Machinist classification to Machinist II could be denied that promotion because it was the practice in the plant to require an interval of work in the Machinist I classification as a preliminary step. The only exception to this practice cited by the union was answered by a showing that the employee had had an exceptional background.

Oxford Paper Company (United Papermakers and Paperworkers, AFL-CIO), 5 AAA 16. Saul Wallen held that foremen could continue to perform bargaining unit work to the extent they had done so in the past, no contractual bar having been agreed upon until after the filing of the grievance. "The previously existing standard of reasonableness, which was apparently the basic standard employed, should be the governing criterion." This case is also discussed in Chapter 5, note 2.

Lebanon Steel Foundry (United Steelworkers of America, AFL-CIO), 3 AAA 12. Donald A. Crawford said that a foreman, returning to the bargaining unit, could be assigned to a job for which he was once scheduled, but which he never actually filled. This was in accordance with "paper" moves which the parties had recognized in layoff and recall procedure in the past. "The company testimony that this practice had been consistently followed in the many layoffs and recalls that have occurred at the plant is not successfully contested by the union," the arbitrator wrote.

[5] See, for example, the award of William J. Fallon in *Tileston and Hollingsworth Company* (United Papermakers and Paperworkers, AFL-CIO), 6 AAA 4, discussed in Chapter 6. Mr. Fallon wrote: "If an ambiguity existed, the intention of the parties could be employed to clarify the ambiguity. Where no ambiguity exists, the prior intentions of the parties notwithstanding, the language must speak for itself. To rule otherwise would constitute a modification and an addition to the terms of the [contract]."

[6] 19 AAA 16.

employees working in excess of eight hours per day would be paid at the rate of time-and-a-half for overtime. Despite this clause, it had been the practice, for many years, to require clerks to perform clean-up operations at the end of the day and to give them no extra compensation for up to ten minutes' work. If, however, they worked from eleven to fifteen minutes, they were paid straight time for the quarter-of-an-hour. Only if they worked more than fifteen minutes did they receive the contractual premium rate.

In 1959, the union filed a grievance, demanding that the contract be applied as written, so that employees would be paid time-and-a-half from the first minute of overtime. As the agreement was "crystal-clear and unambiguous," union representatives argued, the arbitrator had no need to look beyond the "four corners" of the written instrument.

Mr. Seitz rejected this view. "The written contract is, of course, the strongest kind of evidence of what the parties willed, intended or agreed upon," he conceded. "But it is only evidence of that will, intention or agreement. A judge or an arbitrator, under the parole evidence rule, ordinarily will not look beyond its unambiguous language. Where, however, as here, the parties have *unmistakably* demonstrated *how* they themselves have read and regarded the meaning and force of the language, and where the force of the language and this meaning varies from its natural and normal intendment, the judge (or arbitrator) should not, indeed, *cannot* close his eyes to this demonstration. The 'agreement' of the parties is more than the paper on which they express the terms of their understanding. It includes such customs and practices as have been clearly proved to have been given recognition and accepted by both of them."[7]

Mr. Seitz therefore denied the grievance. He reminded the parties, however, that the company could continue the past practice only

[7] See also the decision of Lewis M. Gill in *Linear, Inc.* (United Rubber, Cork, Plastic and Linoleum Workers, AFL-CIO), 4 AAA 16. Mr. Gill wrote: "In general, I am personally inclined to the view that the contract language should govern, if it is absolutely clear and unambiguous, despite a showing of practice to the contrary. What we have here, however, is something more than just a practice of the parties. The uncontradicted evidence shows that at the time the provision in question was negotiated, there was a specific assurance by the company negotiators that it would be interpreted and applied in the manner now urged by the union. The ensuing practice of applying it in that way, in the press room, merely carried out that commitment."

when there was need for clean-up work. The attempt to require employees to work more than eight hours without extra compensation when there was no such need would be an "abuse," which the union would be privileged "to take up in the grievance procedure."

A similar conflict between the plain language of the contract and the contrary practice of the parties came before C. F. Mugridge at *Canada Dry Corporation* (International Brotherhood of Teamsters).[8] The contract clearly required pay for all legal holidays. Nevertheless, Good Friday, one of the legal holidays in that state, was never paid for. The arbitrator found "ample evidence" that the union had "traded out" its Good Friday pay demand for other considerations during negotiations. But the parties apparently found it advantageous not to express their agreement in explicit contract language. The "mutual understanding" of the parties was indicated by their past practice, not their contract, Mr. Mugridge ruled.

In the Introduction, it is pointed out that union contract clauses are sometimes phrased either to create an illusion of a meeting of minds or to conceal the intention of the parties not to carry out the express terms of the agreement. Circumstances of this kind may have been in the background of the *Great Atlantic & Pacific* and the *Canada Dry* cases, discussed above. It may also have explained the case of *Nicolet Industries, Inc.* (Textile Workers Union of America, AFL-CIO),[9] which Eli Rock arbitrated.

For some nineteen years, the parties operated under collective bargaining agreements which, in the recognition clause, clearly covered the truck driver. Nevertheless, during all this time, the truck driver was regarded as one of the classifications outside the bargaining unit. The system of dues check-off was not applied to him, nor were changes in his wage rates over the years made to conform to general wage schedules.[10] During 1959, the union sought, through arbitration, to obtain jurisdiction over this classification. To the union's citation of the recognition clause, which included the truck driver, Mr. Rock replied:

The language of the recognition clause cannot, it seems to the arbitrator,

[8] 24 AAA 3. This case is also discussed in Chapter 7, note 2.
[9] 18 AAA 11.
[10] It appears that the truck driver was a member of an AFL union during the years before the AFL and the CIO merged into one.

offset this contrary, actual fact of the case. Obviously, the parties have had a full understanding, the clear framework of which cannot be disputed in any significant measure, to the effect that [the driver] was not in the unit. There can be no room for doubt that this *was* their mutual agreement. How, then, can it logically be contended that because of a broad and general definition of the bargaining unit, which failed specifically to exclude this single employee, the parties should not be regarded as having intended otherwise?

The right of the company to promulgate rules of conduct unilaterally is seldom questioned, especially where the contract specifically reserves that function to management. But even on so clear a "management prerogative" as this, past practice may override the language of the agreement. At the *West Virginia Pulp and Paper Company* (United Papermakers and Paperworkers, AFL-CIO),[11] for instance, the contract said that "the company shall regulate and prescribe all other working conditions and conditions of employment and operation that do not violate the terms of this agreement." It had been the practice for thirteen years, however, for the employer not to formulate disciplinary rules without negotiating them with the union. When an attempt was made, in 1959, to recodify the rules and to include new rules covering matters not dealt with in the contract, the union objected. The grievance was upheld by the arbitrator, David A. Wolff, who wrote:

In the opinion of this arbitrator, the situation is most unusual, if not unique. The parties have provided that the company shall regulate and prescribe working conditions and conditions of employment and operation that do not violate the terms of the agreement. However, in fact and as shown, since their first agreement in 1946 and up to the issuance by the company of its here challenged October 1959 rules, the parties have always negotiated on the inclusion or exclusion of such rules as a matter of course.

In other words, Mr. Wolff said, the employer's right of "unilateral action" had been made "extremely limited" by the past practice. This did not mean, he said, that the company could not take unilateral action when protection or preservation of the business depended upon such action. In such a situation, however, management would have to show that the need was "pressing and compelling." This was not done in the instant case.

[11] 19 AAA 17.

IRRELEVANT PAST PRACTICE

Not every practice of the past, of course, is of equally persuasive value in union contract interpretation.[12] At *Hitemp Wires, Inc.* (International Brotherhood of Electrical Workers, AFL-CIO),[13] for instance, a past practice in the assignment of stewards to overtime turned out to be of a mere thirteen months' duration. The arbitrator, Thomas A. Knowlton, said this was insufficient grounds for giving stewards a guarantee of overtime work which the contract did not otherwise grant them. "For an arbitrator to give weight to a practice such as is claimed by the union as existing in this case," he wrote, "there must either be a 'past practice clause' in the agreement (there is none) or some lack of clarity in the language of the agreement. In this case, all of the pertinent sections of the agreement are clear, concise and without possibility of misinterpretation."

When a practice can be explained by special circumstances, an arbitrator may be persuaded that it cannot be used to alter the meaning of the contract itself. Such a situation arose before John R. Coleman at the *Erie Forge and Steel Corporation* (United Steelworkers of America, AFL-CIO).[14] The employer was upheld in his assertion that an employee who initiated a transfer from one department to another abandoned his old departmental seniority. The union argued that employees in another plant of the company were permitted to accrue seniority in two departments at the same time under similar circumstances. The facts were accurately portrayed, Mr. Coleman wrote, "but there was a satisfactory explanation for each of those cases." It seemed that a serious record-keeping problem existed in that plant for a time, and it was impossible for personnel department employees to distinguish between voluntary and

---

[12] A past practice which may not be compelling enough to overcome the language of a contract may nevertheless influence the arbitrator's award of a remedy for violations. A case at *Foote Mineral Company* (Oil, Chemical and Atomic Workers, AFL-CIO), 19 AAA 26, discussed in Chapter 5 is an example. Laurence E. Seibel found that foremen had been doing a small amount of forbidden bargaining unit work; but he denied the union's request for a monetary remedy, because such work had been done "for some time" without protest on the part of the union.

[13] 21 AAA 15. This case is also discussed in Chapter 4.

[14] 8 AAA 9.

involuntary transfers. To avoid injustice to any employee, all were credited with dual seniority for that time.

Past practice, no matter how long and consistent, may not be binding if it relates to a matter specifically excluded from the scope of the collective bargaining agreement. That was the finding of Milton D. Green at *Vickers, Inc.* (Allied Industrial Workers, AFL-CIO),[15] where the union protested the employer's offer of inventory work to employees without regard to their seniority. The union showed that seniority had been followed in the past under similar conditions, but Mr. Green said it was irrelevant because inventory work was an activity "not covered by the agreement."[16] Past practice "could not be used to enlarge the scope of the contract beyond its express terms," Mr. Green wrote.

The same principle was expressed by arbitrators in three other cases, involving the discontinuance of long-established privileges which were not required by the contract. The first case was at *The Magnavox Company* (Allied Industrial Workers, AFL-CIO),[17] where the company announced a new rule, permitting employees to use vending machines only during lunch and rest periods. John Day Larkin, the arbitrator selected to resolve the dispute, was not impressed with the union's argument that unrestricted use of vending machines had become "virtually a part of the agreement."

> It may be true that, after permitting the free use of these machines for some eighteen years, the withdrawal of such privileges may have the effect of disrupting the morale of those against whom the action is taken; but that is a risk the management may take if it chooses to take it. The arbitrator has no power or authority to make the Company revoke a rule which we think it has reserved the right to make and enforce.

In the second case, *Charles Lachman Company* (Textile Workers

---

[15] 4 AAA 15.

[16] The contract did not specifically mention inventory work, but it did contain this provision: "The parties expressly declare that they have bargained between them on all phases of hours, wages, and working conditions and that this contract represents their full and complete agreement without reservation or unexpressed understanding. Any aspect of hours, wages, and working conditions not covered by a particular provision of this agreement is declared to have been expressly eliminated as a subject for bargaining and during the life of this agreement may not be raised for further bargaining or negotiation without the written consent of all the parties hereto."

[17] 22 AAA 15.

Union of America, AFL-CIO),[18] the issue was whether, after voluntarily permitting employees to leave work early on the days before Christmas and New Year's Day, for many years, the company could require performance of the full schedule in 1959. John Perry Horlacher said it was within management's rights to do so:

If, as the Union alleges, in prior years a five-hour schedule was worked on the day before Christmas, the company in effect had informally and unilaterally extended the Christmas holiday for three additional hours without pay. This was its clear prerogative under [the management rights clause]. By doing so, it did not vest any rights in the employees to a continuance of this practice although it manifestly produced an expectation of continuance. Although the workers might understandably resent the discontinuance of the practice, they cannot enforce its continuance as though they had collectively bargained such an arrangement, and they cannot predicate a claim for holiday pay upon the discontinuance of a practice in which they have no contractually vested interest.

The third case was of a different kind. Management of the *Pittsburgh Metallurgical Co., Inc.* (United Automobile Workers, AFL-CIO)[19] had drawn up job descriptions, in February 1954, under which truck drivers were required to perform greasing and oil-changing maintenance work on their own vehicles. But it was not until December 1957 that management found it necessary to require actual performance of that work. At that time the union filed a grievance asserting, among other things, that the addition of these duties was barred by past practice. The lapse of time, Bert L. Luskin ruled, did not create a past practice such as would overcome management's rights in this respect. "The fact that the company did not until December 1957 require truck drivers to lubricate their own equipment does not mean that the Company has forever waived its right to require an employee to perform duties specifically covered in an existing job description for a particular classification," he said.

EFFECT OF UNION'S FAILURE TO PROTEST PAST VIOLATIONS

Writing on the effect of past practice, in the case of the *McQuay Norris Manufacturing Company* (United Automobile Workers,

[18] 7 AAA 21. This case is also discussed in Chapter 7.
[19] 6 AAA 6.

AFL-CIO),[20] John F. Sembower said that, to be persuasive, past practice must have three characteristics: (1) it must be unequivocal; (2) it must be clearly enunciated and acted upon; and (3) it must be readily ascertainable over a reasonably long period of time, so as to constitute fixed practice accepted by both parties.

Clearly, these standards are not met when one party is unaware of the practice. In the *Royal McBee* case that occasioned the remarks of Paul R. Hays, quoted above, it appeared that there had been a practice of computing time on layoff as time worked for vacation allowance purposes. But the employer contended that this came about only because of errors in the payroll department. As the union did not know of these errors, management argued, it could not reasonably be said that a past practice had been established which shed light on the meaning of the contract. Mr. Hays answered that the failure of the union to raise any question about vacation computation practices in the past could be held against it only if the employer's practice had been restrictive, rather than liberal. "If the vacation allowance had been reduced by the inclusion of layoff time in the computation," he wrote, "the union would have been made aware of it by dissatisfied members. I conclude, therefore, that by its practice the employer has established a method of computation of vacation allowances on the continuation of which the union has a right to insist."

A similar problem in evaluating past practice arises in discipline cases. Is the union foreclosed from protesting application of a rule or imposition of discipline under that rule by having acquiesced in the past? In cases where such an issue was raised, arbitrators have generally been satisfied that the union had not forfeited its right to protest.

Robert R. France, arbitrator in a case of the *R. T. French Company* (United Packinghouse Workers, AFL-CIO),[21] came to that conclusion, when considering whether the union had waived its right to protest application of a rule governing unreported absences by failing to file grievances over the discharge of five employees under that rule in the past six months. This, he said, "does not establish a past practice," in part because the five discharged em-

---

[20] 9 AAA 7. This case is also discussed in Chapter 7.
[21] 16 AAA 23. This case is also discussed in Chapter 10.

ployees were not interested in being restored to their jobs. He concluded: "The short period of time over which these other releases have taken place and the fact that the union did protest the first such release objected to by the employee involved destroys any company claim to an established past practice."[22]

GENERAL CONCLUSION

"Outside the areas controlled by statute," wrote Archibald Cox,[23] "there is no more important treasury of experience than the record

[22] See also the award of A. R. Marshall, in *Magnavox Company of Tennessee* (International Union of Electrical, Radio and Machine Workers, AFL-CIO), 13 AAA 17, discussed in Chapter 2. Mr. Marshall wrote: "The fact that some violation of the contract has not been protested by the employees or the union does not mean at all that the latter has accepted a procedure whereby the company does not honor division seniority in layoffs arising out of reductions in force."

See also the award of Louis A. Crane, in *Bay City Shovels, Inc.* (United Steelworkers of America, AFL-CIO), 3 AAA 18, discussed in Chapter 8. Mr. Crane wrote: "The acquiescence of the employees involved, who neither negotiated the agreement nor are responsible for the administration, hardly can be regarded as acquiescence by the union. If anything, the failure of those employees to raise the issue merely preserved the question which is raised here."

On the other hand, see *Tri-Part Manufacturing Company* (International Brotherhood of Electrical Workers, AFL-CIO), 15 AAA 17, discussed in Chapter 7. The company pointed out that the union had not objected in the past when holidays falling on Saturdays were not paid for. The union answered that former union officers had "blinked" at contract violations and that past negligence ought not to be held against the union in the instant case. The arbitrator, Louis A. Crane, upheld management largely on the basis of interpretation of the contract. The question of past practice was a minor element in the case. He did say, however, that the union's answer to the company's assertion of past practice was inadequate.

See also the award of Lloyd H. Bailer, in *Perkins Machine & Gear Company* (International Union of Electrical, Radio and Machine Workers, AFL-CIO), 21 AAA 19, discussed in Chapter 7. Mr. Bailer wrote: "The union's failure to challenge past violations does not preclude it from insisting upon compliance with the contract thereafter. The necessary ingredients for a plea of estoppel do not exist here."

See also the award of William J. Fallon, in *Tileston and Hollingsworth Company* (United Papermakers and Paperworkers, AFL-CIO), 6 AAA 4, discussed in Chapter 6 and in note 5, above. Mr. Fallon wrote: "The fact that the union slept on its rights [in a previous incident] is insufficient grounds for a holding that the clear contract language does not apply now."

[23] Archibald Cox, *Law and National Labor Policy*, Institute of Industrial Relations, University of California, 1960, p. 72.

of grievance arbitration. Surely arbitrators have not labored at the administration of collective bargaining agreements for almost two decades without arriving at some generalizations upon which the unbiased can agree, even though partisan interests preclude unanimity."

The search for "some generalization" to guide labor and management in formulating policy and to aid in predicting the outcome of grievances has been going on for many years. The results, from the point of view of those who want infallible rules, have not been altogether satisfying. There are many reasons for this. The first is that arbitrators themselves seldom generalize. Written opinions of arbitrators are usually punctuated with phrases reminding the reader that the decision was based "on the facts of this case." As the grievances reported in this volume demonstrate, an infinite variety of detail is possible in employer-employee relationships. Apparently similar cases may be dissimilar in some respect which the arbitrator may have thought it more tactful not to put into writing. This may happen particularly where subjective factors, such as the credibility of witnesses, are involved. Furthermore, even where contracts in two unrelated establishments contain identical language, it cannot be assumed that they will yield identical interpretations. The history of bargaining may not have been the same; and, as we have seen, parties may be applying the agreement in different ways. Thus, when an arbitrator uses qualifying phrases, making his award applicable only to the situation before him, he is expressing a caution that should be observed by the reader.

Even when an arbitrator seems to state absolute rules of contract interpretation,[24] without the usual qualifications, the perceptive

[24] See, for instance, Alex Elson, in *Fairbanks, Morse & Company* (United Steelworkers of America, AFL-CIO), 18 AAA 10: "It is axiomatic in the construction of a provision of a collective bargaining agreement that it should be considered within the framework of the entire agreement and in relation to other provisions in the agreement germane to it." This case is also discussed in Chapter 2.

See also Frank R. Uible, in *Lovell Manufacturing Company* (United Rubber, Cork, Linoleum and Plastic Workers, AFL-CIO), 23 AAA 9: "In the absence of qualifying or modifying language, we must assume that parties in the use of words in drafting provisions intended the common and ordinary meaning as approved by recognized authorities." This case is also discussed in Chapter 3.

See also Bert L. Luskin, in *Scranton Corporation* (Federal Local Union 23158, AFL-CIO), 14 AAA 16: "Unless an ambiguity exists, the basic rules

reader, familiar with the realities of labor arbitration, will read implied limitations into those rules. The arbitrator does not write primarily for publication. His decision is intended for the two parties who selected him to resolve a particular controversy. Consequently he will, on one occasion, assert an "absolute rule" that past practice cannot alter the meaning of an unambiguous clause. On another, he will state with no less conviction, as arbitrators referred to earlier in this chapter have done, that the past practice of the parties, not the language they chose to use, represented the real agreement. Similarly, an arbitrator may in one case look closely into the history of bargaining, tracing the origin of disputed clauses back to the proposals and counter-proposals made during negotiations. In his very next case, he may rule that all matters discussed during the negotiation leading to the execution of the agreement must be considered to have been merged into the provisions of the contract.

Arbitrators cannot be classified as "strict constructionists" or "liberal constructionists." All are one or the other, depending upon their appraisal of the contract and the bargaining relationship of the parties. It can be argued with merit that the arbitrator forms an impression of the rights and equities of the parties on the basis of all the circumstances of the case, and then selects the "canon of construction" that leads to his conclusion.[25]

---

of contract construction would require that all matters discussed during the negotiation leading to the execution of the agreement must be considered to have been merged into the provisions of the contract." This case is also discussed in Chapter 3.

See also John F. Sembower, in *McQuay Norris Manufacturing Company* (United Automobile Workers, AFL-CIO), 9 AAA 7: "It is an accepted canon of contract interpretation that if particular matters are included or excluded, it is to be inferred that other matters not so included or excluded are not embraced. [Consequently], unless it is clearly established that there are compelling circumstances requiring a special meaning to be attached to the words, they must be given their ordinary meaning." This case is also discussed in Chapter 7.

See also John Perry Horlacher, in *American Can Company* (United Papermakers and Paperworkers, AFL-CIO), 4 AAA 17: "A rule or principle stated in the general form carries with it a presumption of general applicability. This of course can be rebutted but it is not sufficient for rebutting the presumption to prove that the rule grew out of situation X and thereby infer that it applies only to X. This *may* be the case. But if the rule is inclusively framed, the evidence that it does not apply also to Y or Z ought to be pretty clear and convincing." This case is also discussed in Chapter 9.

[25] Clarence M. Updegraff and Whitley P. McCoy (*Arbitration of Labor Disputes*, Bureau of National Affairs, Washington, D.C., 1961, pp. 225–226) ex-

Thus, there are many factors which combine to make every decision by an arbitrator unique. Nevertheless—and this is most important for the stability of labor relations—the area within which the arbitrator's decision will fall is completely predictable. *Ad hoc* arbitrators are not innovators; they do not impose on the parties their own judgment as to how the industrial establishment ought to be managed.[26] In a discharge case, for instance, it may not be known

---

pressed the following "primary" and "secondary" rules of contract interpretation, which they adapted from 3 *Williston on Contracts* (Revised Ed.), Section 618:

"A. 'Primary rules of interpretation' may be briefly summarized as follows: 1. The common or normal meaning of language will be ascribed to the provisions of a contract unless circumstances show a special meaning is justified. 2. Where technical words have been used, they will normally be given the intended technical meaning unless it clearly appears by local usage or otherwise that a contrary intention was mutually agreed by the parties. 3. The entire agreement should be read as a whole, and every part of it interpreted with reference to all other parts. It should be so interpreted as to give effect to its entire general purpose. 4. Consideration should be given to the circumstances under which the writing was negotiated or made.

"B. Certain rules of interpretation which are commonly designated 'secondary' may be put as follows: 1. An interpretation which gives reasonable, lawful, and effective meaning to all manifestations in the writing is preferred to an interpretation which leaves a part of such a manifestation unreasonable, unlawful, or of no effect. 2. The principal apparent purpose of the parties is given great weight in determining the meaning to be given to each manifestation of intention or to any part thereof. 3. Where an inconsistency is found between general provisions and specific provisions, the latter ordinarily qualify the meaning of the general provisions. 4. Words or other manifestations of intention which bear more than one reasonable meaning shall be interpreted more strongly against the party by whom they were written unless their use by him was required by law. 5. Written provisions inconsistent with printed provisions in the same agreement are preferred over the printed. 6. If public interest is affected, an interpretation favoring the public is preferred."

[26] For example, see *American Enka Corporation* (United Textile Workers of America, AFL-CIO), 12 AAA 22, where arbitrator William M. Hepburn refused to disturb a long-standing company policy of charging employees for materials lost through no fault of their own. "As a matter of abstract justice it is not easy to defend a system which imposes on an individual or a group financial 'penalties' without proof of fault or even of actual power to control, unless specifically authorized by the contract or by individual employees," he wrote. But the practice had been in existence for a long time, during which many contracts had been negotiated. "I do not think I should change it in this proceeding. Complaints and dissatisfaction regarding this problem should be referred to negotiation rather than arbitration."

See also comments of James J. Healy, in *Royal McBee Corporation* (United Automobile Workers, AFL-CIO), 16 AAA 7, in Chapter 10, note 1.

in advance whether the arbitrator will reinstate the grievant and, if so, whether back pay will be awarded. But it is a certainty that the award will not order a substitute penalty of, let us say, forfeiture of the grievant's share of overtime. That form of punishment is not part of the industrial relations tradition in the United States. No experienced arbitrator would make it part of his award unless it was sanctioned by the contract or by the practice of the parties themselves.

The primary purpose of every labor arbitration award is to resolve a controversy between the two parties for whom it was written. The lasting contribution of the arbitrators, however, is not merely that they have disposed of grievances, but that, in so doing, they have created a vast body of research material. The arbitrator's insight into the human and technical shortcomings that cause grievances is widely used as source material for the study of industrial relations and for the guidance of labor and management negotiators. It therefore detracts little from the value of reported awards that they do not lead to infallible prediction of the outcome of a pending grievance. What is important is that they point up problem areas in union contract negotiation and administration and show how future grievances may be avoided.

The arbitrator's reliance on the past practice of the parties for many of his decisions and his acceptance of the agreement as his frame of reference make him a conservative and stabilizing force in labor relations. Reform and experimentation are left to the parties. Contract negotiation is an area in which the arbitrator does not participate. Initiative is retained—as is proper in any self-regulatory system—by the parties directly concerned. Arbitration begins with a voluntary act: the agreement to let disagreements be resolved by a trusted third person, a private citizen whose authority depends, not upon power of the state, but upon the original exercise of free choice by the two contesting forces. An agreement to arbitrate, which may seem, at first glance, to involve a temporary surrender of the ephemeral freedom to use economic or physical force in order to win an ephemeral victory, actually lays the foundation for a greater and more permanent freedom for both labor and management.

ARBITRATORS

293

TABLE OF CASES

Bay City Shovels, Inc. (United Steelworkers of America, AFL-CIO), 3 AAA 18:148, 287 n

Bearings Co. of America (United Steelworkers of America, AFL-CIO), 20 AAA 19:138

Belgian Lines, Inc. (Office Employees International Union, AFL-CIO), 8 AAA 5:271

Bigelow-Sanford Carpet Co. (Textile Workers Union of America, AFL-CIO), 4 AAA 1:59

Bird & Son, Inc. (United Papermakers and Paperworkers, AFL-CIO), 19 AAA 6:110; 18 AAA 19:270

Blackford Glass Co. (Federal Local Union No. 22560, AFL-CIO), 11 AAA 20:155

E. W. Bliss Co. (United Steelworkers of America, AFL-CIO), 19 AAA 7:266

Blocksom & Co. (Upholsterers' International Union, AFL-CIO), 7 AAA 18:207

Bonafide Plastics, Inc. (United Rubber, Cork, Linoleum and Plastic Workers, AFL-CIO), 10 AAA 11:162; 10 AAA 12:198

Borg-Warner Corp. (Allied Industrial Workers of America, AFL-CIO), 5 AAA 18:60; 21 AAA 6:84; 13 AAA 11:159; 20 AAA 14:159; 16 AAA 14:206

Borg-Warner Corp. (United Automobile Workers, AFL-CIO), 22 AAA 11:258

Bridgeport Brass Co. (United Steelworkers of America, AFL-CIO), 24 AAA 11:127; 5 AAA 23:200

The Brooklyn Club (Hotel, Restaurant and Bartenders Union, AFL-CIO), 23 AAA 8:116

The Budd Co. (Independent Workers Union of The Budd Co.), 10 AAA 8:84

The Buxbaum Co. (United Rubber, Cork, Linoleum and Plastic Workers, AFL-CIO), 15 AAA 8:194

Canada Dry Corp. (International Brotherhood of Teamsters), 24 AAA 3:112 n, 281

The Cared Corp. (United Steelworkers of America, AFL-CIO), 8 AAA 6:87 n

Celanese Corp. of America (Textile Workers Union of America, AFL-CIO), 14 AAA 2:78

Celanese Corp. of America (United Construction Workers), 3 AAA 15:80

Celanese Corp. of America (United Mine Workers, District 50), 23 AAA 21:83; 23 AAA 20:181; 23 AAA 23:187

Central Die Casting Mfg. Co. (Mine, Mill & Smelter Workers), 23 AAA 13:73 n

Charles Lachman Co. (Textile Workers Union of America, AFL-CIO), 7 AAA 21:117, 284

J. Chein and Co. (United Steelworkers of America, AFL-CIO), 19 AAA 3:119; 19 AAA 2:196

Chesapeake Corp. of Virginia (United Papermakers and Paperworkers, AFL-CIO), 6 AAA 12:278 n

Chicago Rawhide Mfg. Co. (Amalgamated Meat Cutters and Butcher Workmen, AFL-CIO), 10 AAA 18:235

Chief Pontiac Federal Credit Union (Office Employees International Union, AFL-CIO), 19 AAA 9:202

Cities Service Oil Co. (Oil, Chemical and Atomic Workers, AFL-CIO), 18 AAA 12:175; 13 AAA 13:277 n

Cleveland Electric Illuminating Co. (Utility Workers Union of America, AFL-CIO), 3 AAA 1:183

SUBJECT INDEX

work, 212–213; refusal of overtime, 186–190, 201, 230; refusal to cross picket line, 230; refusal to obey work order, 230, 230 n, 241–242; refusal to testify before investigating committee, 247–249; security risk, 247–249; sleeping on the job, 214; unauthorized work stoppage, 69–72, 197; violation of rules, 202–215. See also Discharge and discipline; Disciplinary rules; Discipline, reasons for arbitrators' reversal of.

Discharge and demotion, non-disciplinary: 254–276; abolition of recall rights after long absence, 269–271; difference between discharge and other forms of separation, 25–26, 156, 255; involuntary absenteeism, 254, 254 n; leaves of absence, denial of, 255 n, 271–276; physical disability, 265–269; probationary employees, 255–262

Disciplinary rules: coffee break activities, 203–204; conflict of rules and penalties, 222–224; equal application of, 193–197, 200–201, 214, 215; inconsistent enforcement of, 193–197, 200–201; internal consistency, 215–224, 227; range of penalties for violations, 221–222; reasonableness, 202–215; right of employer to promulgate, 202; statute of limitations in application, 210 n, 215, 242–243. See also Discharge and discipline; Discharge and discipline, causes of; Discipline, reasons for arbitrators' reversal of.

Discipline, reasons for arbitrators' reversal of: added penalty for single offense, 239; arbitrators' views on modifying penalties, 216–218, 216 n, 217 n, 218 n; coercion to obtain resignation, 236–237; denial of contract benefits as a form of discipline, 249–253; discipline intended as an "example" to others, 198–199; inadequate warning, 228–233; inconsistent enforcement of rules, 194–197, 200–201, 219–224, 227; insufficient proof of guilt, 224–227; lack of gradation of penalties, 201

n, 219–220; management's failure to deter violation, 240–242; procedural defects and failure to give contractual notice of discipline, 201 n, 234–242, 242 n; retroactive application of new rule, 228–229; statute of limitations, 210 n, 215, 224 n, 242–243; unclear instructions, 229–233; unequal treatment of employees, 193–197, 200–201, 214, 215; unreasonable application of rules, 202–209, 211–215

Discrimination: for marital status, 202; for union activity, 45, 201, 261–262

Douglas, William O., vii

Foremen and supervisors: 73–95; bumping rights, 91–92; excluded from bargaining unit, 73, 73 n, 74 n; just cause for discharge of, 74 n; performance of bargaining unit work, 73 n, 74–87; remedies for performance of bargaining unit work, 76, 76 n, 83–84; right to bid for bargaining unit jobs, 91–92; right to return to bargaining unit, 87–92; seniority status, 74 n, 87–92; transfer of bargaining unit work to foreman, 92–95

Guaranteed hours, 15, 27. See also Call-in pay.

Holidays and holiday pay: 112–140; call-in pay on holidays, 137–138; computation of holiday pay during irregular weeks, 133–137; conflict with sick leave pay, 117; denial of holiday pay as a form of discipline, 250–251; effect on eligibility of absence on surrounding days, 113–132; effect on eligibility of layoff, layoff notice and vacations, 123–132; effect on eligibility of partial absence on surrounding day, 117–120; effect on eligibility of refusal to work overtime on surrounding day, 120–121; holiday during interval between contracts, 132; holiday on Saturday, 133–134; proof of illness to establish eligibility, 114–115; provisions for pay in collective bargaining agreements, 112; right of